The
TWO O'CLOCK WAR

The
TWO O'CLOCK WAR

The 1973 Yom Kippur Conflict
and the Airlift That Saved Israel

WALTER J. BOYNE

THOMAS DUNNE BOOKS

ST. MARTIN'S PRESS

NEW YORK

THOMAS DUNNE BOOKS.
An imprint of St. Martin's Press.

www.stmartins.com

ISBN 0-312-27303-7

First Edition: September 2002

10 9 8 7 6 5 4 3 2 1

This book is dedicated with love to our five wonderful grandchildren:
Dana "J.D." Teague, Grace Teague, Walter James Coleman,
Charlotte "Lottie" Coleman, and Charles "Boo-boo" Coleman.

Contents

Foreword

IN 1948, THE WORLD WITNESSED two major but seemingly disparate conflicts: a war in the Middle East triggered by the establishment of the state of Israel; and the Berlin airlift, a massive U.S. aerial resupply operation precipitated by the Soviet Union closing all surface access to the former German capital.

Developments spawned by these two seismic events would intersect dramatically a quarter century later during the so called Yom Kippur War launched by Egypt and Syria against Israel in 1973. *The Two O'Clock War* is the story of Israel's desperate struggle against formidable forces that had attacked it during the religious holiday of Yom Kippur, and the unprecedented U.S. Air Force cargo airlift—Operation Nickel Grass—that ultimately provided the difference between Israeli survival and defeat.

Israel, from its amazing victory against overwhelming odds in its 1948 struggle to exist as a state, developed a powerful and prideful armed forces that had enjoyed many military successes during the following two decades. Largely based on its spectacular and overwhelming victory in the Six-Day War of 1967, Israel's leadership had come to seriously underestimate its enemies. By 1973, its military strategy and tactical doctrine had also failed to recognize the significant changes to modern war wrought by new technologies—particularly antiaircraft missiles—that would seriously affect the balance of power in the Middle East.

As a consequence of this hubris and miscalculation, Israel was almost overwhelmed by the aggressive attack of Egypt's newly invigorated forces, which that brilliantly employed the latest Soviet military equipment to cross the Suez Canal with the objective of retaking the Sinai Peninsula lost in the 1967 war. To repel the Egyptians and the simultaneous Syrian and Iraqi attacks on the Golan Heights in the north, the Israelis expended far greater stocks of ammunition than anticipated and experienced wholly unplanned and near catastrophic levels of equipment and personnel losses—particularly tanks, aircraft, and highly trained pilots.

As the desperation of Israel's plight and the extent of the Soviet Union's involvement in provisioning the initial attack and the resupply of Arab forces became clear, the United States launched long-range C141 and giant C5 military freighters to fly continuously, bringing more than 22,000 tons of munitions, spare parts, and even entire battle tanks directly into Israel.

The design of these two highly efficient military cargo planes had evolved from vast U.S. experience in air transport operations during World War II and, in particular, experience gained during the massive Berlin airlift that had barely kept encircled Berlin fed and heated during the 1948 blockade. The C141s and C5s used in Operation Nickel Grass were long-range jet aircraft that allowed rapid loading and off-loading through ramps. Even heavy equipment and pallets of ammunition could be moved from the airfield straight to the battlefield. The handling on the ground was so quick that shells still cool from the long flights from the United States often went directly into the hot breeches of Israeli artillery pieces. Quite simply, the belated success of Israeli arms in the Yom Kippur War would have been impossible if it weren't for Operation Nickel Grass.

The C141s had earned great recognition during the Vietnam conflict, but the jumbo C5 had been highly controversial during its development because of cost overruns and technical problems. But in its first true test, the giant airlifter clearly proved its worth by its unprecedented capabilities to provide global military reach that was impossible until the advent of the C5.

The great accomplishment of the 1973 U.S. Air Force long-range operation to resupply Israel overshadowed the shorter range Soviet airlift in support of Egypt and Syria. The airlift technologies and capabilities displayed during Nickel Grass heralded not only a new age of aerial logistics but presaged an unprecedented U.S. military projection capability that profoundly changed all geopolitical military equations thereafter.

In fact, the aftereffects of the Yom Kippur War and the remarkable air bridge that played such a prominent role in that conflict can be seen clearly today in the continuing strife in the Middle East and recent rapid deployments of U.S. forces around the world. Operation Nickel Grass is a story not only fascinating in its own right but one revealing about the dangers of underestimating new military threats and the effects of America's strategic airlift on international affairs in the twenty-first century.

FREDERICK W. SMITH
Chairman and CEO
FedEx Corporation

Introduction: The War Begins

October 6, 1973, Yom Kippur. 1:50 P.M. (Local Time)

A ROUGH KNOCK ON THE door rouses Yacov Gore from his sleep. Guilt-stricken, he shuts down his record player—forbidden on this holiest of Jewish holidays—and glances out the window. A burly trooper stands at the door, impatient, a paper curled up in his fist—the emergency recall list. Gore, a reporter for the *Jerusalem Post,* pulls off his *kitel,* the white garment worn for Yom Kippur, and grabs his rifle. As always, his kit is in his car; he will drive to his infantry unit at the front.

Ten minutes later a blinding shower of high explosive rains down on Mifriket, a low-lying collection of concrete bunkers and observation posts sunk in the Sinai sand. Artillery and rocket fire from the Egyptian Eighteenth Division upends every inch of the tiny fortress area, turning sand into tiny glasslike meteors. Inside the bunkers, thirty-one Israeli soldiers stare wildly, mouths open to ease the pain of the endless concussive waves, ignoring the chunks of concrete plummeting down from the ceiling. All this for a few yards of dirt overlooking the Suez Canal. Within twenty-four hours, all thirty-one soldiers will be dead or captured.

Simultaneously with the artillery barrage, more than a hundred Syrian air force planes attack targets in the Golan Heights, with MiG-21s flying top cover and MiG-17 and Sukhoi Su-7b fighter-bombers striking defensive positions. Communication centers, antiaircraft batteries, and Hawk missile batteries receive careful annihilating attention. Twenty Su-7bs bomb Brigadier General Rafael Eitan's divisional headquarters. For the first time—but not the last—the cry goes up: "Where is the Israeli Air Force?"

Even as the bombs fall, Egyptian engineers move with

speed and precision as they place the Soviet-built pontoon bridges across the Suez Canal. October 6 is not only Yom Kippur, the Day of Atonement—it is also a day and a time when the tide would be perfect for the bridging operations. One of the best-concealed surprise offensives in history suddenly lunges forward across the canal. Within two days Egypt will have six hundred tanks and one hundred thousand men on the east bank, reclaiming territory lost since 1967, and the Suez Canal can no longer be considered the best "antitank ditch" in the world.

In New York for an annual UN ministers' meeting, Assistant Secretary of State Joseph J. Cisco barges into Henry Kissinger's Waldorf Astoria bedroom at the ungodly time of quarter after six, shouting, "The Israelis say the Arabs are going to start a war today. It cannot be true!"

Kissinger, both Secretary of State and National Security Adviser to President Nixon, listened quietly as Cisco assures him that the shooting has not begun and that he, Kissinger, can resolve the situation with a few phone calls.

Thus began the Yom Kippur War, a savage struggle that Egypt and Syria had little hope for winning but nonetheless came very close—perhaps within hours—to doing so. The October War, as it is sometimes called, was one that the Israelis believed they could not lose—and almost did. It was a war that the Soviet Union promoted but did not want. It was a war that began as a mere annoyance to the Nixon administration, locked in the morass of Watergate, but one that would twice escalate perilously close to a nuclear conflict.

More than anything else, however, the Yom Kippur War is characterized by incredible mistakes by nearly every one of the top leaders of every power involved over the course of the conflict—with one or two surprising exceptions. In stark and shining contrast, it was also a war that came down to superb performances by men in the field and on the firing line. Arab soldiers fought as they had never done before, savagely and with a joyous will to win. It took days of remorseless battle before the Israeli soldiers and airmen recovered from their initial shock—and from the crass political infighting of their leaders—to rally and once again defeat the enemy.

Few people were aware at the time that the Israeli victory was made possible in large part by the heroic and selfless actions of the United States Air Force's Military Airlift Command. Brought into action late in the day, the MAC crews became a tangible symbol of U.S. support and delivered the necessary munitions for the Israel Defense Force (IDF) to survive and then prevail.

Sadly, it was also a war in which all the European nations but one—Portugal—showed their true colors. Terrified by the Arab oil boycott, France, Great Britain, Italy, Germany, and Spain turned their backs on both Israel and the United States, refusing permission for the hard-pressed USAF crews to land on or fly over their territories. If Portugal had not assented to the use of the Azores as a staging base, Israel could not have been rearmed and almost certainly would have lost both the war and the crucial negotiations that followed.

The Yom Kippur War was as much a war of personalities as it was of bullets. On each side of the conflict, bright men and women with huge intellects and even bigger egos clashed in the faces of their enemies. As the following pages will show, certain of them stand out by reason of their contributions—for good and for ill—to the eventual outcome of the war. Among the many towering personalities, four overshadow all the others: U.S. Secretary of State Henry Kissinger; the Israeli Defense Minister, Moshe Dayan; his fearless field commander, Major General Ariel "Arik" Sharon; and the President of Egypt, Anwar Sadat. There were many other major players, but in the end, it is these four who dominate not only the Yom Kippur War but also the world stage. Their actions, aided by misunderstandings and fueled by the Cold War suspicions of the time, would determine the outcome of the Yom Kippur War and twice bring the world incredibly close to nuclear war.

The
TWO O'CLOCK WAR

I   *Hubris and the October War*

THE WAR THAT BLAZED forth on October 6, 1973, would grow swiftly from what looked initially like a minor border skirmish. Its escalation resulted from how the United States and the Soviet Union sought to extend their strength and influence through client states. Both sides used the same techniques: political backing in disputes, loans and gifts of money and other supplies, and, of course, the provision of arms and munitions.

During the Cold War, many client states to the two superpowers received weapons that were surplus to their patrons' need and were often obsolescent. Not so in the Middle East, where the Soviet Union equipped the Arab states with their finest equipment and the United States responded in kind for Israel. The total outlay for this aid was massive, as may be seen by the following table comparing the strength of the opposing forces.

NATION	POPULATION	GNP	TROOPS	TANKS	ARTILLERY	AIRCRAFT
Egypt	35,700,000	$7.5B	260,000	2,250	800	620
Iraq	10,142,000	3.5B	90,000	1,130	700	224
Jordan	2,560,000	.7B	68,000	200	200	52
Syria	6,775,000	1.9B	120,000	1,270	400	410
Total Arab:	55,177,000	13.6	538,000	4,850	2,100	1,306
Israel:	3,180,000	6.9	275,000*	2,000	350	488

*When mobilized[1]

The Arab states knew that they could count on the support of many other anti-Israel partners. This was demonstrated repeatedly during the war by the extension of financial aid, military equipment, and, perhaps most important, support in the United Nations. No fewer than eleven nations directly supported the Arab forces. Kuwait and Saudi Arabia financially backed the war and committed over 3,000 troops. Algeria, Tunisia, Sudan, and Morocco contributed a combined force of 10,000 troops, 150 tanks, and three fighter and bomber squadrons. Lebanese radar operators guided Syrian aircraft and allowed Palestinian terrorists to set up artillery positions within Lebanon's borders.

The table's numbers speak for themselves; more than 55,000,000 Arabs were to be pitted against 3,180,000 Israelis. The armies of the Arab states were vastly superior in manpower, tanks, aircraft, and especially artillery. These facts dictated what had become Israel's permanent strategy: swift mobilization followed by powerful air attacks and a slashing armored offensive. Under Egyptian President Anwar Sadat's clever guidance, Egypt and Syria now sought to undermine that strategy.

It is important to note in the table the gross national product figures. Israel's GNP almost matches Egypt's and exceeds the other three nations' combined GNPs. Israel's GNP depended upon the industry and resourcefulness of its people, many of whom had to do double duty, serving as businessmen or -women while also serving in the reserves. When the reserves were mobilized and the armed forces brought up to strength, business suffered. In contrast, the greater populations of the Arab nations permitted them to maintain sizable standing armies. This was a key difference, one that almost spelled the end of Israel as a nation in 1973.

The qualitative difference between the armed forces of Israel and those of the Arab countries is more difficult to chart. It is of even greater difficulty to measure the degree by which Israel underestimated the Egyptian and the Syrian forces, based on their experience in previous wars. In the War of Independence, the Israeli army was literally born in battle. It was given time to grow and survive by the Arab states, who were unable to coordinate their actions. In 1956, with Great Britain and France as allies, Israel swiftly defeated the Egyptian forces in the Sinai. In 1967 a brilliant preemptive attack by the Israelis utterly routed both Egypt and Syria in what became known as the Six-Day War. After 1967 both sides engaged in a deadly contest called the War of Attrition, which raged until 1970.

During the months leading up to October 1973, Syria's armed forces underwent significant improvement. Under President Hafiz al-Assad's leadership, the army, once rife with corruption, became far more professional, with well-trained officers leading well-equipped and motivated troops. Seven million Syrians created a fighting force that exceeded in numbers and in armor that of many of the major powers of the world, including England, France, and Italy.

But Israel was still a lethal foe. The Israeli Air Force (IAF) was always qualitatively superior by a tremendous degree to the air forces of the Arab nations. This was a matter of discipline, training, dedication, and enormous sacrifice by the Israeli airmen.

The Israeli Army had been formed with the "never-again" philosophy that stemmed from the Holocaust. By 1950 the Israel Defense Force (IDF) modeled itself on a British style of organization and even boasted a new chief of the General Staff, General Yigael Yadin. Only thirty-two years old, Yadin would promulgate five principles that Israel would faithfully follow—until 1973, when the first four were violated. Here are the five:

1. The morale of the country is of the utmost importance.

2. The entire potential of the Israeli community must be fully utilized for war.

3. Unity of command is essential.

4. Israel must operate on the offensive, not the defensive, and must use surprise to the greatest advantage.

5. Israel would need the political support of a major power—most probably the United States—if it went to war again.[2]

To follow Yadin's principles, it became necessary to fulfill the promise of the founder and first Prime Minister of Israel, David Ben-Gurion, to create "a new kind of Jew," by which he meant a Jew who was a fierce, competent soldier. The concept of "dying in the defense of Masada" was pronounced obsolete: losing valiantly was no longer an option. Ben-Gurion took World War II military forces as his model. On the ground he wanted a mobile armored force capable of penetrating far into enemy lines and defeating them as the German Afrika Korps had done in the early days of the desert war. In the air he wanted the hard-hitting precision of the United States Air Forces. Under his guidance, his aims would soon be achieved and Israel was militarily superior to its Arab neighbors.

Ben-Gurion's success came about in large part because of his ability to pick great leaders. First and foremost among these choices was his selection of Moshe Dayan. Dayan personified the "new kind of Jew." Born in Deganya A, the first kibbutz in Palestine, Dayan, balding, one-eyed, and with Spockian ears, would always be the most beloved and the most hated of Israel's politician-generals. No matter what his status, no matter who was in power, Dayan was always a powerful member of the government, a position he had earned by his epic deeds as a soldier and the sheer power of his personality. He maintained the position by savvy political insight and maintaining enough followers to overturn the coalition governments that ruled Israel. It was said that "a large cabinet majority without Dayan is not really a majority."

Moshe Dayan began his military career at the age of four-teen, when he became a member of the Haganah, the secret—and illegal—underground self-defense force of the Zionist movement in Palestine. The Arabs had formed similar groups, and the 1930s were marked by constant reciprocal killings and the cruelest kind of vandalism—despoiling fields, up-rooting orchards, and poisoning water supplies.

Arab violence against both the British and the Jews reached a peak in 1936, at which time Dayan became a *ghaffir,* a member of the Jewish Settlement Police Force, which served as an auxiliary to both the army and the regular police. He was assigned the task of guiding British military units—a Scottish regiment and the Yorkshire Fusiliers—in Palestine in 1937. Later he learned the art of ambush from Orde Win-gate, then a captain and later the leader of the famous "Chin-dits" in Burma.

Imprisoned for sixteen months after being caught on one of his ambush patrols, Dayan went on to fight for the British, losing his left eye in battle during the British invasion of Vichy-French Syria and Lebanon. His vision suffered, but his appearance was enhanced, for the pointy-eared Dayan was pos-itively dashing with his black eye patch.

Dayan's mastery of desert tactics emerged after Israel pro-claimed its independence, when he raised and led the 89th Commando Battalion in daring attacks on Arab positions. His combat experience and his charismatic personality served him well and resulted in his appointment by Ben-Gurion as Chief of Staff. He was the perfect leader to create tough, mobile, and swift-striking armed forces, and as Chief of Staff he would lead his new-style Israeli soldiers to victory in the 1956 Sinai campaign.

Yet the rapid formation of the Jewish state and its armed forces resulted in another "new kind of Jew" being created: the warrior-politician. Dayan was one of these, becoming a member of the Mapai (Labor) Party and serving in the Knesset and in the cabinet. In 1973, Dayan would be one of the principal soldier-politicians who would wreak havoc with the Israeli military machine.

Perhaps more than anything else, however, Dayan's prestige and power stemmed from the deft manner in which he had made Israel into a nuclear power. The infant nation had begun work to this end as early as 1948, when it sent prospectors looking for uranium deposits in the Negev desert. In this endeavor, Israel had been blessed by the leadership of Ernst Bergman, who was a close friend of Ben-Gurion. Bergman developed close association with the French military and scientific community. France had been a world leader in physics prior to World War II but had fallen so completely behind that by 1948 it was on a scientific par with newly emerging Israel. The two nations' needs complemented each other, and France helped build and man the Dimona nuclear facility near Beersheba, in the Negev.

The United States discovered the Dimona facility on a routine U-2 surveillance flight in 1958 and promptly put pressure on Israel not to build nuclear weapons. Ben-Gurion agreed and announced to the world that the reactor would be used only for peaceful purposes. The announcement was palpably false, but then, and forever, the United States preferred to accept Israeli protestations of nuclear probity at face value. Even when Ben-Gurion demonstrated that he was prepared to execute his *ein brerra* (no alternative to first strike) policy at a moment's notice, his word on the peaceful use of nuclear power was not officially questioned.

Israel and France continued to work hand in hand, with Israeli scientists making notable contributions to both nations' programs. The nuclear tests conducted in 1960 that formally introduced France into the ranks of the nuclear powers also brought Israel to that status. Israel soon adopted France's concept of *force de frappe,* meaning that it would work to achieve the ability to strike at the Soviet Union independently, without using the United States as a nuclear umbrella.

Many Israeli leaders were influential in the nuclear program, but none more so than the former Prime Minister Shimon Peres, who saw to it that Bergman's plans were followed in the development process. However, once Israel was nuclear-capable, no one had his hand deeper in the pie than Dayan. It was Dayan, as Minister of Defense, who had two primitive but effective nuclear bombs assembled prior to the 1967 Six-Day War, where the swift turn of events did not require their use. And Dayan was almost solely responsible for the decision to begin serial production of the nuclear warheads in early 1968.

Every Israeli Prime Minister, from David Ben-Gurion on, backed the Israeli development of nuclear weapons, as well as the don't ask, don't tell policy of "nuclear ambiguity." The Israelis viewed their nuclear capability as their single best guarantee for preventing another Holocaust. "Never Again" meant "Never Again at Any Price," and no one was more fervent in this view than Moshe Dayan.

All of this contributed to the effect Dayan would have on the October War. Much of the blame for Israel's surprise was attributed to him, and he used his role as Defense Minister to both intervene and interfere at every turn. Yet it was Dayan who was responsible for Israel's having a nuclear capability, the threat of which may well have stopped the Syrian advance and averted the loss of the war.

Dayan's chief rival for public attention was Ariel Sharon, who was born in 1928 in Kfar Malal, some fifteen miles northeast of Tel Aviv on the coastal Plain of Sharon. His parents, Samuil and Vera, were stoic farmers who wrested a meager living from the barren soil. Samuil was an ardent Zionist but, unlike others in the community, not a socialist.

By the age of thirteen, Ariel Sharon was not only a veteran farmer but also a member of the guards who protected the fields from Arab predators. By fourteen, he was initiated into the Haganah and soon became a member of an elite unit of the underground army, the "Signalers." There he practiced with the small arms that were available, and spent hours learning the desert terrain.

During the War for Independence, the solidly built Sharon distinguished himself as a platoon leader in crucial battles around Latrun, during one of which he was badly wounded. After the war he suggested the formation of an Israeli commando unit and was selected to command it. Fedayeen (suicide squad) raids were becoming more frequent. The fedayeen killed about 1,000 Israelis between 1951 and 1955, and Sharon fought them with his special Unit 101—a foreshadowing of his tactics fifty years later. Actions like this made him a favorite of Ben-Gurion. As Chief of Staff in 1953, Dayan, who had initially opposed special units, merged Unit 101 with the paratroops and placed Sharon as commander of the new force.

Sharon led the unit in some brilliant raids but got into trouble by exceeding his orders during the ill-starred Suez Crisis. There were excessive Israeli casualties as a result, and Sharon's career was temporarily halted.

The political climate changed in 1967, when Yitzhak Rabin became Chief of Staff of the IDF. Sharon was reinstated and promoted to major general. In June of 1967 Sharon distinguished himself in the Six-Day War by commanding a key division.

By 1973, Sharon was out of political favor again and left the army to enter politics. He helped form the Likud Party, and his politics were part of the problem when he returned to command a division in the Yom Kippur War. He was always an aggressive fighter, never hesitating to question— or ignore—orders that he felt were unwise. He was immensely popular with the people and with his troops, but not with his military peers.

Given commanders like Dayan and Sharon, it was not surprising that Israel was successful in war. Nor was it surprising that the brilliant Six-Day War of 1967 gave its citizens and its leaders pride and confidence in the Israeli armed forces.

There was, however, a certain hubris also born of Israel's success that would lead to the early miscalculations that took place that October. As matters transpired, Israeli hubris was most pronounced in exactly the place where it was most dangerous, the vaunted Israeli intelligence system.

Despite the nation's short history, Israeli intelligence operations had achieved world renown, not only for their operations in the Middle East but also for their excursions into Europe, the United States, and Asia. The Israelis pursued the full spectrum of intelligence work, from basic tasks such as creating target folders for future attacks, to influencing elections in foreign countries, to savage assassinations of those perceived to be Israel's enemies.

Like all of Israel's armed forces, its intelligence corps began operations on an ad hoc basis. Some of its first operations occurred before the May 15, 1948, Independence Day, including purchasing arms in Czechoslovakia and using a Douglas DC-4 to smuggle them to a clandestine desert airfield. Only a few weeks later, Israeli intelligence put together the plan that saw the first Israeli fighter planes (Czech-built versions of the Messerschmitt Bf 109) attack an Egyptian tank column nearing Tel Aviv.

After independence, Israeli intelligence services were soon well organized, achieving a professional status that was respected, envied, and feared. The organization was unique in many ways. It was comprised of two main elements. First was the infamous Mossad, which conducted foreign intelligence operations and was responsible for actions that ranged from assassinations to stealing state secrets. It also avenged itself upon anti-Israeli terrorist operations and established a reputation for swift, merciless, and skillfully executed reprisals. The second was the less widely known Directorate of Military Intelligence (called AMAN), which conducted internal intelligence operations that spanned routine military matters to the more demanding assessment of the military capacity and intentions of both friendly and unfriendly nations. AMAN was responsible for preparing the National Intelligence Estimate, which perforce dictated Israeli strategy and foreign policy.

Intelligence functions are vital in every country, but Israel's unique style of government immeasurably enhanced the importance of the AMAN. As Israel was literally pulled from the womb of war by its soldiers, it is not surprising that its governmental positions have been dominated by the presence of the military. The names of soldier-politicians dominate its history, including Dayan, Sharon, Rabin and more. Because of this, the Israel Defense Force has a position unique in democracies, being almost an expression of the government itself. As a military force, it is responsible to the civil government—but the civil government is often indistinguishable from the IDF. The top positions (the Prime Minister and the cabinet) are often held by former Chiefs of Staff or retired generals, who, in time of war, might well relinquish a cabinet position to assume command of a large military unit.

Within this ultramilitary environment, the Director of Military Intelligence had virtually become a cabinet post itself.[3] The DMI nominally reported to the Minister of Defense, but was often called upon to put forth intelligence directly to the Prime Minister and the cabinet.

The brilliant operations that led to the massive success of the Six-Day War (see "Appendix: Born in Battle") enhanced the prestige of the Directorate of Military Intelligence just as it did the prestige of the IDF and IAF. The proper assessment of targets, the split-second timing, and the follow-up attacks all spoke to the harmony between the intelligence service and the fighting arms of the IDF. Not even the long decade of pinprick attacks by Arab forces, many terrorist attacks, or the costly War of Attrition (again, see Appendix) served to diminish the sense of confidence and well-being of the IDF.

Confidence soon gave way to a sense of inevitable victory. Both Israeli intelligence and the IDF believed that no matter what the Arab nations did, they would be defeated soon after the war began. It was considered simply impossible that any combination of Arab effort could defeat the Israelis. The most important element in this belief was in the air supremacy guaranteed by the IAF and demonstrated frequently in combat against the historically inept Egyptian and Syrian air forces.

By 1973 it became a given among Israeli leaders that its intelligence operations would give at least two days' warning of an Arab attack and that this was more than sufficient to mobilize the reserves, bring up the armor, and poise the IAF for devastating air strikes. The Egyptian leaders were generally accepted as rational men who would consider a war possible only when the Egyptian Air Force became powerful and proficient enough that it could launch a surprise attack on Israel and knock out the IAF on the ground. Even with massive Soviet aid and training, this seemed impossible for the moment and improbable for many years to come. It thus became an article of faith to Israeli leaders that war did not make sense for Egypt, for it could not win, and therefore it would not attack. Syria was written off as unable to proceed without Egypt. The Israeli leaders understood that Egypt would continually undertake threatening military maneuvers but these actions were believed to be intended solely to maintain the morale of the armed forces.

All of these factors merged into a single hubristic philosophy: Israel cannot be defeated. All of Israel's military and civilian leaders *knew* that the IDF was invincible in any war against any combination of the Arab states. The Israeli principles of obtaining air superiority and fighting a swift offensive armored war in enemy territory was accepted as a given. And they believed this single-minded philosophy so strongly that they assumed that the Arab leaders, being intelligent men, also believed in it.

This blind faith in the soundness of Israeli intelligence and in the invincibility of Israeli arms was raised to the highest—and most dangerous—level in the person of the director of military intelligence, Major General Eli Zeira. A charismatic leader whose powerful personality governed the way AMAN was run, Zeira had a strong relationship with the minister of defense, Dayan, and was widely respected for his brilliance.[4] Over the years, Zeira crafted AMAN's relationship with the Prime Minister and the cabinet in such a way that allowed him almost to dictate the course of the government in military matters.

When Zeira reported to the cabinet, as he did frequently, he presented a carefully crafted decision paper that offered the results of AMAN's research as a unified point of view. He did not give expression to the opposing minority in his report. His counterpart in the Mossad, Major General Zvi Zamir, was often not invited to cabinet meetings, especially if he disagreed with Zeira. Conducting his briefings in a quantitative style that would have appealed to Robert McNamara, Zeira dazzled everyone with his intimate knowledge of enemy strength and dispositions, reciting the Arab formations by name and evaluating their capability, often down to the number and type of tank in each area. Similar expositions followed on enemy air and naval strength. Zeira salted his briefings with quick flashes of rough military humor, usually a slashing putdown of an Arab leader or, if he was confident enough, a gentler dig at an Israeli colleague. Zeira's listeners had to be impressed, for if he was this knowledgeable about enemy capabilities, it followed that he must be equally knowledgeable about their intentions.

Internally Zeira ran a taut ship and permitted no dissension within AMAN, which had a monopoly on raw intelligence. Any AMAN analyst who volunteered a contrary opinion, even informally to a close friend, would find his career abruptly sidetracked.

Confidence in Zeira's judgment reached an all-time high in the spring of 1973, so much so that Zeira was considered to be almost a member of Golda Meir's cabinet. The Egyptians, as they had done so often, appeared to be preparing for war, but Zeira assured everyone that it was just another bluff. He informed Prime Minister Meir that any attempt by the Egyptians to force a crossing of the Suez Canal would be well known to the Israelis several days in advance. The Israeli Chief of Staff, Lieutenant General David "Dado" Elazar, disagreed, and his deputy, Major General Israel Tal, supported his position. Rough-hewn in appearance, Elazar was a thoughtful man who had been instrumental in building Israel's armored force into a potent weapon. Almost as articulate—if not nearly so handsome and dashing—as Zeira, Elazar saw that Anwar Sadat might have internal political considerations that would force him to go to war knowing that Egypt could not win a complete military victory. It was possible, in Elazar's view, that Sadat might be impelled to go to war simply by the passage of time. Sadat was maintaining hundreds of thousands of soldiers on salary—he might simply have to use them to justify their existence and his tenure of office. Zamir, the chief of Mossad, generally agreed with Elazar, but his opinions were not as widely disseminated as Zeira's.

In May 1973, after weighing all the options, Elazar ordered a partial mobilization, part of a plan called Blue-White, intended to defeat a combined attack by Egypt and Syria.[5] Just as Zeira predicted, the Egyptian threat failed to materialize, and Elazar was castigated for prematurely mobilizing, an exercise that cost Israel by some estimates as much as $35 million. Elazar suffered a serious loss of face, even receiving a public reprimand from the finance minister, who bemoaned the man-hours lost to the economy by the mobilization. (Calling up reservists took them away from their jobs, and the proportion was so great that the economy faltered with each call-up.) Meanwhile, Zeira's reputation—and ego—soared.

Some later analysts believe that Elazar had been correct, despite disavowals by Sadat in his autobiography. The claim has been made that Egypt had in fact intended to go to war in May but did not when the Soviet Union pressured Sadat to postpone the operation. The pressure came directly from Premier Leonid Brezhnev, who did not want his attempts to achieve détente with the United States to be interrupted by a Middle Eastern war.[6]

For the next five months, Zeira would continue to play into the hands of Anwar Sadat, whose guile, duplicity, and capability were equally underestimated by the Israelis and the world. From 1967 through August 1970, the two nations had waged what became known as the War of Attrition, in which both sides tested weapons, installed new equipment, and launched every sort of attack upon each other. Some of the battles were mere firefights between opposing infantry units; others were massive artillery battles, with as many as a thousand guns belching fire. In the air, the IAF had difficulty counteracting the ever-increasing numbers of surface-to-air missiles (SAMs) and antiaircraft artillery (AAA) of the Egyptians. To offset the potential for an Egyptian invasion, the Israelis constructed what became known as the Bar-Lev line, a system of fortifications designed to delay any Egyptian military incursion until reserve forces could be brought forward. (For more details, see "Appendix: Born in Battle.")

A general pattern had developed in which the Israelis would react with massive retaliation to every Egyptian initiative. Sadat had become convinced that Egypt might as well make the heaviest possible all-out attack, because it would receive a vicious Israeli response no matter the degree of engagement. And despite the influx of Soviet weapons and technicians, Sadat and his key military men had no doubts about the superiority of the IAF and the excellence of the IDF's armored formations. Yet in February 1972 offsets to both these problems were provided by the Soviet Union.

It was suggested to Egypt's Minister of War, General Ahmed Ismail Ali, during his visit to the Kremlin that year, that a sufficient number of a variety of missile types would shift the balance of power. The Soviet military advisers believed that the Israeli air superiority might be countered by the establishment of a massive "missile wall" along the banks of the Suez Canal and the Golan Heights. If sufficient SA-2, SA-3, and SA-6 missiles were available, supplemented by the new handheld SA-7 Grail missile launchers and heavy anti-aircraft batteries, the IAF could be countered and Egyptian forces would be able to operate without the devastating losses incurred in every previous campaign. Additional SAMs would also be sent to Syria, to counter Israeli air operations there.

The SA-2s were Mach 3.5 missiles effective at altitudes up to and beyond 60,000 feet and had a slant range of about 23 miles. The SA-3s flew at Mach 2.1, had a range of up to 13.7 miles, and operated at altitudes from 50 to 50,000 feet. The SA-6 Gainful missiles were designed for lower altitudes. A SA-6 system consisted of a radar/fire-control unit and four transporter/launcher vehicles, each carrying three missiles. The missile itself had a slant range of 17 miles against low-altitude targets. The heat-seeking SA-7 was inexpensive and could be provided by the thousands. It weighed only twenty pounds and carried a 5.5-pound warhead. With a speed of Mach 1.5 and a range of about 4,000 yards, the SA-7 could be fired in barrages against low-flying aircraft.[7] The SA-7 proved very successful against U.S. aircraft when used by the North Vietnamese in their Spring 1972 invasion of South Vietnam.

The missile systems had a perfect complement in the ZSU 23/4 antiaircraft system, which was built on the same tracked chassis as the SA-6. Its four water-cooled 23mm guns could put out 4,000 rounds per minute to defend the missile sites against low-level threats. Ground-controlled intercept for fighters had long been a Soviet strong point. These missiles and guns were integrated into a defense network using multiple radar systems and command centers that provided extremely good protection from Israeli air attack. And to offset the threat of long-range raids by Israeli aircraft, which had proved so devastating to morale in the years since the Six-Day War, the Soviet

Union offered SS-1C Scud and FROG (free rockets over ground) surface-to-surface missiles, which would be able to strike Israel's major cities from Egypt. The Syrians fired more than twenty FROG missiles during the October War, killing a number of military and civil personnel.

It was believed that the presence of Scuds would be a deterrent to Israeli air raids. And if they did not deter, they could exact some modicum of revenge. The Scud, which would become notorious in the Iraq-Iran and Persian Gulf wars, was a primitive descendant of the German V-2. It had a range of about 200 miles and carried a 1,800-pound high-explosive warhead. As primitive as it was, it was a weapon of great importance to Sadat, and it convinced him that he could now go to war, even though the Soviet Union wisely decided to retain control of the use of the weapons.

The third leg of the Arab missile triad consisted of the introduction of massive amounts of antitank weapons to neutralize Israeli armor. In addition to superb Soviet artillery and tanks, the Arabs were provided with thousands of shoulder-fired rocket-powered grenades, AT-3 Sagger missiles, and BRDM-2 armored missile-carrying vehicles. The RPGs were the direct descendant of World War II bazookas and panzerfausts and fired a five-pound shaped high-explosive charge over a range of 545 yards. The AT-3 Sagger missile was a medium-to-long-range wire-guided antitank missile carrying a six-pound warhead and delivered at speeds up to 267 mph. The BRDM-2s were swift wheeled scout cars, capable of up to 60 mph speeds and carrying six Sagger missiles.

None of these weapons was revolutionary, and their counterparts could be found in armed forces around the world. What was different was the massive numbers of these armaments with which the Egyptians and Syrians would be equipped. The shoulder-fired RPGs were found in quantity at platoon level, while the BDRM-2s and Saggers filled battalions and brigades with the immense firepower necessary to dominate tank battles.

With this abundance of weaponry, the Soviet Union helped Egypt and Syria offset three major advantages the Israelis had previously enjoyed and still counted on: air supremacy, armored supremacy, and deep strikes into Egypt. Now all Sadat needed was the element of surprise to make sure of the success of his plans.

Anwar Sadat, dark-hued (so dark that his Egyptian enemies conferred the nickname Black Ass upon him) and with a flashing smile and penetrating gaze, was not taken seriously by Western leaders for many months after his becoming President of Egypt after Nasser's death on September 28, 1970. Even so astute an observer as Henry Kissinger thought that Sadat was an interim replacement, one who would in turn be displaced by a stronger leader.

Sadat was born on December 25, 1918, in the small village of Mit Abul Kum in the Nile Delta, his mother the daughter of a freed Sudanese slave. Smart and energetic, he attended the military academy and rose to the rank of Lieutenant Colonel. Violently opposed to British influence in Egypt, he joined with Nasser in the group of Free Officers who seized power on July 23, 1952. Sadat served Nasser effectively but built no political power base for himself. Once Sadat was in power, however, his intelligence and energy quickly consolidated his position.

In his memoirs, Kissinger recalls Sadat as "a great man," an accolade he does not often give. Kissinger particularly admired Sadat's psychological discernment, noting that he handled the four U.S. presidents that he dealt with (Nixon, Ford, Carter, and Reagan) with great skill. Sadat was in fact forceful and decisive and able to keep his own counsel. In the manner of many wise people, he masked his shrewdness with what seemed to be naïveté.

Yet Sadat was still unproven in 1971, which he regarded as his year of decision. It was then that he determined to liberate the Sinai even if it cost 1 million Egyptian lives, and one part of his plan was providing disinformation not only to his enemies but also to his friends, as Syria and the Soviet Union would discover. The principal Egyptian disinformation campaign was directed against Israel, and it was masterful, playing in each instance to the Israelis' overweening confidence in themselves and their scarcely veiled contempt for their Arab enemies.[8]

The disinformation plan was convincing because Sadat remained bellicose, always proclaiming his intention to go to war with Israel. He stated so publicly in April 1973 and repeated it often thereafter, to the point that he began to lose support and credibility among other Arab nations.[9] Behind the scenes, Sadat attempted to overcome this by promising that an Arab-Israeli war would permit Arab nations to invoke the "oil weapon" effectively for the first time. With oil production reduced and oil prices skyrocketing, the West would think twice about aiding Israel. In a single stroke, the Arab world would be united even as it was made rich by huge oil revenues. In this thinking, Sadat was absolutely correct; when war came, the European NATO nations resolutely refused to assist Israel in any way. Fortunately, Portugal would be an exception, allowing the USAF the use of Lajes Airfield in the Azores.

In early 1973 Sadat established a special disinformation staff. Some of its members established elaborate ruses to soothe Israeli suspicions; for example, notice was given in the newspapers of hundreds of army officers going on leave to make a religious pilgrimage. Egyptian and Syrian troops were encouraged to play soccer in view of the Israelis or to swim or fish in the Suez Canal. Others on this special staff were tasked to monitor comments from Israel and around the world. Their technique was then to leak information to foreign correspondents that confirmed rather than denied any material disparaging Egyptian and Syrian capability. Israeli leaders, including Dayan and Rabin, repeatedly expressed their opinion that Egypt and Syria were not going to go to war. In each case, Sadat's special staff backed them up with carefully leaked stories that emphasized how unprepared Egypt's armed forces were. It should also be noted that Israeli and U.S. intelligence worked hand in glove and their estimates were almost always closely aligned. This was natural enough, for the United States had great respect for the Israeli intelligence capability. It recognized that Israel was more focused on Middle Eastern problems than the United States could be and generally tended to rubber-stamp Israeli assessments.

Meanwhile, Sadat played Ziera and the AMAN like a violin. He carefully stroked Israeli egos and fed them what they wished to hear. Israel's intelligence eventually found itself in a position where it could rationally explain every Egyptian and Syrian action, no matter how threatening. As a typical example, the IAF had given the Syrian Air Force a drubbing on September 13, shooting down a dozen Syrian aircraft without losing a single Mirage. Later in the month, when the Syrian army began a tremendous buildup in the Golan Heights and Syrian Su-7 and Su-20 fighter-bombers were flown into advanced bases near Israel, the actions were explained as being merely indications of "fear of Israel" and responses to the September 13 air battle.

In a similar way, the huge buildup of Egyptian forces along the Suez Canal, which included the assembly of bridging equipment on an unprecedented scale, was explained as being "just another maneuver" and another expression of Egyptian "brinkmanship." When a brash young officer, Lieutenant Benjamin Siman Tov, analyzed Egyptian maneuvers and predicted war, his report was not only ignored; it was also pigeonholed—until the postwar investigation of the intelligence fiasco.

The most carefully thought out portion of Sadat's disinformation campaign was the skill with which he handled his relations with the Soviet Union. After having expelled some twenty thousand Soviet military advisers from Egypt in June 1972, Sadat allowed the USSR to woo him with ever larger promises of equipment beginning in February 1973. He even permitted some fifteen hundred highly skilled Soviet advisers back to supervise the installation of the advanced missiles and to train the Egyptian forces.

All during this period, Sadat had maintained an unusual commodity for Arab forces: secrecy. Only a handful of top leaders knew that war was planned for October 6. Sadat's concern for security extended even to his Syrian ally; he did not inform Syria of Egypt's true war plans until well after the war had started. He also did not inform his patron, the Soviet Union, that he had maintained a secret line of communication with the United States since 1971. So clever was Sadat in this regard that he soon identified Henry Kissinger, then only the National Security Adviser, as the man who had Nixon's ear instead of the Secretary of State, William Rogers.

In effect, Sadat mesmerized Israel, openly proclaiming his intention of going to war and moving vast forces to the Suez Canal, forces of such a size and nature that their capability, if not their intent, could not be concealed. Even casual analysis, if made without the blinders of overconfidence, would have revealed that the buildup was larger than ever before. More important, the buildup showed evidence that the Egyptians had learned the lessons of the War of Attrition, for the assembly of SAMs was unprecedented. Yet Israel remained blind to the threat even when the Soviet Union suddenly moved units of its fleet from Egyptian ports and began evacuating Soviet citizens from Cairo via a massive airlift on October 3.[10] Sadat had reacted furiously to this, accusing the Soviet Union of deliberately giving away the fact that war was imminent. And indeed they had—but the oblivious Israelis simply discounted this as they had all the other warning signs.

The triad of missiles so lavishly supplied by the Soviet Union had provided the Arab forces with a counter to Israeli air and armored superiority. Sadat's successful disinformation campaign had now deprived Israel of its most essential commodity, the time to mobilize. The date to open the war, October 6, had been chosen for three reasons. First, the tides and currents would be favorable for bridging the canal. Second, as Yom Kippur was the holiest Jewish holiday, many people would be on leave, there would be no television or radio broadcasts, and mobilization would be slowed. Third, October 6 happened to fall on the tenth day of Ramadan, historically the date upon which the Prophet Muhammad had begun his preparations for the Battle of Badr, which enabled him to return to Mecca. The Egyptians used the name Operation Badr for their planned assault into the Sinai.

The exact time to start the war had been the subject of much discussion between Sadat and Assad. The Syrians wanted a morning attack, so that the sun would be in the eyes of the Israelis; the Egyptian wanted a late-afternoon attack for the same reason. A compromise was reached: the war would begin at 2:00 P.M.[11]

2   A New Kind of Arab Soldier

ON OCTOBER 6, AN AVALANCHE of one hundred thousand
artillery shells began at 2:00 P.M., hammering the Israeli
positions for two hours and sparing no one. In the thinly
manned Bar-Lev line along the Suez Canal, the Israeli commanders at strongholds Orkel, Lahtzanit, Ketuba, and Hi-
yazon were killed in the first barrage, along with many of
their deputies. Dozens of others died, some in prayer
shawls, some in battle jackets. Younger noncommissioned
officers stepped forward to take command and to hold on as
loaded rafts crammed with Egyptian soldiers began to
plunge across the canal. Though the Egyptians had not
learned that war was coming until that very morning, many
were exalted with a religious joy, their hopes buoyed by the
obvious surprise they had obtained. Their mission was simple: they were going back to reclaim their land, stolen from
them and profaned by the Israelis. Eight thousand troops
swarmed ashore, putting down a covering fire on the Israeli
strongholds and establishing bridgeheads that would allow
armor and manpower to come streaming across into the territory. Soon several pontoon bridges were in place, supplemented by thirty-one ferries churning back and forth like
water beetles. More would follow.

Hafiz al-Assad, the President of Syria, had long planned
for this day, which he intended to be the pinnacle of his long
career. Assad, born in 1930 in a tiny village in the northwest
of Syria, had been a career air force officer, a pilot. He worked
his way up in the military and, after a series of coups, seized
power to become Prime Minister of Syria in 1970, assuming
the presidency in February 1971.

An extremely hard worker who put in long hours covering

the most detailed minutiae of his office, Assad was highly disciplined, a vegetarian who drank no alcohol. He built up a Stalin-like cult of personality that saw his smiling visage on posters everywhere. His propaganda emphasized that he was the first man from the peasant class to rise to become Syria's leader, and his people liked the idea. Assad ruled with an iron hand, steadfastly and cruelly suppressing any domestic opposition. In one instance he reportedly stifled incipient resistance by killing twenty thousand of his own people in the Syrian town of Hama.

Assad was nonetheless a Syrian patriot who had the courage of his convictions and pursued policies he considered to be in Syria's interest, regardless of Arab or world opinion. He was the only Arab leader to ally himself with Iran in its war with Iraq, a courageous move, given Iraq's long border with Syria.

An extremely tough man with whom to negotiate, Assad followed every argument closely, sought definitions for every word, and never conceded anything that might be in Syria's interest. When foreign dignitaries visited, it was his habit to meet with them alone at first, using the visitor's translator if necessary. Assad would go through all the essential points of the meeting, down to the finest detail. Then, with a clear idea of the approach he wished to take, he would call in his own advisers and translators and repeat the entire meeting. It was his custom in negotiations to always present a position that was impossible for the visitor to accede to and which far exceeded his own requirements. Having done so, he would reluctantly "concede" points, moving back toward a position that actually met his needs.

Although a tough negotiater, Assad had a mordant sense of humor that he used even when discussing the most serious subjects. Sometimes the cruelty of his jokes could be read in the nervous reactions of his staff, for whom these jokes had a meaning all too real.

Assad was determined never again to have a debacle like the 1967 war, and his harsh methods had a tonic effect on his armed forces, which were by 1973 better trained and equipped than at any other time in Syria's history. And while he viewed all nations, including his Arab allies, with suspicion, he felt that his interests were parallel with those of Egypt's Anwar Sadat. Although other Arab countries, Jordan and Iraq in particular, professed their desire to go to war once again with Israel, Assad did not count on them. He believed that Egypt and Syria had sufficient military might to achieve his objective, which was to take back the Golan Heights.

Although Assad was a micromanager, prudence dictated that he delegate the conduct of the war to Major General Yusuf Shakkur, who could be assigned the blame if things did not go well. Shakkur mustered what amounted to seven divisions. He planned to use his overwhelming superiority in tanks (some 1,200 deployed along a fifty-mile front) and 600 pieces of artillery to isolate the Israeli forces in the Golan Heights from reinforcement and then systematically destroy them.

In the north, Shakkur followed Soviet military doctrine, laying down a fifty-minute artillery barrage. Forty-five minutes after the shelling began, four Soviet-built Mil Mi-8 helicopters landed elite Syrian commandos of the 82nd Parachute Regiment and captured the strategic Mount Hermon in a feat reminiscent of Hitler's 1940 attack on the Belgian Fort Eben Emael.[1] The Israelis were shocked by the precision and daring, for it did not jibe with their concept of the Syrian army. From the assault on Mount Hermon, the war immediately took on a totally different tone.[2]

The commandos of the 82nd were the toughest, most reliable troops in the Syrian army and had been perfectly briefed on their target.[3] The 9,232-foot Mount Hermon, called the Eyes of the State of Israel, was a massive, arrogant insult to Syrian sovereignty. It was Israel's key electronic-warfare outpost, theoretically able to read, track, or jam Syrian communications at will. Despite its importance, Mount Hermon was weakly defended, with only a few troops and a large contingent of noncombatant technicians. There were no heavy weapons and only a few light machine guns available for its defense—a telling indictment of Israeli overconfidence.

The main battle lasted for less than an hour. The Syrians gained possession of the mountaintop, and the Israeli defenders withdrew into the bunkers below, splitting up as they went, fighting a Stalingrad-like battle, room by room, hallway by hallway. Eventually the Israeli commander led a subterranean breakout with twenty of his men—only nine of whom would reach Israeli lines. Among the prizes captured by the Syrians were documents that compromised Israeli military codes. The sophisticated electronic gear on Mount Hermon was promptly shipped to the Soviet Union for analysis.

The defeat, coupled with the utter ignominy of a commander escaping and leaving some of his troops behind, was the first of a series of blows that would devastate Israeli morale. Israel had suffered defeats before, but always in a fight to the death. Never had a position been abandoned by a commander with troops still fighting. Was it possible that the IDF had somehow lost its will to win?

Back in Tel Aviv, the entire fabric of General Zeira's blanket assurances of peace had come unraveled at 4:00 A.M. October 6 when he received a call from a trusted Mossad agent that stated Egypt and Syria were going to launch a war "late that afternoon."[4] Zeira immediately informed Prime Minister Golda Meir, who called a meeting for 7:00 A.M. with her Minister of Defense, Dayan; the Chief of Staff, Elazar; Yisrael Galilli, a minister without portfolio and part of Meir's kitchen cabinet; and Deputy Prime Minister Yigal Allon.

It would characterize the opening phase of the war that the Minister of Defense and the Chief of Staff would immediately disagree on what to do. Elazar was furious with himself that he had not insisted on mobilization in October as he had done in May—he was now in the position of being on the wrong side of the fence twice.[5] He now recommended an immediate mobilization of the IAF and the equivalent of four divisions—meaning almost total mobilization of the army. His boss, Dayan, opposed this. He insisted that the Egyptians could not cross the canal in less than twenty-four hours and thus called only for the mobilization of the IAF and of two divisions, one each for the Northern and Southern fronts.[6] Dayan, like Elazar, was in an intolerable position for a man with a strong ego: all of his advice on the probability of war had been wrong, and now he had to redeem himself with superior diplomatic insight.

Elazar and Major General Bennie Peled, the argumentative head of the IAF, had met earlier, at 5:00 A.M. They were certain that a preemptive strike in the style of the Six-Day War was necessary. Peled had sent out preliminary orders to prepare an attack for noon, but to pull off comprehensive strikes in both Egypt and Syria they had to have immediate government approval. Dayan was in favor of a lesser degree of mobilization and against a preemptive air strike because he felt that it would portray Israel as the aggressor to the world. Meir agreed about the preemptive strike but allowed Elazar to mobilize 100,000 men, twice the number that Dayan had proposed.[7] In any event, Elazar called for the mobilization of almost 200,000, counting on the fog of war to cover his bending Meir's instructions.

Meir still clung to the hope that diplomacy might somehow avert war. A hard but fascinating life had given her a remarkable personality, at once commanding and warm, capable of being stern but blessed with a sense of humor, even in the tough times of 1973. (On one occasion she was able to quip that she was disappointed in Moses, complaining that he had traversed the desert for forty years with the Jewish people, then led them to the one spot in the Middle East that had no oil.) Born in Kiev, Russia, in 1898, she spent from 1906 to 1921 in the United States, before moving to Palestine with her husband, Morris Meyerson. She had become a magnificent fund-raiser for the Zionists and a leader in the Jewish independence movement. In 1948, at the height of the struggle, David Ben-Gurion sent her, disguised as an Arab, to negotiate with King Abdullah of Jordan. She became the first Israeli ambassador to the Soviet Union in that same year.

As time passed, her quick mind and fluent speech won her a place first in Israel's Knesset and then in cabinet posts. When Prime Minister Levi Eshkol died suddenly in 1969, she succeeded him, becoming the second female Prime Minister in the world, after Indira Gandhi.

Throughout Meir's career, personal diplomacy had been her strong suit, and now she contacted the U.S. ambassador to Israel, Kenneth Keating. She told him that Israel would not make a preemptive strike but begged him to have Washington inform Egypt, Syria, and the USSR that Israel was aware of their intentions. Her forlorn hope was that if Egypt and Syria knew the element of surprise was lost, they might yet pull back.

News of the imminent war ricocheted around the world like a bullet, caroming from one diplomat to the next. Kissinger's surprise has already been noted, and the reaction in Moscow was not far different. The Soviets knew the war was imminent but had hoped until the very last that Sadat would somehow listen to reason. Now both superpowers began maneuvering to limit their exposure while at the same time obtaining as much diplomatic advantage as possible. Like a bickering married couple, the two superpowers would swap strategies more than once as the military situation changed.

The Kremlin viewed the war with deep misgivings. Relations with the Arab nations had never truly solidified and depended primarily on bribes and a cornucopia of supplies, equipment, and training to maintain the fragile and unlikely alliance of communism and pan-Arabism. The war was inevitably a no-win situation for the Soviet Union. If the Arabs won a striking victory, they would only become more independent and have less need for Soviet aid. If they lost, Soviet client states would have been defeated by an ally of the United States. In either case, the détente with the Americans that Brezhnev regarded as his crowning achievement would be destroyed.

This fact became of singular importance. While Brezhnev was inclined to compromise and save détente, President Nixon and Henry Kissinger were not. Kissinger especially regarded the removal of Soviet influence from the Middle East as far more important than the preservation of détente. This key difference would become almost a controlling factor all through the war and particularly when the timing of a cease-fire became the paramount issue.

The Soviet ambassadors to Egypt and Syria, Vladimir Vinogradov and Nuritdin Mukhitdinov, respectively, had been given warnings that war was imminent, but the first actual word of war received by the USSR was a telephone call from Kissinger to Soviet ambassador Anatoly Dobrynin in New York, at 6:40 A.M. EST on October 6. Dobrynin, as was so often the case with Soviet politics, was caught completely by surprise. His rivals in the Kremlin had not passed along the information garnered from Vinogradov, Mukhitdinov, and elsewhere. Dobrynin was not even aware that Soviet families had been evacuated from Egypt two days before.[8]

The initial communications between Washington and Moscow were both circumspect and accommodating. Each side assured the other that it was gathering information and that it hoped that the conflict could be localized and the peace quickly reestablished. The Americans passed on Prime Minister Meir's assurance that there had been no preemptive strike by the Israelis, a touchy point given the results of the Six-Day War.

Kissinger began a marathon series of telephone calls to key diplomats, including the chargé d' affaires at the Israeli embassy, Mordechai Shalev; the Israeli Foreign Minister, Abba Eban; the Egyptian Foreign Minister, Mohamed el-Zayat; and the Secretary-General of the United Nations, Kurt Waldheim. (Kissinger could not contact anyone in the Syrian embassy—the phone rang unanswered.) Sadat's secrecy had been superb—everyone Kissinger called was caught off guard by the attack.

Kissinger enjoyed being at the center of the global diplomatic network, and it was a role he played well. With President Nixon sorely preoccupied with Watergate and the growing scandal of Vice President Spiro Agnew, Kissinger was in a position to make decisions not ordinarily given to the Secretary of State. His authority was enhanced by his retention of his role of National Security Adviser, which allowed him to "suggest" how U.S. military forces should be employed in reaction to the crisis.

In the meantime, casualties were mounting in the Middle East.

General Hosni Mubarak was Commander in Chief of the Egyptian Air Force and future President of Egypt. An expert pilot, Mubarak had an innate aura of command, a dignified solidity that lent credence to his words. He had moved rapidly up in rank to take command of the EAF in 1972. Mubarak masked a somewhat dour nature with a big grin that he turned off and on like a searchlight. His military bearing and good looks were enhanced by his knack for pleasant conversation, all qualities that would stand him in good stead on the diplomatic circuit.

Mubarak was pleased by the first two hours of attack. Egyptian planes had destroyed Israeli Hawk missile sites and radar installations as well as airfields in the Sinai.[9] In the course of the day, Mubarak's greatest satisfaction would come from the 450 sorties flown in support of the bridging operations taking place at eleven points along the Suez. When the IAF had attempted to intervene in the crossing, it suffered severe losses from the SAMs already in place.

Mubarak relished the fact that Tel Aviv would be struck

by his modern cruise missiles. Late that afternoon, his swift twin-jet Tupolev Tu-16 Badger bombers, the Soviet equivalent of the Boeing B-47, had launched AS-5 Kelt guided missiles. The results from these Kelt attacks were not as promised. The Kelt had originally been designed as an antishipping missile, but its massive 2,205-pound warhead and 120-plus-mile range made it a serious threat to Tel Aviv. During the course of the war, twenty-five Kelts were launched against Israeli targets. Israeli fighters and antiaircraft destroyed twenty of these. Two of the remaining five made direct hits on Sinai radar sites, destroying them and giving rise to speculation that they had been equipped with an antiradiation seeker. The other three landed in unpopulated areas. The Egyptian army complemented the cruise missile effort by firing FROG missiles against Israeli command posts. The FROG was not very accurate but carried a 1,000-pound warhead over twenty-five miles and was devastating when it hit Israeli fortifications.

Mubarak personally planned the first air strike against Israeli airfields with an armada of 222 fighters and fighter-bombers. His MiG-17s, MiG-21s, Sukhoi Su-7s, and Su-20s were joined by Iraqi Hawker Hunters. All took off at different times from a number of different airfields, but all crossed the canal at exactly the same time, a point of pride with Mubarak, for it demonstrated the EAF's discipline and training. As further evidence of Arab success at secrecy, only the pilots flying the strikes knew they were going to war. Their mechanics did not find out until the planes returned damaged or with their gun ports blackened.

The Egyptian fighters hit eight different Israeli airfields. The squat-looking MiGs and Sukhois would roar in at a low level, then pop up to rip holes in the runway with "dibber bombs," which, unlike most of their weapons, were built in Egypt. Parachute retarded, the dibber bomb had a rocket engine that fired the bomb deep into the subsurface of the concrete runway. Delayed-action bombs were also dropped, to hinder runway repair. The force also attacked radar installations, missile sites, and fuel dumps. They were greeted with a barrage of antiaircraft fire (most from Soviet equipment captured from the Arabs, ironically enough) and missiles that managed to shoot down four Su-7s while two F-4s accounted for seven MiGs. Overhead, MiG-21s, tiny silver triangles in the October sky, flew their combat air patrols, ready to dive on any Israeli aircraft that got off the ground. At the end of the day, only five Egyptian fighters had been lost. While the damage inflicted on Israel did not compare to that received by the Arabs during the first hours of the Six-Day War, it was substantial, particularly to the IAF runways.

The only significant Egyptian defeat on Yom Kippur was the loss of fourteen of the workhorse Mi-8 helicopters launched at dusk and used to carry commandos to the Mitla Pass in the Sinai. They fell to Israeli fighters and antiaircraft guns. The news was welcome in Tel Aviv, as it was about the only positive event in the course of a tortured day.

Nevertheless, the first air attacks vindicated Sadat's faith in the EAF and moved Mubarak to center stage in the military/political hierarchy. In 1981 he would succeed the assassinated Sadat as president of Egypt.

Missions against Israeli targets and, indeed, vital incursions into its territory were made easier by the tiny size of the country, surrounded on almost every side by enemies. When it won its independence in 1948, it measured only 275 miles long from its extremities in the north and the south. Its width varied from a maximum of 75 miles to a minimum of about 15 miles—or forty-five minutes in a tank—where Jordan's border edged close to Tel Aviv. The successful Six-Day War in 1967 provided Israel for the first time with some breathing space. In the north, the occupation of the Golan Heights added only about 12 miles in depth but gave the security of the high ground. On its eastern front with Jordan, Israel established a line extending along the Jordan River, so that Tel Aviv was now 50 miles from the border. But the most important area was the 23,500 square miles of the huge Sinai Peninsula wrested from Egypt. Israel's border now extended to the Suez Canal and the Gulf of Suez. Israel's territory had grown from 7,992 square miles to approximately 38,500 square miles.

Yet in an air war the distances were still short. Israel's greatest length ran from a point inside the Golan Heights to the Sharm al-Sheikh at the tip of the Sinai Peninsula—a distance of about 400 miles, or just forty minutes in a jet airplane. At its greatest width, Israel spanned 200 miles at a point between Jordan's Aqaba in the southeast and Egypt's Port Said in the northwest—twenty minutes in a jet. Tel Aviv remained terribly vulnerable, only a few minutes away from an attack by Jordan and less than twenty minutes from an attack by Egypt.

Unfortunately for the Arab air forces, the war would soon become more difficult when surprise was no longer a factor. While providing the most advanced modern hardware, Moscow had declined to provide the essential electronic devices, including chaff and flares, which were necessary for combat. The Soviet rationale, while perhaps difficult to understand, was totally consistent with their Middle Eastern policy. While they wanted their Arab clients to have sufficient weapons to deter an Israeli attack, they were less willing to provide them with all they needed to initiate a war. In this way, the Soviets completely misjudged Sadat, despite his clear warnings. Sadat was willing to go to war with the weapons he had in hand, even if they were not perfect.

When Prime Minister Meir turned down the request for a preemptive attack, General Peled found himself in the position of Admiral Nagumo in the Battle of Midway: his aircraft were armed with one type of weapons when another type was suddenly called for.[10] The offensive bombs and missiles had to be off-loaded and the aircraft reloaded with air-to-air missiles.

Despite this, thirty minutes after the first Egyptian strike, the IAF launched a sweeping counter against Egyptian bridges and troop concentrations. Raids on Egyptian airfields would not take place until the following day, and these were disappointing, for Israeli 500- and 750-pound bombs bounced off the individual concrete aircraft shelters the Egyptians had built at almost every airfield. Where in 1967 the Israelis had gutted the enemy's air force in the first wave, most of the Egyptian first-line equipment was now well protected.

As frustrating as the airfield attacks proved to be, they were far better than the next series of sorties, delivered against the ever-growing horde of Egyptians racing across the military bridges that crossed the canal. It was here that the IAF met with disaster, one that shook the confidence of the Israeli government and had even the most audacious Israeli leaders concerned about the future.

Major General Muhammad Ali Fahmi commanded the sophisticated Egyptian air defense system. Fahmi had 75,000 men in his air defense command, compared to only 25,000 in the entire IAF.[11] His men operated more than 150 SA-2, SA-3, and SA-6 SAM batteries, plus many thousands of SA-7 shoulder-mounted missiles and antiaircraft guns. Sixty of the SAM batteries were stationed along the canal. The SA-6s would prove to be the most dangerous, for they were swift, hard to see, and impossible to jam with standard IAF electronic counterwarfare equipment.

The IAF flew straight into the heart of the storm, sending 200 sorties against the bridges (some of which were decoys). On the surface it seemed like a routine, if admittedly difficult, attack, much like those executed during the War of Attrition. In fact, it was far different, because of the intensity of the Egyptian defenses and the skill with which the Egyptians repaired damaged bridges. In the first 200 sorties, the Egyptians claimed twenty-seven aircraft downed while the Israelis officially admitted to the loss of four aircraft. It would not be until the following day that aerial losses would constitute a significant portion of Israeli strength and, worse, a tremendous share of their best and most qualified pilots. Almost every loss was from SAMs or antiaircraft fire. The news would stun Meir and Dayan and immediately create a demand for swift aid from the United States.

The Israelis, so expert in the Rommel style of slashing tank attacks in the Sinai, elected to use a Rommel defensive tactic on the austere but strangely beautiful plateau that was the Golan Heights. The most useful products of the inhospitable heights, ripped by valleys and covered with dust and low desert shrubs, were the stones it yielded to build defense works. Wrested from Syria in the Six-Day War, the heights extended some forty-five miles from the now-captured Mount Hermon in the north to the Yarmuk River in the south.

Heavily outnumbered in both tanks and manpower, the Israelis had assumed that their air force would be the third and decisive dimension in their intricate defense plan. On the ground, the Israelis had built elaborate tiered defenses to provide cover in the terrain that separated them from the Syrians. These ramparts, keyed to a low ridge of volcanic rock on the west side of the valley, would not have been out of place in Roman times, but instead of mounting catapults they concealed Israeli tanks, just as Rommel had concealed his in North Africa. It was much closer to Maginot Line theory than the Bar-Lev line and was to be defended at all costs. These ramparts used an antitank ditch, mines, and fortifications to channel enemy armor into the desired spots. The Israelis planned to bleed their Syrian opponents with defensive tactics and air attacks. When sufficient damage had been done, the IDF tanks would lash out in mobile ground attacks, supported, as always, by the IAF.

The Syrians, however, were very well equipped. The Soviets had excelled in building first-rate tanks since World War II, and they had lavishly supplied the Syrians with some fifteen hundred T-54, T-55, and T-62 tanks. The very similar T-54s and T-55s were 80,000-pound monsters, armed with excellent 100mm cannon and capable of speeds of up to 30 mph on the flat stretches of the valley. The T-62 was a far more sophisticated weapon, introduced in 1962 and equipped with a 115mm cannon, but considered by many to be more vulnerable than the earlier models. All three tanks were somehow sleeker and more sinister than their Israeli counterparts, who were equipped with a mixed bag of British Centurion, U.S. Patton, and upgraded but aging U.S. Sherman tanks. The Centurion and Patton tanks were heavy, at 115,000 pounds and 108,000 pounds, respectively. The Sherman was lighter at 72,000 pounds. All three had been equipped with 105mm cannon, which outranged the guns mounted on Syrian tanks by as much as 1,500 feet. Israeli strategy was to dig their tanks in along the ramparts so as to have a maximum field of fire and expose as little of their surface as possible. Knowing that they would be outnumbered, they invested time and money in training their gunners for sharpshooting work. It was a clever and economic strategy—as long as the Syrians did not break through their lines. If somehow they did create a breach, the plan was to use mobile reserves to prevent them from bursting across the River Jordan into the heart of Israel. Unfortunately, the surprise attack precluded the arrival of those reserves.

The war in the Golan Heights was divided into two sectors. The Syrians positioned three infantry divisions—the 5th, 7th, and 9th—forward, each one equipped with 200 tanks and other supporting armor. Crouched in the rear were the 1st and 3rd Armored Divisions, each with 250 tanks. Another 400 tanks were split up among independent brigades and reserves. No fewer than 1,000 artillery pieces supported the attack. The Israeli forces in the Golan had been reinforced, but they were still heavily outnumbered, with only 170 tanks and 60 artillery pieces divided between two armored brigades, the 7th toward the north and the 188th back closer to the south. The 7th was the elite of the Israeli army, while the 188th—called the Barak Brigade—was somewhat under strength and had a large reserve component.

The Syrian plan of attack called for a massive effort to overrun Israeli positions in the north and to split the 188th Brigade in the south on the first day of battle.[12] The following day they were to regroup and drive on to the Sea of Galilee.

In the northern sector of the front, huge masses of Syrian infantry waited as the seemingly endless ranks of armor poured forward in parade-ground style to form two main elements. The first element moved to the north, then split to attack Israeli positions at Nafekh and Kuneitrah, both already worked over by air and artillery attack. The second engaged the Israeli positions toward the southern end of the Golan Front.

The Syrian tanks maintained an open formation as they clanked their way to war. They moved implacably, concealed by a curtain of dust hanging across the battlefield like a shroud and constantly renewed by the thousands of shells pulverizing the rocky valley floor. There were many more Syrian cannons than there were Israeli military targets, so the artillery barrage also set its sights on the tiny villages behind the Heights.

The Purple Line, so called from the way it was inked on maps, marked the boundary of Israeli-occupied territory in the Golan Heights. Fifteen fortified outposts had been built, but like the principal one, Mount Hermon, they were neither strongly manned nor well equipped. The Syrian tanks moved forward unimpeded until they bumped into a monumental error, one of those classic foul-ups that punctuate warfare. The Syrian engineers had not yet bridged the huge Israeli tank trap with its massive minefield that blocked their way. The tanks lurched to a halt with the curious, almost elephantlike rocking that characterized Soviet armor, to make way for the belated engineers who hurried forward with their bridging tanks and crossing equipment.

All of the no-man's-land between Israeli and Syrian lines had been carefully registered by artillery experts, and the crack Israeli gunners had practiced often. Now they conducted a master-sniper campaign, picking off the engineering vehicles and bridging tanks first, then turning their attention to the stationary battle tanks, "cooking them off," in the cliché of tank warfare.

A tank is inhospitable even in peacetime: Quarters are cramped, the noise is deafening, and temperatures can shoot up to 140 degrees during the day, then drop to near freezing at night. The air is filled with fumes—fuel, oil, human, and, if there is some practice firing, gunpowder. But in war, life aboard a tank is brutal. The tankers sweat in the unbearable heat, their hearing dulled from the impossible noise, and except for the tank commander they are almost unable to see. All of the tankers, without exception, are wracked by fear, for as thick as the armor seems, they know they are vulnerable to cannon and missile attack. A quick hit on a tank track would be a blessing; if the tank is disabled, they might be able to scramble out and perhaps survive the Israeli machine-gun fire. But even a glancing hit might mean the explosion of the fuel tanks or of the ammunition carried inside and sometimes strapped outside, setting off a blazing fire from which escape was improbable. The worst possibility of all was a direct hit, when the enemy shaped charge pierces the tank armor as if it were cloth, entering as a jet-fast, jet-hot stream of molten metal that sprays over the interior, incinerating everyone at their posts.

Thus it was with the Syrian tanks. One after another, the mottled gray-green tanks "brewed up" into orange flames as the Israeli 105mm armor-piercing shells found their mark, either killing the crews outright or roasting them to death in a firestorm of fuel-and-ammunition-fed flames. The fiasco at the antitank ditch had deprived the Syrians of their initial and seemingly unconquerable momentum, as their attacks broke down into isolated thrusts by individual units.[13] The

Moroccan Brigade, a token unit there to demonstrate Arab solidarity, pushed thirty tanks into the Israeli defenses, only to have them chewed up by the lethal fire from the Centurions. The pattern was repeated across the front: dug-in Israeli tanks, sometimes supplemented by an additional four or five tanks rushed from another position, ambushed the Syrian invaders and turned them back. But the Syrians would regroup to continue fighting through the night. Their best effort finally came with a breakthrough in the southern sector.

The Israeli defenses were stretched razor-thin. Only four Israeli battalions, two infantry and two tank, were deployed against the massive Syrian onslaught. All four battalions were under the temporary command of Colonel Yitzhak Ben-Shoham. The regular commander of all IDF forces in the Golan Heights, Major General Yitzhak "Haka" Hofi, was that day in Tel Aviv. Ben-Shoham, whose customary command was just the Barak Brigade, was buoyed by initial successes and made a fundamental error by assuming that this was just another border clash. On the evening of October 6, he sent his forces forward to the dispersed firing positions, where they were systematically destroyed that night by Syrian forces equipped with night-vision equipment that the Israelis lacked. During the night attack the Syrians penetrated twelve miles beyond the Six-Day War cease-fire line. By morning Ben-Shoham was killed and most of his brigade destroyed. The triumph was so substantial that President Assad himself came to plant a victory flag upon the Golan Heights in one of the most satisfying moments of his life.

Dayan watched events unfold in the Golan with mounting concern. When the Israelis seemed upon the point of breaking, he would intervene in his usual abrupt, chain-of-command-be-damned manner. He did exactly that at six o'clock the following morning, when he ordered Major General Dan Laner, a division commander responsible for the southern half of the Golan Front, to go down to the Jordan River and prepare the bridges for demolition.

More than three thousand miles away, United States Air Force air crews were occupied with their usual routines, unaware that in a little more than a week they would be called upon to supply an airlift to Israel.

The end of the war in Vietnam in 1973 meant the end of the fighting for the United States—but it did not mean the end of the work for the airlifters of the USAF's mighty Military Airlift Command. In the previous decade they had carried millions of tons of equipment to the Southeast Asian conflict, and MAC was now heavily engaged in bringing the most critical elements back home. The Lockheed C-141 Starlifters and the newer Lockheed C-5 Galaxys were now running round-the-clock missions to evacuate the most expensive and/ or most sensitive commodities, but at the end of the day billions of dollars in supplies would be left behind in the huge open-air warehouse complexes in Da Nang, Saigon, and elsewhere. For the crews involved, their duties involved long flights across the Pacific, with hurried refueling stops at Hawaii and the Philippines, and a swift turnaround in South Vietnam. No one talked about it, but there was a subtle change in feeling. Before, the long flights had been purposeful: they were delivering key materials to American soldiers. Now, it was a little humiliating, salvaging material out of a country the United States had left to be overrun by the Communist forces of North Vietnam.

One saving grace to these runs was the equipment. The C-5 was a monumental aircraft, with a wingspan of greater than 222-feet and a gross takeoff weight of 769,000 pounds. It was a comfortable aircraft to fly, particularly for those brought up on "Old Shaky," the Douglas C-124, which had once been the primary big-cargo carrier. Loading was simplified on the C-5 by both nose and rear ramps. The cavernous fuselage could carry anything up to and including the army's main battle tank. Four huge engines propelled the behemoth through the air at a maximum speed of 571 mph, but cruising flight was done at about 540—still faster than most passenger airliners.

The C-5 had been born into controversy, accused of being yet another one of the "billion-dollar blunders" that the press liked to pin on military procurement. Senator William Proxmire had awarded it his infamous Golden Fleece award, and Lockheed executives had spent as much time before Congress as they had behind their desks, trying to explain the rise in costs and drop in performance estimates.

The explanations were difficult, primarily because the government was at fault as much or more than the contractor, having insisted that the aircraft be procured under the "Total Package Procurement (TPP)" process. TPP was a bureaucratic nightmare, one that penalized the contractor at every turn and prohibited the contractor from exercising judgment on how to avoid costs. It was ultimately recognized as such and abandoned in 1969 (when its principal proponent, Secretary of Defense Robert S. McNamara, left his post), but not before wreaking havoc on several weapon systems.[14] The devastating TPP debacle with the C-5 almost bankrupted Lockheed when the Pentagon reduced the procurement from 115, with the prospect for more, to 81. (Fifty additional C-5Bs would join the fleet, but not until the late 1980s.)

To the crews lucky enough to fly C-5s, however, the arguments were moot. The C-5 had proved its worth in the last few months in Vietnam, or so thirty-eight-year-old Lieutenant Colonel Harry Heist felt. As the shells of October 6 were falling on Israeli lines, Heist was taking off in his C-5A, carrying cargo from Patuxent Naval Air Station, Maryland, to Andersen Air Base in Guam. Heist, of middle height and build but extremely wiry and strong and possessed of a great sense of humor, would spend the next eight days navigating his C-5 from Patuxent to California, Hawaii, and Guam and back to Maryland on October 14. En route, he would be providing training to a new navigator and, thinking about retirement after twenty years, would make a mental list of chores that needed to be done on his house in Dover, Delaware.

While Heist and his crew flew west, the airlift that the U.S. C-5s could provide became a symbol of survival in Tel Aviv. A massive USAF airlift of supplies would signal many things. At the tactical level it would allow existing Israeli reserves of armor and ammunition to be used up with no thought of tomorrow. Strategically it would mean that Israel's sole ally was rallying to its cause. In Washington, the question of an airlift became a political football tossed between Secretary of State Kissinger and Secretary of Defense James Schlesinger, a game at which Kissinger would prove to be more adept by far.

Back in the Sinai, Israeli defenses on the southern front were under the command of Major General Shmuel "Gorodish" Gonen, a rough, native-born Israeli who had superseded the dynamic and temperamental Ariel Sharon. It was not a happy change of command, for Sharon openly complained to Dayan that Gonen was not up to the task. When war came, neither Sharon nor Gonen would forget their differences—and this time Sharon would be under Gonen's command. Gonen was a harsh, intimidating disciplinarian who did not hesitate to throw things at his subordinates. He ruled by fear and had the reputation of being a "bicycle rider," one who presses down on those below him while looking up for approval to his superiors.

Nonetheless, Gonen had his hands full, for Israeli complacency and decreased military budgets had cut back the forces he had available for the vast area of the Southern Command. The IDF was short on everything from big-ticket items such as artillery, tank transporters, and armored personnel carriers (APCs) down to individual equipment such as binoculars and stretchers. This was in part because of budget restrictions but also because of Israeli doctrine that called for tanks, tanks, and more tanks. Despite his shortages, Gonen had nothing but contempt for his Arab enemies, whom he considered both inept and cowardly.

Israel's principal defense in the Sinai was the 110-mile-long Suez Canal. The fabled and crucial waterway, a prize long sought after, by the Germans in World War II and Britain and France in 1956, averaged about 660 feet in width and 60 feet in depth. Dirt embankments, some more than 100 feet high, had been erected on the Egyptian bank to conceal military operations. Behind the embankments, the land was flat and arid, permitting the easy assembly of bridging equipment, rubber boats, and ferries by which the soldiers and armor would cross. There the wily Sadat had quietly deployed no fewer than five infantry divisions, three mechanized divisions, and two armored divisions, all backed up by specialized independent brigades. A total of 200,000 Egyptian men were assembled in the desert by the Suez, a troop movement that could not be concealed, but Israeli intelligence dismissed it as mere "maneuvers."

On the opposite bank, the Israelis had built an earthen embankment reaching as high as seventy-five feet running parallel to the canal. The canal was kept under observation from the Bar-Lev line, which originally had consisted of thirty-one minifortresses. Under Elazar's command, fifteen of these had been deactivated, as had the elaborate system by which petroleum was to be released into the canal and ignited. Now the infamous trip wire was manned by a total of 451 Israeli defenders, mostly reservists, backed up by a tank brigade near the canal and a tank division farther to the rear. These happy few were supposed to observe and report, and when war came they held out as long as they could. All but one of the forts fell, almost all of their defenders dying in the process. In addition, the principal armored reserves for the Bar-Lev were supposed to be within ten miles, but in recent months Gonen had them withdrawn to positions at least twenty miles away to avoid Egyptian artillery—a disastrous error in planning.

In creating their defenses at the edge of the canal, the Israelis had built a network of roads. There were two principal "highways" running north and south for the entire distance of the canal. These two-lane highways were code-named Lexicon and the Artillery Road. The latter was intended to be the basis for a second line of defense. The two roads were separated by a five-mile interval of terrain that ranged from salty marshes in the far north to the typical arid desert terrain of the Sinai. On a map the roads resembled a fragile ladder, with the steps being rough cuts in the desert that connected Lexicon and Artillery to the many fortifications, AAA sites, and munitions depots. The roads were built to facilitate Israel's mobilization plan, allowing the stream of reservists to flow quickly to the important assembly points.

Israel's plans for countering an invasion had been called Operation Shovach Yonim (Dovecote), which was based on forty-eight hours' advance notice of an invasion.[15] During this time large armored units would come forward to strengthen the Bar-Lev line, followed by infantry formations. When war came, the reserves were supposed to be in position, ready to counterattack after the Egyptian forces had been pinned down and destroyed by Israeli airpower.

By 10:00 P.M. on October 6, it was abundantly clear to the Egyptians that whatever the Israeli defensive plan may have been, it had failed. The Egyptian commanders had anticipated suffering as many as 25,000 casualties in the initial crossing, with perhaps 10,000 being killed. Instead, the total fatalities were just over 200. The only setback had been in the operation of the special high-velocity water cannons that the Egyptians had employed to wash away the Israeli earthen ramparts. In some areas, where the nature of the soil varied, instead of breaching the ramparts the water cannons created a quagmire that could only be traversed after rudimentary plank roads had been laid down.

That same hour in Tel Aviv saw the early-morning consternation give way to two points of view. Initially Dayan, perhaps in denial but still hoping to salvage his reputation, felt that things in the Sinai were not going too badly. He was deeply aware that while the situation was critical because of the number of enemy troops who had crossed the canal, at that moment life in the Golan was far more dangerous. There were miles of desert in the Sinai, but none in the north, where the Golan Heights overlooked one of Israel's most heavily populated areas, including villages such as Amir Shamir, Yesod Hamaala, Kfar Hanasi, Almagor, and Tel Katzir.

Dayan's immediate subordinate, Dado Elazar, felt differently. The Israelis sent to the south had been committed piecemeal to battle and were being chewed up. The first reports of the extraordinary antitank firepower of the Egyptians were just coming in. There was already mounting evidence that the Israeli commitment to tanks at the expense of artillery and auxiliary arms was a major error. Even worse, within days it would become painfully clear that quartermaster predictions on ammunition use were completely wrong. Ammunition was being fired at an unprecedented rate, and to no apparent effect. The essentials for replacing the ammunition were well-stocked depots and plenty of transport, but these were already obviously inadequate. To Elazar, the south looked much worse while the reports he had from the north were vaguely comforting—Syrian tanks had been destroyed and the momentum of the enemy advance checked.

While the war raged on two fronts, a third battle erupted between Dayan and Elazar in the Israeli underground command post, the Pit, as it was called. Dayan criticized Elazar for remaining in the command post, coordinating efforts, instead of personally visiting the fronts. For his part, Elazar resented Dayan's hovering presence. Dayan and Elazar argued in the stilted manner of senior commanders, each one being careful to respect his opponent's official title but unable to conceal his personal feelings. Nor were these the only quarrels—bickering had become a way of life at Israeli head-quarters. The differing views of the Israeli leadership led first to arguments and then to accusations, and these, like a white-hot fuse train, sped down the line of command, causing morale problems and creating confusion at every level. Despite the open hostility, an air of unreality pervaded the IDF, almost as if it were clinging to the illusion of peace eight hours after the Egyptians and Syrians had attacked.

Over the course of the night, the mixture of the military and politics further poisoned the atmosphere of the Pit. Dayan ran an open shop, and retired generals, many of them members either of the government or the opposition, were permitted to wander in and kibitz. While the IDF prided itself on its initiative and informality, these admirable qualities were taken past the limit in the Pit and created an awkward and confusing situation.

Early-morning reports of October 7 on the highly successful use of night-vision equipment by the Syrians alarmed both Elazar and Dayan.[16] The enemy tanks had been able to engage and destroy Israeli armor during the night and had now penetrated deep into the Israeli lines. It was too much for Dayan, who left for the Northern Front at 5:00 A.M., leaving Elazar in the command post at a time when he had to make two crucial decisions. The first of these was how to employ the IAF in the next few hours. Should he throw it against the Syrian armor in the north or the Egyptian missile sites in the south? The second dilemma was the deployment of his armored reserve: Should it go to the Golan, which it could reach in a few hours, or march toward the Suez? Within hours, Dayan would relieve Elazar of the burden of one decision.

At 6:00 A.M. on October 7, Dayan roared into the advance headquarters of the Northern Command to find out that the night-fighting Syrians had punched through one Israeli brigade.[17] Some three hundred Syrian tanks were within five miles of the Bnot Ya'akov Bridge, in position to break through to the Jordan River. It was here that Dayan demanded that all the bridges over the Jordan be wired for immediate demolition. When, back in Tel Aviv, Elazar learned of Dayan's instructions, he immediately countermanded them: no bridges were to be mined.

Unaware that the Syrian tanks had outstripped their supplies and were waiting for fuel and rations to come up, the Israelis had been mustering scattered units of armor, one and two tanks at a time, and positioning them so that they could hold until reserve forces could arrive. Dayan knew that the Israelis had run out of territory and luck. By his eye there was only one solution: continuous strikes by the IAF.

Instead of working through Elazar and the commander of the Golan Front, Hofi, Dayan ignored military protocol and called Major General Bennie Peled, the head of the IAF, demanding an immediate strike on the Syrian tanks. It was not an order—Dayan as Defense Minister could not issue orders and always referred to his instructions as "ministerial advice"—but Peled understood and accepted Dayan's advice. Over the early morning, Douglas A-4s and Dassault Super Mysteres ceaselessly attacked the Syrian tanks, taking heavy losses from the tightly integrated air defense network that had moved into position with the armor. The IAF suffered so much from the ZSU-23 AAA and SA-6 Grail missiles that it had to regroup to begin defense suppression attacks. Two flights of four McDonnell F-4 Phantoms were sent in around noon, and six were quickly lost. In the sky above, Israeli fighters had a field day against their Syrian opponents, but the victories were meaningless compared to the battle on the ground, where Syrian armor continued to advance.

By noon, the battle on the Golan Front began to be stabilized and the first full reports of the debacle in the Sinai began trickling in. In Moscow and Washington, analysts peered over reports of the fighting and tried to correlate them with the flood of diplomatic overtures coming from Damascus, Cairo, and Tel Aviv. Within twenty-four hours Assad would let it be known that he wanted an immediate cease-

fire. He had come into the war solely for the purpose of re-
gaining the Golan Heights for Syria, and he felt that this was
nearly done. Now he wanted his gains ratified and made permanent by a UN cease-fire.

In his *Years of Upheaval,* Henry Kissinger described October
7 as "a day of stalling." Convinced that the United States was
in an excellent position to dictate the ultimate outcome of
the war, he preferred to let the situation "develop" so that the
maximum gain might be exploited. The peripatetic Secretary
of State was unduly confident that Israel would triumph. He,
like most of the U.S. military men he consulted, believed that
there would be a quick repeat of the Six-Day War. This opinion was shared not only by Moscow but by most of the Arab
world as well. The Arab countries had a dilemma. They
wanted an Arab victory—but not at the price of winning
through Soviet arms and thus being drawn more into the
Soviet orbit.

Further, Kissinger felt that Brezhnev's desire to maintain
détente was a trump card—he was certain that the Soviet
Union would not sacrifice good relations with the United
States to Sadat's advantage. Finally, even the political nightmare of the American presidency played to Kissinger's advantage. Nixon's utter preoccupation with the rising tide of
the Watergate scandal would allow Kissinger to be the Met-
ternich of the Middle East.

Kissinger had dropped the diplomatic bait at 9:35 A.M. on
October 6, when he suggested that the United States and the
Soviet Union make a joint proposal to the UN Security Council that a cease-fire be put into effect, with all forces withdrawing to the prewar boundaries. Inveterately—and
rightly—suspicious of Kissinger's intentions, Moscow had
delayed replying until late in the day, and when its message
came it said only that it would take no action until it had
received word from the Arab nations. The reply enabled Kis-

singer to set the hook. When Moscow reopened the subject, he would be able to delay in turn, so that he could choose the moment when it was best for the interests of the United States to agree to seek a cease-fire. And that moment would come when Israel had defeated but not yet humiliated the Arab forces.

At midmorning on October 7, Kissinger received a message from Prime Minister Golda Meir assuring him that although the fighting was difficult, Israel would prevail when the reserves were fully mobilized. She asked that no cease-fire be arranged until October 10 or 11, when Israel would have assumed the offensive on all fronts. And for the first time, Meir asked for an airlift of critical supplies, including heat-seeking air-to-air missiles. Over the coming days her requests become increasingly urgent. Nixon, Kissinger, and Schlesinger quickly agreed to her initial request and arranged with Ambassador Simcha Dinitz that El Al aircraft, their national markings painted out, could pick up eighty Sidewinder missiles and additional ammunition at Naval Air Station Oceana, Virginia.[18] It was the beginning of an abortive attempt by El Al Airlines to conduct an airlift with passenger planes converted to cargo duty.

Late on the evening of October 7, the "back-channel" communication with Egypt confirmed the validity of Kissinger's plan. Sadat sent word rejecting the idea of a return to prewar boundaries and stating that Egypt's war aims were limited to securing a foothold on the east bank of the Suez Canal. For Kissinger, Sadat's message made the entire day one well spent—and well stalled. Ironically, he now had information that President Assad desperately needed—but did not have. Assad expected Sadat to maintain pressure on the Israelis by forging ahead through the Mitla and Gida passes. If Egypt stopped pressing forward, Israel could transfer its forces to the Golan Heights, and this could well mean disaster for Syria.

Back at the Pit, the battle reports that flooded in from both the Northern and Southern fronts were turning nightmarish. The impossible was happening: the IDF was losing battles at every level. Counterattacks had been made in a piecemeal fashion, and Israeli tanks had been wasted in useless, old-fashioned charges. Casualties were high and supplies were low. Worst was the sense that the command decisions had been wrong from the start.

On the Southern Front, a shaken General Gonen faced disaster.[19] All of the Bar-Lev fortresses either had fallen or were surrounded. One-third of the Israeli tanks had been lost, many to the RPGs and Sagger antitank missiles. Fully aware of Dayan's disapproval, Gonen followed prewar planning by dividing his front into three sectors. Major General Avraham "Bren" Adan received the northern sector, where the swamps would at least guard his right flank. In the center, the old warhorse Sharon was placed in command of a reserve division. He promptly went to the depots and began driving his armor forward, disdaining the use of tank transporters and disregarding the wear on the tanks. He wanted action, and he wanted it now. He would get it, in the form of broken-down tanks that left his reserves open to the Egyptian onslaught.

In the southern sector, toward the Gulf of Suez, Major General Avraham "Albert" Mandler regrouped the battered remains of his two armored brigades. Lacking the expected forty-eight-hour warning of the war, Mandler did not have his tanks in position when the fighting began. When he finally moved them forward under fire, the losses were staggering. On October 6 he had 110 miles of front, with 294 tanks; now he had fewer than 130 tanks left, his armor was as shredded as his reputation, and he was extremely vulnerable to Gonen's bullying style. Mandler, within the week, would be killed in action.

Hearkening back to its guerrilla origins, the IDF had a reputation for informal efficiency and a sensible approach to military proprieties that allowed affectionate nicknames to be bestowed not only on individuals but also on the units they commanded. Yet placing Sharon and Adan under Gonen was a significant mistake. Both Adan and Sharon were senior to Gonen, both had far more combat experience, and both heartily disliked him. Their dislike and distrust was mutual, and while Adan remained militarily correct, Sharon did not bother to conceal his contempt for Gonen's failure to repel the Egyptian thrust across the canal.

When Defense Minister Dayan made a hasty inspection trip to the Southern Front, he was appalled at both the losses and the disposition of the forces. There were only three divisions available, with no reserves. He flew back to Tel Aviv for yet another showdown with Elazar. The two met with Golda Meir and her other ministers, none of whom were prepared for the bad news.

Dayan shocked them with a proposal to abandon the canal front and establish a second line of defense to contain the Egyptians when they burst forward from their newly won positions. The Defense Minister was proposing to reject the traditional style of Israeli warfare for a defensive strategy totally unfamiliar to the IDF.

The Chief of Staff, Elazar, agreed to form a second line of defense—any prudent commander would have—but proposed that any withdrawal be postponed until after a counterattack had been made. Sharon and Adan were going to be in position to attack within hours, and Elazar hoped that they could save the situation. Dayan protested, concerned with the current loss rate and knowing that in a prolonged war of attrition the Egyptians were bound to prevail. He also insisted that demands be made both upon the United States and, if possible, in Europe, for the immediate supply of aircraft and tanks.

He lost his point. Meir and her ministers were determined to have good news, and Elazar had promised to provide it. That and their faith in the IDF were enough.

Among all the leaders of the Arab world, only Syria's President, Hafiz al-Assad, had been taken into Anwar Sadat's confidence—and then to only a limited degree. New in office, still unsure of himself, Assad had succumbed to Sadat's pressure to join the war against Israel. Assad came to the decision, however, only after a Soviet agreement to bring fifty batteries of SA-2 Guideline missiles to defend Damascus. As a pilot, Assad understood the efficiency of the IAF, and he did not want to see the events of 1967 repeated.

On the evening of the second day of the war, Assad saw that his Syrian troops had broken the Israeli defenses in the Golan and had an advanced unit within a few miles of the Jordan River. Israeli air strikes were already under way, and Assad knew that a counterattack was inevitable. With the wily cunning that had enabled him to seize office and hold it, he hedged his bets, summoning the Soviet ambassador, Mukhitdinov, and asking for the Soviet Union to seek an immediate cease-fire in place.[20] The cease-fire would confirm the military victory and leave Syria in an excellent negotiating position to regain the Golan Heights—its prime objective in the war.

The gray, faceless bureaucracy of the Kremlin responded to Assad's request with alacrity, preparing a cease-fire resolution for presentation to the United Nations by the Soviet representative, the dour Yakov Malik. Then the old survivor of Soviet domestic politics Foreign Minister Andrei Gromyko intervened, insisting that Sadat be informed of Assad's appeal and that any subsequent resolution receive Brezhnev's approval.

Vinogradov, the Soviet ambassador to Egypt, met with Sadat and stressed the Soviet support of Assad's request for a cease-fire. Sadat was indignant, cataloging both the Egyptian and the Syrian victories and stating flatly that Assad could quit the war if he wished, but Egypt would fight on. Sadat reasserted Egypt's intention to exhaust the Israelis by ceaseless combat and indicated that it would soon seize the key Mitla and Gidi passes, which controlled access to the Sinai. When these two military feats—Israel's exhaustion and the control of the two passes—had been accomplished, the time would be ripe for negotiations. Until then, Sadat insisted that the Soviet Union not propose a cease-fire at the UN Security Council.[21]

At 8:00 A.M. on October 7, for differing reasons, Sadat, Kissinger, and Meir agreed on one thing: no cease-fire. The situation would soon change. In Moscow, a significant decision was made: Egypt and Syria would be resupplied by air, a gesture that would show Arab/Soviet solidarity and perhaps induce the Israelis to negotiate.

3 *Black Monday*

BY THE MORNING OF OCTOBER 8, the people of Israeli were eager to learn of victories in the usual IDF style, poised to hear of smashing armored attacks that had destroyed the Egyptian invaders and sent the Syrians reeling back to Damascus. Instead, October 8 would prove to be a day of utter confusion, punctuated at nightfall by the radio and television broadcast of Major General Aharon Yariv telling them in somber tones that "this was war and not a picnic."[1]

As sobering as Yariv's broadcast had been, it was tame compared to what Dayan had intended to say. Meir was determined not to have Dayan's views made widely known, and she had insisted that Yariv deliver the message instead. Yariv was straightforward and serious but far more upbeat in his assessment than Dayan had intended to be.

For the IDF, the calamitous results of October 6 and 7 lent themselves to excuses—the failure of intelligence, the arrogance of Dayan, the perfidy of the Arabs. However, the disasters of October 8 would belong to the IDF alone.

It all started with Dado Elazar, the Chief of Staff, making a decision to redeem the disasters on the Southern Front with a counteroffensive that would destroy the Egyptians on the Israeli side of the canal as a preparation for crossing the canal in force.[2] Bren Adan's division was to attack first, although it could muster only four pieces of artillery. Adan's instructions were inherently contradictory: He was to drive south, keeping at least three kilometers east of the canal except when he could dart west to rescue any units still holding out in the Bar-Lev line. When Adan reached Sharon's division at Hamutal, the two were to join forces to attack the main Egyptian body. Elazar gave both Adan and Sharon explicit orders *not* to cross the canal without further instructions from him.

Unfortunately, when Adan reached Hamutal, Sharon's division was on a southern plunge of its own, ordered by Gonen to capture Suez City.[3] Gonen was also pressing both men to cross the canal and establish bridgeheads as soon as possible. He began issuing a series of often-contradictory orders that placed his subordinates in impossible positions. When questioned, Gonen took the position that "things are going better than expected; we can take the risk." He had determined this without going forward to the front himself to understand the situation, an unusual error for an Israeli general.

Even without Sharon in support, Adan turned west and began one of the famous Israeli tank charges that had always smashed the enemy in the past. Adan expected to attack the Egyptians and see them flee, for all of Gonen's messages had indicated that the enemy was collapsing. Instead, the Egyptians stood their ground, then came forward in overwhelming numbers. Expecting air and artillery support and deficient in infantry, Adan committed two brigades sequentially, instead of combining them into a single force. The results were disastrous, with each wave being engulfed by Egyptian infantry using the Sagger and RPG antitank weapons that cooked Israeli crews in their tanks. By 5:00 P.M. on October 8, Adan had to order a fighting withdrawal. Of his 170 tanks, 70 had been destroyed and another 25 were abandoned in enemy territory.

Around midnight, the exhausted, exasperated leaders of the Israeli military met in the Sinai. It was a cauldron of mutual animosity, for there were old personal scores to settle, not least of which was Elazar's recent request of Sharon that he retire from the army. Dayan and Elazar were barely talking, confining their remarks to those essential for winning the war, Gonen was nearly apoplectic, for the Egyptian enemies he had so scorned had bloodied his nose. He also knew that his conduct of the war had been terrible and that he was being

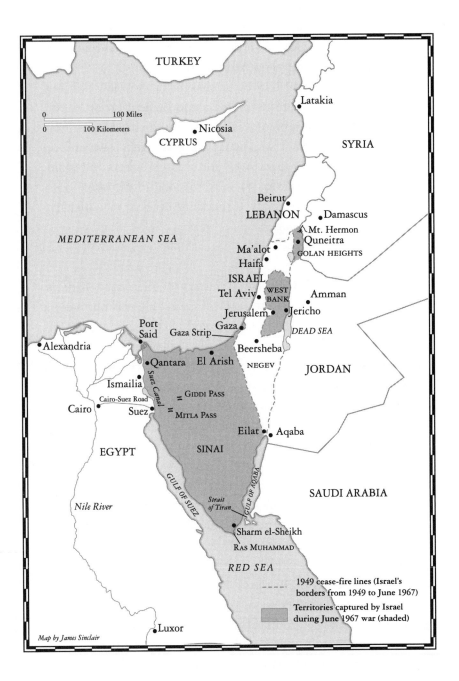

TURKEY

0   100 Miles

0   100 Kilometers

•Nicosia

CYPRUS

SYRIA

•Latakia

MEDITERRANEAN SEA

Beirut•

LEBANON

•Damascus

Mt. Hermon

•Quneitra

GOLAN HEIGHTS

Ma'alot•

Haifa•

ISRAEL

Tel Aviv• WEST BANK

Jerusalem• •Jericho

Gaza

Gaza Strip

DEAD SEA

Amman

Port Said

•Alexandria

•Qantara   El Arish•

Beersheba•

NEGEV

JORDAN

Ismailia•

Suez Canal

Cairo-Suez Road

= GIDDI PASS

Cairo•   •Suez

= MITLA PASS

EGYPT

SINAI

Eilat• •Aqaba

GULF OF SUEZ

Nile River

GULF OF AQABA

SAUDI ARABIA

Strait of Tiran

•Sharm el-Sheikh

RAS MUHAMMAD

RED SEA

1949 cease-fire lines (Israel's
borders from 1949 to June 1967)

Territories captured by Israel
during June 1967 war (shaded)

•Luxor

Map by James Sinclair

judged severely by both superiors and subordinates. Sharon, Adan, and Mandler were boiling with anger, more furious with their leaders for the orders they had received than they were with the enemy who had fought so well.

None of them had bathed or shaved for two days and few of them had had more than an occasional field ration to eat. They listened, faces blank, as Elazar stated that Sharon's division, exhausted as it was by its pointless trek down and up the canal, would prepare itself for a thrust across the canal. Adan's and Mandler's forces were to take up defensive positions and rest, preparatory to backing up Sharon's offensive when it was launched.

The failure of the Israeli counterattack on October 8 had apparently reduced Dayan to utter despair.[4] He was normally a military pulsar, radiating energy and enthusiasm, always eagerly assessing the next battle for the triumphs it would bring. Now he was just the opposite, his face gloomy with defeat and his eyes downcast. In a private conversation with one of Elazar's advisers, Dayan said that there was not a single tank between Tel Aviv and the Israeli lines in the Sinai. It was, he said, the ruin of the Third Temple, a prediction of Israel's destruction. (The First Temple had fallen to the Babylonians in 586 B.C.E. The Second Temple was destroyed by the Romans in 70 A.D.) He believed that the real problem was not just the loss of terrain but also the terrible attrition rate that subtracted hourly from Israel's total of tanks, planes, soldiers, and pilots. Simple mathematics made it certain that Israel could not sustain a prolonged defensive war. Unless she won a decisive victory soon, the Arab armies were certain to grind her into the ground. Dayan believed he knew what had to be done to gain that victory.

While the Defense Minister's gloomy concern, as presented in his own memoirs and those of Meir, Kissinger, and others, was sincere, there is a strong possibility that he was painting

the situation as dark as possible to set the stage for his request
to use nuclear weapons. He had brought those weapons into
being and had allocated the resources to build the delivery
vehicles. He believed in their use when at war, and many
believe that he wanted to use them.[5]

Under his leadership, Israel had enough nuclear matériel
prepared for as many as twenty-five nuclear weapons. Thirteen, of an estimated twenty-kilo-ton yield each (about the
size of the bomb dropped on Hiroshima), are reported to have
been placed into operational condition. Some were to be fired
by the Jericho missiles that Israel had clandestinely developed. The Jericho, with its single-stage rocket and 1,000-to-
1,500-pound warhead, was a stunning technological coup,
created, like the nuclear weapons themselves, in cooperation
with the French but drawing heavily on freely available technology in the United States. According to investigative reporter Seymour M. Hersh, the Israelis paid $100 million to
the Dassault Company to develop twenty-five missiles, each
able to deliver a miniaturized nuclear warhead over a distance
of three hundred miles.[6]

Additional missiles were produced in Israel, despite ongoing problems with guidance and control. The missiles were
reportedly stored at Hirbat Zachariah in the foothills of the
Judean mountains west of Jerusalem. Mobile missile launchers were also developed.

The Jericho missile could be used for deterrence, and, from
1971 on, the world's intelligence communities were well
aware of Jericho's capabilities—and their deficiencies. Israel
saw them as a more than effective counter to the Scud missile
being supplied the Arabs. (The Jericho has long since been
improved, and the latest models have an estimated range of
1,500 miles. The development program has also led to the
deployment of submarine-launched missiles stationed on Israeli submarines built by Germany, one of the more bizarre
ironies of history.)[7]

Other nuclear warheads were to be dropped by eight specially configured McDonnell F-4E Phantoms. The F-4s had the range to reach the combatant Arab capitals—Cairo, Damascus, Aman, and Baghdad. Some sources mention one-way missions to Moscow, but this seems improbable. In 1973 the Soviet air defenses were still in good order, and the range would have been too much even for a Phantom with four auxiliary fuel tanks. The F-4s' exact targets are unknown and probably never will be known, but they would have included not only the primary military headquarters in the Arab capital cities but also the most dangerous troop concentrations facing Israel.

The Phantoms were naturally manned by the best pilots. It was an expensive luxury for Israel, for risking the nuclear-capable Phantoms and their crews on dangerous and costly nonnuclear combat missions during the October War could be justified only as a last resort.

Dayan returned to Tel Aviv to meet with the Prime Minister at 7:20 A.M. on October 9. He had three main tasks. Sheer protocol required that he first ask if she wanted his resignation, given the extent of the military debacle. He undoubtedly knew that she would refuse to accept it, and she did, later remarking that she never regretted it, evidence of Meir's forgiving heart. Dayan and Meir knew already that their careers were forfeit, along with those of Zeira, Lieutenant General Chaim Bar-Lev, and others who had allowed the terrible Arab surprise to come about. It took courage and character, for which Meir was famous, not to attempt to shift the blame to Dayan.

Once his resignation was refused, Dayan next put forward his recommendations on the use of nuclear weapons. The implications of an Israeli nuclear attack for the rest of the world were unknown. With John F. Kennedy's warning on attacks of Cuba still ringing in their ears, the leaders of the Soviet Union might have decided that a retaliatory attack with nuclear weapons against Israel might also require a first strike against the United States as a preventive measure. Deterrence having failed, the United States would have responded with its surviving forces, and the fate of the world might have been decided in *On the Beach* fashion in a few hours.

Meir was well aware of the zero-sum possibilities. She vetoed an immediate strike but almost certainly approved that all necessary steps be taken to be prepared for one last-ditch salvo. The title of author Seymour Hersh's book *The Sampson Option* clearly defines the mind-set of Meir and, indeed, of most Israelis. Israel would fight to win a conventional war, but in the awful event that sheer defeat loomed, they would emulate Sampson and bring down the walls of the Arab world with nuclear assaults. With the Third Temple destroyed, what happened elsewhere in the world would be of no concern. The Jews believed that victorious Arabs would engage in another Holocaust, and few national slogans have been so deeply felt as the simple two words "Never Again."

On an immediate, practical level, Meir recognized instantly that an explicit warning that nuclear weapons of last resort were being readied would spur Washington to intensify its efforts to have the emergency airlift of ammunition and supplies begin. She hoped that the inevitable leak to the Soviet Union might convey a sufficient threat to deter Egypt and Syria from further military excursions. Events later in Syria proved that she was probably correct, for the Syrian advance halted just when it seemed unstoppable.

With the major overriding questions behind him, Dayan settled into his twin role as defense minister and adviser. His first request was the simplest, to direct Elazar to relieve Gonen of command. (After the meeting, Dayan suggested that Gonen and Sharon swap positions, but Elazar balked, deciding instead to recall the former Chief of Staff, Lieutenant General Chaim Bar-Lev, and place him in a position over Gonen. It was a bad decision, adding a layer of command, offending Gonen without relieving him, and infuriating Sharon, who was Bar-Lev's bitter political and military enemy.)

Dayan next asked Meir for permission to have a "stand or

die" order issued to the forces in the Golan Heights. It did not matter if every Israeli tank and man was lost—the Syrians had to be stopped before they debouched across the Jordan into Israel. He also suggested that the Syrian use of artillery and FROG missiles against Israeli settlements called for retaliatory air strikes on Damascus. The Prime Minister agreed and approved each request.

Meir, weary but composed, evidence of too much coffee and too many cigarettes floating like a cloud around her, next surprised Dayan by suggesting that she was going to fly to Washington to speak directly to President Nixon. She had a threefold mission, the first of which was most dire: confirm the possibility of a last-ditch nuclear response to Nixon directly, without the Kissinger filter intervening. This would, she hoped, ensure the success of her second mission: an immediate airlift of arms to offset the terrible losses already incurred. Third, she wanted a major demonstration of U.S. support announced to the world. When Kissinger learned of her offer, he declined vehemently, saying that it would be interpreted as hysteria or blackmail and he could not afford either.[8] The last thing he wanted was a face-to-face meeting with a powerful, emotion-driven Meir and Nixon, who, given his crumbling psyche, might have responded in a way Kissinger had not sought.

Nonetheless, Dayan saw her suggestion as the first bright spot in a long black day that had seen cherished Israeli beliefs come tumbling down. The Egyptian soldiers had not run at the first sight of Israeli armor, as they had been expected to do. Instead, they proved to be what Sharon called the first modern infantry, equipped and trained not only to fight tanks but also to hunt them down. The Egyptian soldiers hunkered down in the sand and with their long-range Saggers and short-range RPGs popped off Israeli tanks like firecrackers.

Perhaps in an effort to prepare public opinion for the ultimate use of nuclear weapons, Dayan at 7:00 P.M. on October 9 presented an ominous future in a briefing to the Committee of Newspaper Editors. In a lugubrious fashion he listed the difficulties and stated that not only might there be a general withdrawal in the Sinai, back as far as the Mitla and Gidi passes, but there would probably also be a withdrawal of several miles in the Golan Heights. To newsmen accustomed to one victory announcement after another, Dayan's gloomy visage and discouraging words were unprecedented. Further, Dayan again wanted to make a television address to the nation, informing the public of just how extensive the casualties were. Once more, Meir vetoed the idea.

The final act of Dayan's day of woe was with the officers of the General Staff. While it is almost certain that he discussed the nuclear option with them, there are no reports of this in any account. What is reported is that his comments took on a Custer's last stand air as he proposed the creation of an Israeli Volkstrum." There was to be an emergency mobilization of elderly people and youngsters below the age of the draft. He proposed arming them and, indeed, the entire Israeli populace with mass-produced bazookas like those the Egyptians employed. Their job: stop Egyptian armor from entering Tel Aviv.

None of these suggestions was put into effect or even, for the most part, taken seriously. But Dayan's demeanor left, as one author termed it, a Masada mood in his wake. It was a profoundly jolting experience for officers who had previously only known victory. Yet unbeknownst to Dayan or to them, a significant measure of victory was already in process.

As bad as the events of October 7 and 8 had been, those of October 9 and 10 would seem even worse. Despite this, there was a bright spot that would go unrecognized until October 11—the deadly effects of the actions of the IAF.

The IAF had become a fire brigade, flying mission after mission, and switching its activities between the Northern and Southern fronts. The ground crews worked furiously to rearm and refuel while the pilots were hurriedly and all too often inadequately briefed. The failure of Israeli intelligence procedures now extended to IAF operations. It soon became apparent that complacency had resulted in inadequate liaison between army intelligence and the IAF. Vital information on Arab airfields, missile sites, and antiaircraft batteries was missing, and the shield of Soviet missiles had sealed off reconnaissance efforts. The IAF was forced to improvise, picking up its intelligence on one combat mission for use on the next, the hardest and most costly method. The result was the highest casualty rate in IAF history as strikes against missile defense systems continued to be subordinate to the vital close air support missions.

The courage of the Israeli pilots was incredible, for an improvident government had deprived them of the weapons they needed, the electronic counterwarfare pods and the antiradar missiles. As a result the Skyhawks would fly in at high speed and low level, hoping to avoid the SAMs, only to be caught in the murderous antiaircraft fire. If the AAA drove them up, they were exposed to SAMs. Yet, despite losses on almost every pass, they came, time after time, trying to succor the Israeli armored forces.

Their efforts were beginning to pay of, for on the morning of October 9, the missile systems would be worn down to the point that the IAF could conduct, for the first time, strategic air operations against Syria.[9] The first success came when the vitally important El Burak radar facilities in Lebanon were destroyed. The installation's elimination made the next steps easier. The IAF struck key military targets in Damascus, including the Syrian air force headquarters and the transmitting facilities of Radio Damascus. There followed a series of pinpoint raids against the electrical power grid, petroleum facilities, and military depots. Syria begged for Egypt to counter with air raids against Israeli civilian targets, but the request was denied.

The IAF's key tactical effort was put forth in the southern flank of the Golan Heights where virtually every Israeli tank had been destroyed and the defense depended solely on close air support. Israeli Skyhawks flew incessantly, striking missile sites when they could but concentrating on stemming the tide of Syrian armor. In the morning on October 9 a flight of eight Phantoms, en route to Damascus with fifty-six tons of bombs, had to abort the mission because of the weather. They were diverted to a pickup air strike against a Syrian tank column advancing against weak Israeli positions. The avalanche of bombs stopped the Syrians in their tracks, giving the Israeli defenders just enough time to breathe until their own reserve tanks arrived. All in all, the IAF lost thirty-five aircraft to Syrian fire during the first six days of the fighting, most from the savage SA-6.

Airpower was almost equally important on the Sinai Front, where F-4 Phantoms defied SA-2, SA-3, and SA-6 barrages to take out seven of the fourteen Egyptian bridges across the canal (although some of the bridges were decoys). When the bridges were rebuilt, the Phantoms came back and destroyed those as well. For twenty-four precious hours, the Egyptian Third Army had *no* bridges across the southern length of the canal, relying on ferries for resupply.

But the exhausting effort came at great cost. The IAF had been forced to attack tanks and bridges before it had destroyed all the SAM sites, a stark violation of tactical doctrine. Late in the afternoon of October 8, General Peled, the IAF commander, ordered that no aircraft were to come within twenty-four kilometers of the canal unless they were on a priority mission. By the end of the third day, nearly fifty aircraft had been lost, almost all to SAMs.

The efforts of the IAF and the arrival of mobilized reserve forces combined to stiffen Israeli resistance just when Dayan and others thought that the war might be lost. As dark as the situation seemed, from October 9 on no more Israeli territory was given up. And while the tide had not yet turned, the grumpy, disagreeable, disobedient, and cantankerous warhorse Sharon had discovered a chink in the enemy's armor.

Even as the Arab and Israeli armies struggled like scorpions trapped in a bottle, the hot line between Washington and Moscow sang with dulcet tones of amity as both Nixon and Brezhnev sought to minimize the danger of the Middle Eastern war destroying détente. Each continued to put forward his client state's opinion. Nixon suggested that an immediate withdrawal be made by Arab forces to the prewar boundary lines, while Brezhnev preferred that Israel abandon all occupied territory.

Yet both men had been surprised by the extent of the Arab success, and Nixon, concerned about Arab relations with the United States in case of an Israeli defeat, became more conciliatory, even suggesting that détente could be furthered by the Soviet Union helping smooth Arab/U.S. relations.

In this polite diplomatic charade Nixon had a major advantage over Brezhnev, for his Secretary of State, Kissinger, had enjoyed a private line of communication with Hafiz Ismail, Anwar Sadat's security adviser, for almost two years. Kissinger would remain the only person in the diplomatic circuit to have contact with both of the warring sides.[10] Just the knowledge that Sadat intended only to cross the canal and hold a small but symbolic strip of land—knowledge still concealed from his Syrian allies—allowed Kissinger to shuffle the diplomatic cards to the advantage of the United States while aiding Israel at exactly the right level for his own purposes.

Not that helping Israel was easy. Kissinger later wrote that because the United States was its only friend and supporter, Israel had to maintain an air of fiery intransigence and independence. Otherwise it would have appeared to be just a submissive satellite state, serving the United States as Bulgaria or Romania served the Soviet Union. Golda Meir had already sent Kissinger a tart message telling him that Israel's current plight was due to its not having launched a preemptive air strike, implying his pressure had forced this decision. The Israeli-U.S. ambassador, Simcha Dinitz, continued to put forward his repetitive demands for support, with little ceremony and at all hours of the day and night. For the first two days of the war, Dinitz had been determinedly upbeat, insisting that the Israeli forces had already rebounded and were on their way to victory. All that went by the boards with his first call to Kissinger on October 9, at 1:45 in the morning. Kissinger, exhausted by the previous day, listened quietly as Dinitz explained that Israel was now desperately short of supplies, had suffered heavy losses, and was near defeat. An emergency airlift was absolutely imperative. At Meir's urging, Dinitz called again at 3:00 A.M., straining Kissinger's civility to the breaking point.

In Kissinger's memoirs, these calls were dealt with in a delicate, faintly humorous manner that speculated that the reason for Dinitz's calls were to prove to the Israeli cabinet that "he could get me out of bed at will." Kissinger was fond of Dinitz and regarded him as a friend, admiring his wit and intelligence even as he had to put up with his belligerent, almost defiant methods. It is evident, however, that even in 1980, as the memoirs were written, Kissinger could not reveal the full import of the calls. The most that he gives away is that something was seriously wrong.

In fact, the calls were almost certainly the first intimations of Meir's decision to resort to nuclear war if defeat was imminent. Kissinger put Dinitz at the top of his schedule, arranging to meet him at 8:20 A.M. in the Map Room on the ground floor of the White House. Despite Dinitz's obvious concerns, Kissinger still believed firmly that Israel would prevail and was willing to give all the assistance the Israelis wanted and more, but things had to be done as quietly as possible and with the best efforts not to inflame the Arab world. The Arab oil weapon had been used as a threat before and now loomed as a reality. Kissinger was not as concerned about the effects of an oil embargo upon the United States as he was about its effects upon the NATO allies. Events would soon prove this calculation to be valid.

At the early-morning meeting, Dinitz and his military advisers briefed Kissinger that the Israeli losses were frightful: forty-nine aircraft down, with fourteen Phantoms among them. But the figure that staggered Kissinger was the tank losses—almost five hundred destroyed in less than four days of fighting. No nation, not the United States, not even the Soviet Union, could make up such losses if the rate was sustained.

It was then that Dinitz delivered a private and much more important verbal message, of which no record can be found. However, the sequence of events and the facts that have since become known make it almost certain that Kissinger was informed that Israel's decision to defer, but not rule out, the possibility of using nuclear weapons depended upon the effectiveness and rapidity of U.S. aid. Kissinger's reaction can only be speculated about, but one thing can be sure: he did not share the fatalistic view of Meir and Dayan. Instead, Kissinger began to turn the heat up on the problem of acquiring supplies and airlifting them to Israel—a task that faced internal opposition from his open rival, the Secretary of Defense, James Schlesinger, and had to also overcome the normal bureaucratic inertia of the Pentagon.

The crisis in Israel resonated around the world, stirring reactions from those with obligations, such as reservists, and from those who simply felt a kinship with a nation in difficulty. More than twenty thousand reservists and volunteers would arrive via El Al Airlines before the war ended. One of them was a young man from Detroit, twenty-two-year-old Harry Cohen, a newly licensed pilot with two hundred hours' flying time and a recent graduate of Washington University in Saint Louis. An activist, Cohen had marched in the civil rights movement, supporting Martin Luther King Jr. Cohen was learning his family's consumer products distribution business from the ground up. But on October 8, when it first became general knowledge that the war in the Middle East was not going rapidly in Israel's favor, Harry decided that he, for one, was not going to stand for it. With the faint hope of being able to fly for the IAF, perhaps in one of their Cessna liaison aircraft, he purchased a ticket for Tel Aviv on El Al Airlines. He told his parents nothing about his plans, knowing they would protest. They found out when El Al called his home for security reasons to confirm his intentions—and while they did not want him to go, they understood and relented.

Within a day after his arrival at Lod International Airport, Cohen was in a processing line with other volunteers. When he got to the front of the line, he pressed for a flying job. Weary and hard-eyed, the civil servant behind the desk ignored Cohen's request, saying only, "Come back tomorrow."

Since the start of the war, the Syrian infantry and tank forces had conducted an unceasing battle for ninety-six hours, hurling themselves against Israeli defenders all along the Golan Front. Barely allowing themselves time to regroup and reform, the Syrians had attacked four to five times a day, their nighttime assaults being the most difficult to counter. The Syrian armor had suffered heavily from air attacks and from the pinpoint accuracy of Israeli gunners, but still they came, their courage reinforced by the knowledge that failure to advance meant a firing squad. By Tuesday afternoon the Syrian tanks had broken through Israeli lines along the southern part of the front and the war had turned into a contest between the invaders and surrounded Israeli tanks.

The Israeli 7th Armored Brigade, an elite unit, had fought hard since the beginning of the war. Nights had been particularly bad, for without night-vision equipment the Israeli tankers had been forced to resort to a primitive strategy to identify friend from foe. On signal, they would simultaneously shut down their engines; by default, any tank with its engine running was an enemy and had to be engaged. It was a rinky-dink way to run a war.

The 7th's losses were so heavy that the entire battle on the center sector of the Golan Front now hinged on the purely serendipitous and totally improbable arrival of Lieutenant Colonel Yossi Ben-Hanan. A battalion commander, Ben-Hanan was on his honeymoon in the Himalayas when the war broke out. By incredible effort and luck in transportation he arrived in Israel in time to lead a pickup force into battle in the Golan.

In classic crisis style, Ben-Hanan combed the hospitals and supply centers for men to crew thirteen hastily repaired tanks, then led them to a sector in the front lines where the remains of the beleaguered 7th Brigade—seven tanks and a handful of men—were about to retreat. Ben-Hanan joined the two forces into a twenty-tank fist that plunged into the exhausted Syrian armored forces.[11]

It was a successful charge. By then the Syrians had lost more than 500 tanks, and this sudden arrival of 20 tanks turned the tide. It was the Syrians who now retreated, fighting all the way. Ben-Hanan followed at a close but guarded distance until the enemy had crossed the Purple Line that marked the previous no-man's-land boundary and adopted defensive positions. (Ben-Hanan would soon prove to be too offensive-minded—driving forward, he would lose many of his tanks in a Syrian minefield.)

Over the years, the anecdotes about the exploits of Ben-Hanan have imparted an ever more heroic quality to his attack. Yet the Syrian retreat was difficult to explain, for their forces were still far stronger than their opponents'. The numbers simply do not add up, particularly given the fierce Syrian resistance found in many places. To some, the real explanation

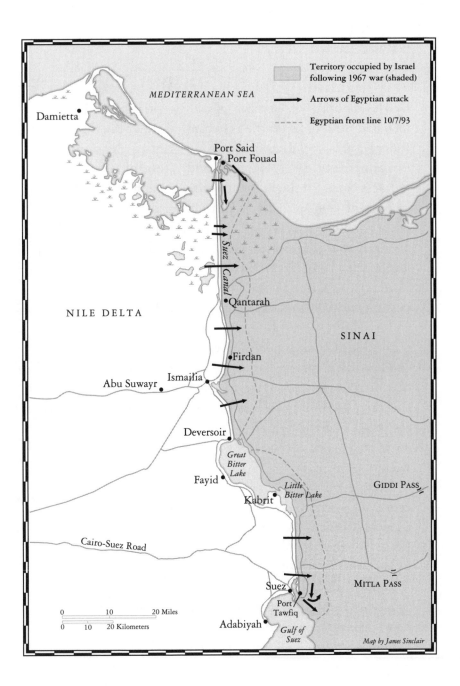

MEDITERRANEAN SEA

Territory occupied by Israel
following 1967 war (shaded)

Arrows of Egyptian attack

Egyptian front line 10/7/93

Damietta

Port Said
Port Fouad

Suez Canal

•Qantarah

NILE DELTA

SINAI

•Firdan

Abu Suwayr   Ismailia

Deversoir

*Great
Bitter
Lake*

Fayid

*Little
Bitter Lake*

GIDDI PASS

Kabrit

Cairo-Suez Road

MITLA PASS

Suez •
Port /
Tawfiq

Adabiyah •

*Gulf of
Suez*

0   10   20 Miles
0   10   20 Kilometers

Map by James Sinclair

is that the retreat was due to the rattling of Israel's nuclear saber. If so, Dayan had once more saved Israel—even as his personal star was falling.

By the morning of October 9, the Egyptians had 100,000 men and 800 tanks on the east bank of the canal. They also had two armored divisions, two mechanized divisions, and two armored brigades, equipped with a total of 900 tanks, on the west bank. President Sadat was raging at his Chief of Staff, Lieutenant General Saad el Din Shazli, to break out of the pocket and race to the Gidi and Mitla passes.

Shazli was a dedicated professional officer, a charismatic leader who combined charm and daring with meticulous planning. As Chief of Staff, he had done the seemingly impossible, forced the close coordination of Egypt's air, ground, and naval forces. It was Shazli who had planned the crossing of the Suez Canal, supervising every element of its planning and execution. Shazli, knowing full well that the existence of his forces depended upon coverage by the SAM batteries shielding them, argued against the breakout plan. It was an argument that the increasingly stressed Shazli could not win, for if he did not advance he would be fired and if he did he would be defeated.

Shazli's opposite number, the equally stressed Dado Elazar, could not worry that his own career was in jeopardy, as were those of other top Israeli leaders, including Meir, Dayan, and Zeira. For the moment, Elazar's job was to run the Pit, and to keep the General Staff operating.

Elazar's philosophy for fighting in the war was directly opposite Dayan's.[12] Elazar did not believe new defense lines depended upon surrendering territory, particularly in a war fought with armor. Rather than pull back on any front, he wanted to hold every inch of ground and grind the enemy down. Elazar felt that the greatest weight of effort should be against the Syrians, who he thought could be defeated by the

IAF and by the augmentation of the reserve forces. The intense battle of armor was to be complemented by an air strike on Damascus. Once the Syrians had been defeated, all effort could be applied against the Egyptians. He had already designated the units that would carry the war back across the canal, but he wished to wait and see before agreeing to a cross-canal operation.

Although he was not yet fully aware of it, by October 9 Elazar's philosophy was proving itself. His strategy was basically the same for the Southern Front: no retreat. Elazar wanted the Egyptian armor to attack again and be worn down by Israeli resistance so that the ratio of forces would not be so heavily in Egypt's favor.

By noon, Elazar had reviewed all the action on both fronts and one fact was appallingly clear: the Israelis were running short of ammunition, particularly artillery shells. The tank losses were terrific, but while tanks might be replaced in the short term, dead crews could not. The most dangerous situation was in the air force. So many aircraft had been lost or damaged that the infamous "red line" where there was no longer enough aircraft to conduct operations had been reached. Immediate help from the United States, particularly the delivery of Phantom aircraft, was imperative. Then, after eighty-three hours with virtually no sleep, Elazar folded and took a three-hour nap. In that interval, the maverick Sharon disobeyed his explicit orders and engaged in offensive action, moving his division into position to cross the canal.

Most Americans prefer to forget the shame of the dying days of the Nixon administration, which were such a contrast to its glorious beginning. Then Nixon had scored one of the greatest electoral victories in American history in 1972, defeating George McGovern by 520 electoral votes to 17 and losing only Massachusetts and the District of Columbia. There was no quibbling over the popular vote, nor any need for a recount, as Nixon gained a clear 60.69 percent with 47,169,911 votes to McGovern's 29,170,383. While Nixon never had been seen as a warm or sympathetic personality, his foreign policy had been innovative. Nixon's February 1972 visit to China had shattered precedents and seemed to foreshadow a new era for U.S. policy in Asia. In a similar way, his engagement with the Soviet Union had resulted in the era of détente and furthered the Strategic Arms Limitations Talks (SALT) process. Yet 1972 would be filled with woe, for the war in Vietnam was dragging on and protests were getting ever more violent. The force of these protests, which had driven Lyndon Johnson from office, combined with domestic political pressures to bring out the worst in Nixon and his colleagues.

One situation was merely embarrassing and undignified. Nixon had chosen Spiro Agnew to be his Vice President in 1968 and ran with him again in 1972, despite Agnew's rampant unpopularity. In the summer of 1973, Agnew came under intensive investigation for criminal activities during his time as governor of Maryland. He was accused of extortion, bribery, and income tax violations and faced federal indictment on these charges. On the night of October 9, Agnew and his staff were in the midst of preparations for his resignation as Vice President—only the second U.S. Vice President to resign, the first to resign due to criminal charges. Yet the embarrassment of Agnew was minor compared to the growing furor over an inept burglary of the Watergate offices of the Democratic National Committee on June 17, 1972. The burglary was clumsily covered up, with the participants no match for the unrelenting investigative reporters who pursued them. In April 1973 Nixon denied any personal role in the cover-up and allowed his top aides to resign, hoping to create a firewall against the rising tide of indignation. Things went from terrible to catastrophic as it became evident that Nixon had indeed participated in the cover-up. On the night of October 9, the political events swirling around him began to include serious talk of impeachment. With his judgment perhaps impaired by the advice of his counselors and the unceasing personal attacks in the media, Nixon began a cover-up of the cover-up, fighting to retain control of tape-recorded conversations that confirmed his participation.

Yet despite all this Nixon remained in full control of his faculties when it came to addressing the crisis in the Middle East. For all of Kissinger's gamesmanship, when it got down to the crunch it would be Nixon who made the crucial decisions.

Named for Corporal Frank S. Scott, the first enlisted man to be killed in a flying accident, Scott Air Force Base combined the old-army charm of stately redbrick buildings and residences with the ceaseless bustle of a worldwide military airlift operation. Located east-northeast of Belleville, Illinois, Scott was the headquarters for MAC.

The people who flew military airlift aircraft were a special breed, inured to long trips away from home and at ease with the idea that while all the glory went to the fighter and bomber boys, the serious spadework of war was conducted by the airlifters. In the past, the airlift equipment had always been less than adequate, usually comprised of airline passenger planes redesigned for cargo use. That had changed somewhat with the 1953 introduction of the piston-engine Douglas C-124, which was slow and vibrated so much that it was fondly referred to by its crews as Old Shaky. The C-124 continued to do satisfactory work in the Vietnam War, but the crews were grateful that it had been superseded by two truly modern jet aircraft, the Lockheed C-141 in 1965 and the C-5 in 1970. The efficiency of the new aircraft was enhanced on the ground by the 463L equipment handling system and in the air by the global control exercised from the MAC Headquarters at Scott.

General Paul K. Carlton, Commander of MAC, was also

the Executive Director of the Single Manager Operating Agency for Airlift Service, a position intended to make airlift more efficient and to reduce competing and redundant efforts. Carlton was a powerful man, six feet, two inches tall and weighing more than two hundred pounds, and blessed with an acute sense of humor. Yet no one gets to be a four-star general without being demanding, and Carlton fit the bill. At the same time, competent personnel found him easy to work with and he handled people well. He had come to MAC from the Strategic Air Command (SAC), where he had learned the importance of planning and procedures that anticipated every conceivable mission that might be required. That October, he recognized that the MAC personnel were fully up to his standards and well experienced in the work that they were about to undertake.

General Carlton was keenly aware that MAC would be called in to supply airlift to Israel, and he had begun making the initial preparations for it on October 7. He was supported in this effort by the Air Force Chief of Staff, General George S. Brown. Many people have credited Brown with anticipating the President's decision to send munitions and even F-4s to Israel. (Ironically, only one year later Brown would be pilloried by the Jewish War Veterans and the Anti-Defamation League of B'nai B'rith for comments he made in an address at the Duke University Law School. Brown had remarked upon the undue influence of the Jewish lobby in Congress. Then, in what he later termed as "poorly chosen words," he went on to comment about the extent to which Jews were represented in the ownership of banks and newspapers. The ensuing storm of criticism almost forced his resignation. The government of Israel took a dispassionate view, with Prime Minister Yitzhak Rabin commenting on December 6, 1974, that "General Brown probably helped Israel in the last war more than anyone else.")[13]

Without clear instructions from the Department of Defense, Carlton called for the creation of a variety of plans that enacted a wide range of operations. At the lowest level of MAC effort, supplies would simply be airlifted to the East Coast for pickup by El Al aircraft. A medium level of effort would call for the supplies to be airlifted to the East Coast, from which U.S. commercial aircraft would carry the matériel to Israel. Another effort, a notch up, would see MAC aircraft picking up the supplies and flying them to Lajes, in the Azores, for transshipment to Israel via El Al aircraft. Finally—and with his keen foresight Carlton felt that this would be the selected option—plans were made for MAC aircraft to fly directly into Israel, via Lajes.

What was important to Carlton was that Brown had begun the process of assembling the munitions and missiles that Israel would need so desperately at standard MAC pickup points around the country. Within days this process would take on a life of its own as depots were scoured for equipment and factories were sent into triple shifts to produce matériel. But if Brown had not jump-started the process, the airlift would not have had enough to deliver in the first crucial days.

The hand-in-glove manner in which Carlton and Brown had foreseen the requirement for an airlift and had tactfully and quietly given the initial orders to establish it reflected their years of experience. Both combat veterans of World War II and long experienced in the Cold War, they were good men to have at the helm in an emergency. Both men were aware that many of the items on the list were crucial to USAF strength, which had been so depleted by the Vietnam War. Among these were air-to-air missiles, electronic counterwarfare pods, and a number of F-4 Phantoms.

One of Carlton's principal concerns was to make sure that involvement in the Middle East would not devour MAC's assets to the point that it would be unable to fulfill its other worldwide commitments.[14] He hoped that at least some of the airlift load might be handled by the Civil Reserve Air Fleet, an organization by which U.S. civil airlines could participate in military operations, backing up MAC's efforts. In the next few days he would find that the commercial airlines had no desire to participate, not wishing to divert their aircraft from lucrative passenger work and absolutely unwilling to offend the Arab nations. Their concern about Arab feelings was twofold. They needed the Arab airlines as partners in carrying passengers to and from the Middle East, and they wanted, at all costs, to avoid the increase in fuel prices that the Arabs were threatening.

Well aware that the Soviet airlift was already under way, with the first landings to be made in Egypt and Syria on October 10, Carlton mentally compared that operation to the rather feeble efforts of Israel to carry equipment in 707 and 747 passenger planes. The disparity was too great; he knew that within days MAC would be given the task to fly into the combat zone. With his staff, he continued preparations for what would be the single biggest airlift challenge since the Berlin Blockade.

It was a 4:45 P.M. on October 9, uncomfortably near the cocktail hour, when the second most decisive U.S. meeting of the Yom Kippur War took place. Henry Kissinger was already exceptionally annoyed because of news that the Soviet Union was urging King Hussein of Jordan and President Houari Boumedienne of Algeria to enter the war against Israel, promising complete support. This more than anything confirmed Kissinger's opinion that there could be no request for a cease-fire until Israel was obviously gaining the upper hand. He was also terribly concerned that, despite his admonitions to the contrary, Golda Meir might decide to come to the United States and make her plea to the President— and the public. Overriding all of these considerations was the Israeli threat to use nuclear weapons unless overwhelming support from the United States was immediately supplied.

President Nixon presided over the meeting, which included Kissinger; Brent Scowcroft, Kissinger's deputy in the

National Security Council; General Alexander Haig, Nixon's new Chief of Staff; and one of the early spin-meisters, Ronald L. Zeigler, chief of the White House press office.[15] As preoccupied as he was with Watergate, Nixon came straight to the point, announcing that Israel must not lose the war. He ordered that the deliveries of supplies, including aircraft, be sped up and that Israel be told that it could freely expend all of its consumables—ammunition, spare parts, fuel, and so forth—in the certain knowledge that these would be completely replenished by the United States without any delay. There was no need for Israel to hold back its reserve stocks, as it had already begun to do. This simple assurance, as undramatic as it was vital, was key. Over the next few days, the Israeli consumption rate of ammunition was staggeringly high, and without U.S. resupply it would in a few days be unable to fight.

Ambassador Dinitz had supplied Kissinger with long lists of the needed equipment. After a brief perusal, Nixon approved almost all of them, including electronic countermeasures equipment but excluding laser-guided bombs. Emphasis was placed on the replacement of losses in the Patton tanks and A-4 and F-4 aircraft. While under ordinary circumstances the tank replacements would not arrive in any substantial quantity until after the war, Kissinger promised that in an emergency they would be delivered immediately. The flow of McDonnell F-4 fighters would begin without delay, two a day to begin but more as they became available.

In one of the high-level blunders that typified the conduct of the war in every country, the meeting closed with the understanding that the airlift into Israel would be conducted exclusively by El Al aircraft. This was an inexcusable mistake, for the sheer quantity of equipment required was obviously far beyond El Al's capability. The failure stemmed from the inability of the meeting's participants to comprehend the magnitude of Israel's requirements or the immense effort that would be required of MAC to meet them. At

MAC Headquarters at Scott AFB, those requirements were recognized, and under Carlton's direction there began the process of gearing up for an operation that would dwarf the Berlin Airlift in terms of the rapidity of the sorties, the tonnage, and the logistics and navigation difficulties.

No one at Scott, including General Carlton, knew it, but the outcome of the Middle East war and preventing the outbreak of a nuclear war now depended upon the simple mathematics of airlift: how many tons of cargo could be delivered and how swiftly it could be done. Implicit in this formula was a question: Could MAC deliver supplies to Israel more swiftly and more efficiently than the Soviet air force could deliver supplies to the Arab nations? For the moment, the advantage lay with the Soviet air force, for it had clear orders from the Kremlin to gather up the requisite supplies from all over the Soviet Union and the Warsaw Pact nations and get them posthaste to Egypt and Syria. The distances the Soviets had to fly were shorter, and the routes that had to be flown were over friendly countries.

The U.S. aircrews and the aircraft involved would answer the question.

4 Arab Euphoria

THOUGH IT WAS NOT YET apparent from the Pit, the gloomy subterranean command post in Tel Aviv, October 10 would be a day of transition, one in which the strength and motives of the Egyptians and Syrians would have to be reassessed while endless debate nearly paralyzed Israel. Yet before the day ended Chief of Staff Dado Elazar would make one of the key decisions of the war.[1]

The continuing prospect of a cease-fire in place meant that any change in Israeli positions—for good or bad—would have profound political effects during the negotiations that would take place after the cease-fire. For that reason, Elazar was determined to stick to the chain of command and to get all of his major decisions ratified by Minister of Defense Dayan and, of course, Prime Minister Meir and her cabinet. This was not, as it might appear, merely an attempt to cover himself in case things went wrong. Elazar would have far preferred to have acted on his own, as he had done to his glory in the Six-Day War when he commanded the Northern Front. A political realist, he simply wanted to do the best he could for his native land, making the recommendations he felt best but acceding to political dictates of which he might have no knowledge.

There was no question that Dayan would be a problem; he was already excusing himself with unnecessary visits to the fronts and trying to distance himself from Elazar's decisions. It was difficult to understand—Dayan's career was also almost certainly at an end, as was that of Golda Meir. But Dayan still clung to his image and still sought to somehow rise above the debacle that had in his own words almost overthrown the "Third Temple."

Elazar was fully conscious that military disaster after disaster had bred an unwonted caution among Meir's advisers. Unfortunately, caution was exactly what Israel could not afford, for time was clearly on the side of the Arab enemies. The cold term *ordinary wastage* is military jargon that means the number of soldiers, sailors, and airmen killed daily when no major offensive or defensive operations are being conducted. Israel had reached the point where "ordinary wastage" could not be tolerated. Although the Egyptians were now much less active than anticipated, they were extracting a toll every day, and though the Golan was somewhat quieter, people were still being killed with appalling regularity.

The IAF was a critical factor; the most optimistic estimates gave it only four or five days more of operations at the current rate, and then its strength would decline precipitously and reach what the Israeli leadership called the red line. This was the point beyond which full-scale operations could not be conducted. It was blindingly obvious that if the IAF was grounded, the war was unsalvageable.

Elazar was bowed but not broken by his wrong decisions and the surprising skill of the Arab armies. His dark and rough-hewn features were those of a pugilist, and he often barked his orders like a drill sergeant. No one would have gained the impression that he was an extremely sensitive man. Like all top military leaders, he had the air of command, and in the Pit, with its crowds of high-ranking hangers-on and advisers, Elazar was often outspoken and rude. Yet at headquarters they soon learned one unwritten rule. While he obviously had to be informed daily of the number of killed and wounded—there were close to five hundred dead by the evening of October 9—it was soon understood that the names of those killed were never mentioned to the Chief of Staff.[2] Only in those instances when command reasons dictated—as with the soon-to-come death of Major General Avraham Mandler—was Elazar to be given the names of the dead. The staff learned that one area was particularly sensitive. The men who had fought the Arabs from 1948 on were fighting them again, but this time there was a signal difference. For the first time, many of them had sons who were also fighting, and their losses were particularly hard for Elazar to bear.

The morning of October 10 was exceptionally challenging for Dado, who had to juggle the myriad requirements of both fronts along with those of the air force. He could do little about the battles currently being waged, but upon his decisions rested all the possibilities of success for tomorrow and beyond. He was faced with an either-or situation. Either he would mass forces to attack in the Golan Heights, risking both the danger of intervention by Jordan and the expected appearance of an Iraqi tank brigade, or he would have to attack in the south before determining Egyptian intentions.

Yet even before arriving at the key decision on the next day's attack, he had three immediate problems to solve in the early-morning gloom. One was tactical, and the other two involved high-ranking personnel. The tactical problem was easiest. Soviet aircraft were due to start landing in Syria, and he gained permission from Dayan to bomb the runways before they arrived.

The personnel problems were stickier. The first was getting Major General Gonen to accept the fact that he was being superseded by an old and hated rival, Lieutenant General Bar-Lev.[3] The second was to placate his Deputy Chief of Staff, Tal, who wanted the job that was being given to Bar-Lev.

The men were a study in personal contrasts. Elazar was articulate and outgoing, easily familiar with superiors and subordinates alike. Bar-Lev was immensely focused and, slow to speak but emphatic when he spoke. If Elazar was a quarterback, then Bar-Lev was a linebacker, ready to crush opposition on the battlefield or in the conference room. Tal, small of stature, was a technical genius who had twice won the Israel Prize for his inventions. An extremely strict disciplinarian, he was an international expert in armored warfare.

Yet Tal (or Talik, as Dado called him) was a disappointment in his role as Deputy to the Chief of Staff. In the heat of battle and at the height of emergency, he would come to Elazar with self-interested arguments about rank and position. This seemed inappropriate to Elazar, who expected more in the way of self-sacrifice.

Information supplied by Major General Peled of the IAF helped Elazar decide where to attack next. Peled was confident that he had knocked out a substantial part of Syria's missile defense system and absolutely certain that the IAF had defeated the Syrian air force in the air. When Zeira, the Chief of Intelligence, reported that a mutiny had broken out in the Syrian 1st Armored Division, Elazar's mind was virtually made up. Rumors of a UN cease-fire request abounded. An attack in the north would gain Syrian territory, a bargaining chip against the section of the Sinai now held by Egyptian forces. The offensive would be kicked off by an extensive bombing attack of Syrian airfields.

Late in the evening on October 10, Elazar and Dayan squared off once again, with Dayan letting his political/ diplomatic views dominate his military thinking. He was against an offensive in the Golan Heights because its success might threaten Damascus—and this might bring the Soviet Union actively into the war to protect Syria. Elazar countered these arguments by stating that the IDF would advance only to an easily defensible line where Israeli long-range artillery could threaten Damascus. It would then stop and await developments. Dayan reluctantly agreed.

The Arabs once again showed surprising resilience, repairing the effects of the airfield bombing from Israel in short order. Then, in a vivid demonstration of resolve and efficiency, eighty Soviet air force Antonov An-12 and An-22 transports, supplemented by twenty transports drawn from Aeroflot, made landings in Palmyra and Aleppo in Syria and in Cairo, Egypt, on October 10.[4] The airlift showed considerable planning, for the flights had originated at a number of bases in Europe and the Soviet Union. Some came through Warsaw Pact capitals, including Budapest and Belgrade, while others had flown from bases in the Caucasus and the Ukraine. The Arab forces had been using ammunition at the same profligate rate as the Israelis, so these initial cargoes were primarily munitions and missiles.

The Arabs also received reinforcements of heavier equipment, such as tanks and MiG-21 fighters. These came by sea, embarking at Rostov, Mykolayiv, Odessa, and Kerson, plodding first across the Black Sea and then into the western Mediterranean. Much of the heavy equipment had been scrounged from Warsaw Pact sources.

The airlift aircraft were the pride of the Soviet air force. The Antonov An-12 was a four-turbo-prop high-wing transport with a maximum payload of over 44,000 pounds, corresponding roughly to the U.S. Lockheed C-130 Hercules. The An-12 was not as sophisticated as the C-130, as its cargo area was unpressurized and it lacked internal ramps for loading and unloading. However, it was very rugged and had a good turn of speed (412 mph cruise) and a good range—2,236 miles with a maximum payload.

The An-22 was a much larger aircraft, with four huge 15,000 ehp (equivalent horsepower) turboprops each driving two four-bladed contrarotating propellers. With a 90,000-pound payload it could fly at close to 400 mph for more than 3,000 miles. Most important, it could carry T-62 tanks, which were in short supply among the Arab armies.

Fortunately for the Arabs and the Soviet crews, the distance from the Soviet staging areas to the Arab airfields was only about 1,700 miles at the longest, with some routes being as short as 400 miles. And unlike the U.S. crews, the Soviets could fly direct routes over their allies in the Balkans to reach their destinations.

When President Nixon decided that there would be an American airlift, the Israelis had less than a two-week supply of ammunition. By the time the airlift arrived, the IDF had munitions for little over a week.

The Israelis, knowing that the go-ahead had been given on October 9, expected aircraft to start arriving on October 10. It was not to be, for despite the prescient preparations of Generals Brown and Carlton, there were still hazards and red tape to be cleared at the highest levels.

The first and greatest difficulty was the sharp divergence in views between Secretary of State Kissinger and Secretary of Defense James R. Schlesinger. Over the years and through a glut of memoirs and papers, the rivalry of the two men has been continuously discounted by both of them, but no one who worked with either has ever been in doubt of the degree of their animosity. Personally, their similarities were as striking as their differences. Both were born Jews, although Schlesinger converted to Christianity. Both had received doctorates from Harvard. Both had distinguished themselves in a variety of governmental posts. Both had deep defense interests. Kissinger, born in 1923, was six years older, but in 1973 both men were dealing with older superiors and peers.

Each was personable in public and difficult to deal with in private. To say that both had tremendous egos would belabor the obvious. Of the two, Kissinger had better rapport with the media. The two men's views, egos, and skills came into sharp divergence when it came to aiding Israel in the Yom Kippur War. Schlesinger wanted to distance the United States as much as possible from the conflict. He was certain that Israel would win its fight in relatively short order, and he did not wish to antagonize the Arab nations into using the "oil weapon." In particular, he feared that fuel supplies to the Sixth Fleet in the Mediterranean might be compromised. To this end, he repeatedly postponed meetings with Israeli Ambassador Dinitz.

Kissinger, as we have seen, was determined to assist Israel, but only when absolutely necessary and only to the degree required to preserve it from Arab domination. He absolutely did not wish to have Egypt so humiliated that it would refuse postwar attempts at a genuine peace treaty. To him the war offered a parlay: the removal of Soviet influence in the Middle East and an improvement in relations with the Arabs that would lead to the dominance that supplying arms always brings. Because Kissinger saw himself emerging as the arbiter of the coming armistice/peace talks, he felt that Schlesinger was obliged to assume the "bad-cop" role in regard to any delays in airlifting aid to Israel. Schlesinger, reasonably enough, refused to do this.

Ironically, in the end there was enough blame to go around for the delay—which turned out not to really matter very much. Had Kissinger and Schlesinger put aside their personal motivations to act in perfect accord and had they assessed the input from Carlton and others accurately, they could have perhaps expedited the airlift by two or three days, so that it might have started on October 11 or 12. The delay was caused in almost equal parts by the Department of State and the Department of Defense. At State, it was delayed because of Kissinger's desire to avoid U.S. involvement until he had made sure his motivation was understood in both Moscow and the Arab world. At the DOD, it was delayed by Schlesinger's reluctance to immediately acquiesce to Kissinger's request and a desire to investigate the use of civilian commercial air carriers if possible. This led to a delay in seeking the necessary diplomatic permission for a full-scale military airlift from the United States' NATO allies. Ironically, both Kissinger and Schlesinger were comfortable with the delay because of their joint belief that Israel would prevail in any case.

The relationship with the NATO allies went back through World War II and extended forward through the Marshall Plan and the protection provided by the United States' nuclear umbrella. However, gratitude for all these measures did not displace the politics of self-interest. Fearing the oil embargo, each of the NATO allies immediately distanced itself from the war in the Middle East. Despite the Presidential order that the airlift begin, NATO dragged its heels, refusing not only landing and refueling but even overflight of NATO member territory. The MAC airlift would not begin until October 13.[5]

Yet in retrospect, this delay was not as crucial as it might seem, for the very promise of an airlift permitted the Israeli forces to use their stores of munitions at the rate they desired. But the most important factor, a hard reality too often overlooked, is that the airlift became *decisive* for the outcome of the war long before the first MAC airplane landed at Lod. It was decisive because it demonstrated that the United States was going to support Israel directly, not just through the United Nations or NATO. The effect on both the Arab world and the Soviet Union was tremendous, so great that Sadat could later say without embarrassment that "Egypt was more than willing to fight Israel, but it could not fight the United States." Israel expressed its gratitude profusely at the time, but in later years, in keeping with its reputation for intransigent independence, the importance of the airlift has been downplayed. However, one thing can never be forgotten: had the United States, for whatever reason, subsequently reneged on the airlift, an isolated Israel, alone against the world, would have been vulnerable to Arab victories on the battlefield and at the diplomatic bargaining tables.

General Carlton's preplanning would pay off, but there was still much to be done. The Joint Chiefs of Staff directed that three C-5s and fifteen C-141s be loaded with supplies and ready to take off the moment the final decision came down. The Deputy Secretary of Defense, William P. Clements Jr., approved the decision but still wished to find if there were any other possible means of delivery before the release order was given. (Clements would later be accused by Ambassador Dinitz of having ties to oil companies that made him deliberately sabotage the efforts to get the airlift started.) By the night of October 10, MAC was girding for a colossal effort on a worldwide basis.

The battle in the southern sector of the Golan took longer than the fight in the north but netted the same results. Major General Moshe "Mussa" Peled, acting on Elazar's decision of October 7, had rushed a division from the Jordanian border to a position bordering the Sea of Galilee. (The Israelis had three General Peleds on active service—the IAF's Bennie; another armored division commander, Elad; and Mussa.) On October 10, Peled's 19th Brigade had launched a midday attack intending to take the Syrian headquarters operating at Tal Kudne. The Syrians' 9th Division opposing him was still full of fight, however, and Peled's brigade incurred heavy losses. Peled was ordered to assume a defensive position that would serve as the anvil for the hammer of Major General David "Dan" Laner's reserve division. Caught between Laner's and Peled's forces, Tal Kudne was turned into a killing ground as bloody as the 1944 Battle of the Falaise Gap. In twenty-four hours of continuous fighting, the Israelis ground the Syrians almost to extinction, then pushed the remnants back to their starting point.

Over four days, the Syrians had lost 1,400 tanks and armored personnel carriers to Israeli armor and Israeli air attacks.[6] Of these, hundreds had been abandoned in near working condition, mostly the older T-54 and T-55 types. By the night of October 10, the Syrians were a spent force, conscious that the Israelis would pause only briefly before the inevitable counterattack that would be very difficult, if not impossible, to contain. President Assad wanted a cease-fire now more than ever, even though his request had been called treasonous by Anwar Sadat.

Along the Sinai Front, the war was beginning to run more in the style to which the Israelis had become accustomed. The Israelis were now under the command of General Bar-Lev, which pleased Adan and infuriated Sharon. Gonen accepted the change with more grace than could have been expected, concealing his bitterness with humor. When told that Bar-Lev was to function as Deputy Chief of Staff, Gonen responded, "Thanks a lot. And I am to be an administrative officer."

Sharon's reconnaissance had revealed that there was "an open seam" between the Egyptian Second and Third Armies that could be exploited by a cross-canal attack.[7] As evening fell, one of Sharon's reconnaissance battalions had arrived at the Lexicon Road, just a few hundred yards from the Great Bitter Lake. Some twenty-eight miles long and ranging from nine miles to a few hundred yards in width, the Great Bitter Lake connected the two man-made lengths of the canal. At that point in the road, scouts discovered that the Egyptians had not fortified the Second Army's southern flank. It was an incredible military blunder. Sharon recognized at once that it was the opportunity of a lifetime.

Sharon radioed Gonen that he was near Bitter Lake. Instead of praising him, Gonen raged that he was disobeying orders. Uncharacteristically, Sharon held his temper, calling back in twenty minutes to urge that a crossing be made. Less than half an hour later, Gonen's deputy called back, telling him to forget the attack and bring his troops back. Infuriated, Sharon was certain that Gonen did not want him to have the glory of leading an attack across the canal.

Forgetting for once the political enmity that divided him from Bar-Lev, Sharon now went to the new commander to advocate an attack into the seam that divided the Egyptian forces. In his mind's eye, Sharon could see the Israelis splitting the two Egyptian armies and then cutting off and surrounding the Egyptians on the east bank. It would be a belated replay of the Six-Day War. His idea was totally consistent with the Israeli doctrine of attacking whenever possible.

Yet Sharon found another naysayer. Bar-Lev vetoed Sharon's suggestion, to no one but Sharon's surprise. The Israelis had only about six hundred tanks available, and Bar-Lev stipulated that at least one thousand were required if they were to hold their current positions and also cross the canal. Adan supported Bar-Lev, in part because he agreed with him and in part because he felt Sharon was a showboater who had let him down for the past two days. Not incidentally, Adan wanted his division to be the one to cross the canal and defeat the Egyptians.

Fortunately, the tank resupply effort was progressing and it did not look as if the buildup would take long. More Pattons and Centurions were arriving hourly, along with units using captured equipment. (Captured T-54 and T-55 tanks had been reworked with 105mm cannon and U.S. engines and redesignated TI-67S.) Other tanks were being repaired by the retrieval and repair crews, a task at which the Israelis excelled and the Arabs were less proficient. The Israelis were equally adept on the personnel side, taking armor reservists arriving from abroad, crewing them up, and mating them with newly repaired tanks. That October it was not unusual for a reservist to step off an El Al airplane at Lod and within twenty-four hours be at the front in command of a refurbished tank.

The Israeli commanders put aside their personal differences to share what they had learned about armored warfare in the last three days. New tactics were evolving in which armored personnel carriers—"Zeldas," in Israeli parlance—were loaded with infantry and sent forward ahead of the tanks to deal with the Swagger-and-RPG-armed Egyptian infantry. The Zeldas were U.S.-made FMC (Food Machinery Corporation) M113A-1 tracked vehicles.[8] Capable of reaching 42 mph with a crew of two and eleven soldiers, the Zelda's

215-horsepower Detroit Diesel engine gave it an enviable re-
liability. Originally designed to be both amphibious and air-
transportable, the M113s were built in a bewildering variety
for export over the years. The Israelis eventually decided they
did not need the amphibious capability for desert operations
and installed a battery of machine guns and, when available,
antitank missile launchers. This was a positive change in tactics, yet there were too few Zeldas, reflecting once again the
improper emphasis that had been placed on the acquisition
of tanks.

Another new but costly tactic, one that made U.S. aid absolutely imperative, involved the concerted use of artillery
with tank movements. Whenever possible, the Israeli commanders learned to send their tanks forward surrounded by
"artillery boxes" that protected their front and flanks with a
rolling barrage of shells that kept enemy heads down. Inside
the barrage, ahead of the tanks, the Zelda's four machine guns
laid down a withering fire on any bit of ground cover that
might conceal a lurking Arab infantryman and his antitank
weapons. The constant spray of shells made this a difficult
and costly way to fight a war, and it would not have been
possible if the U.S. airlift had not been promised.

For the present, and as much as it galled them, the Israelis
remained in defensive positions, turning back pinprick attacks by the Egyptians all along the front. All hoped for and
expected a major attempt by the Egyptians to break out and
reach the Mitla and Gidi passes. But both sides knew that
such an attack meant moving out from under the Egyptian
SAM shield, the very event that the Egyptian Chief of Staff,
Major General Shazli, was fighting desperately to avoid.

For the moment, the trenches were dug in and all was quiet
on the Southern Front—at least compared to the Golan.

In retrospect, it is difficult to reconcile the hesitation and
indecision in the United States to initiate the airlift with

the speedy decisions generated by the geriatric Politburo in Moscow.

In October 1973 the Politburo was headed by General Secretary Leonid Brezhnev, the sixty-six-year-old former political commissar of the Red Army and protégé of Nikita Khrushchev. In the typical manner of Soviet politics, Brezhnev remained loyal to his mentor until 1964, when it was opportune to betray him. In the fashion of the time, the change in power was softened by the creation of a collective leadership with Premier Aleksey Kosygin, and with Nikolai Podgorny, who as chairman of the Presidium was the formal head of state.

With a powerful often overbearing personality, Brezhnev was a curious mixture of opposing traits. In the course of a single meeting he could be both boastfully belligerent and terribly insecure. When drinking—and he often drank heavily—he mellowed and kept his company laughing with a repertoire of naughty jokes. He had two primary tactics in diplomacy: either bully the opponents into submission or cajole them with heavy humor and flattery.

Brezhnev took upon himself the duties of foreign and military affairs, delegating internal tasks to others. He traveled extensively within the Soviet bloc and exerted an iron hand when necessary, as with the summary crushing of dissident opinion in Czechoslovakia in 1968. After the ruthless suppression of Czechoslovakia, he enunciated his infamous "Brezhnev Doctrine" in a speech in Poland in which he stated that the only road to real socialism was that of the Soviet Union. Any talk of national self-determination—Alexander Dubček's sin in Czechoslovakia—was contrary to the interests of communism and, in Brezhnev's warped view, to the nation seeking it. National interests had always to be subordinated to the international interests of the Communist Party, as defined by the Soviet Union.

For the most part, Brezhnev's foreign and military policies were quite successful. He opposed U.S. policy throughout the world, especially in Southeast Asia, where Soviet Union supplies and support enabled North Vietnam to force the United States from the war. At the same time, he sought and obtained better relations with the United States and considered himself the personal architect of the détente that resulted from his summit meetings with President Nixon in 1972 and 1973.[9] Although he was relatively modest in his private life, Brezhnev was a lover of luxury items, especially extravagant automobiles. Try as he would, however, he was not successful in his efforts to improve Soviet trade or its domestic economy. The greatest failures were in agriculture and in the production of ordinary consumer goods such as soap, toilet paper, tampons, and other necessities.

By the fall of 1973, Brezhnev saw the October War as a means to shed the last trappings of "collective leadership." The silk-covered walls of the Kremlin began to tear at the cracking of his whip. In the process he had many able allies, the most stalwart of whom was the cautious and stony-faced survivor Foreign Minister Andrei Gromyko; the physically imposing Minister of Defense General Andrei Grechko; and Yuri Andropov, the head of the KGB and future successor to Brezhnev.

These three men, so unlike in most respects, were united on one thing. They all disliked dealing with the Arabs and in particular with Sadat, who they felt suffered from megalomania. They believed the war was a major political error on the part of the Arabs, who in their minds had no chance for victory. All three were traditionally anti-Semitic and ardently anti-Zionist. Brezhnev took advantage of the fact that the emigration of Jews from the Soviet Union had turned into a business that generated large sums of hard currency from those lucky enough to leave, largely obtained from wealthy American Jews. It was difficult for any Jew to leave the Soviet Union. A declaration of intent to leave resulted in an immediate job loss and other penalties. Yet anti-Semitism was such a fact of Soviet life that emigration became the only hope for hundreds of thousands of Jews. In the meantime, the Soviets used the Jewish population as a scapegoat to explain the miserable domestic economy.

Despite this climate of distaste and gloom, Brezhnev sought to make the best of it by working toward cooperation with the United States to achieve some sort of bilateral agreement for a cease-fire. Working the customary dual diplomatic track, Brezhnev himself on October 6 immediately approved both the airlift and the unlimited supply of arms and munitions to the Arabs. Although the Soviet air force had anticipated the airlift, it still took time to get under way, and the first landings did not occur until four days later. Nonetheless, by October 10 the skies over Egypt were filled with contrails and a heavy Soviet transport landed almost every thirty minutes.

It was also Brezhnev who helped to unite the Arab world against Israel, sending confidential personal messages to all the major heads of Arab states. One of these backfired, for his message to Algeria's President Boumedienne was published in the press. Brezhnev was furious and certain that it would undercut his efforts to assure Nixon of his desire for peace in the Middle East. As it happened, the event was scarcely noticed in the United States.

The surprising military successes of the Arabs early in the war had revealed a number of things that would affect Brezhnev's thinking. One of these was the excellence of the Soviet arms, including not only SAMs and the antitank weapons but also the auxiliary equipment such as bridging gear, antiaircraft guns, and the invaluable armored personnel carriers. This made it seem to him that a continued Soviet presence would unquestionably be desired by the Arab world, regardless of the outcome of the war.

Offsetting this was the increased awareness of how poorly the Soviets understood Arab strategy and politics—or perhaps the lack thereof. This was a tremendous disadvantage in deciding what further steps to take, one that Brezhnev tried to remedy personally. He had his military people constantly urging Sadat and Assad to coordinate their military actions much more closely.

By October 10, however, the euphoria of the Arab success began to be eroded by the news from the Golan Heights and the relative inactivity of the Egyptian forces that had crossed the canal.[10] Soviet military leaders, particularly Grechko, charged that the inept Arab military leaders were going to throw away all that had been won. The sharp antagonism of the Syrian and Egyptian military commands was evident, as was the cold suspicion with which Assad now regarded Sadat.

For Brezhnev, however, there was no turning back. Only that morning Ambassador Dobrynin had conveyed his message to Kissinger, stating that the Soviet Union would not block a cease-fire in-place resolution in the UN Security Council. There was no concession on the question of a return to previous battle lines. But now even that slight degree of accommodation was no longer possible. The Israelis had bombed the Soviet Cultural Center in Damascus on October 9. The press now had a clear line to follow, as the Israelis were to be portrayed as aggressive murderers who must be defeated. Brezhnev elected to make his feelings known in a strong message to President Nixon. Neither man would recognize that this was the first step leading to the nuclear confrontation that both desperately wished to avoid.

To his disappointment, if not to his surprise, there would be no flying for Harry Cohen. Instead, he was assigned with another dozen volunteers to a factory building at Netanya, a coastal city north of Tel Aviv. Told that the group was freeing reservists for active duty at the front, Cohen had accepted the assignment with good grace. He had known all along that a flight assignment was highly improbable.

Harry's first nights in Netanya added to his motivation. The city was completely blacked out as London had been during the Blitz, giving way to a spectacular night sky, with the stars brighter than he had ever seen before. It was almost as quiet as it was dark, for the streets were empty, with the silence occasionally interrupted by the roar of Israeli jets going on patrol.

The first day on the job tested Harry's motivation. Rather than turning out bazookas or mortars, his group had been assigned to a factory making cots for recently arrived refugees from the Soviet Union. Harry's task was to use a primitive lever device to stretch wire coils across the frame, connecting the spring's hook to holes drilled in the frame's flange. When the line of coils was connected, he had to lift the 75-pound frame to a stack near the loading dock, where a truck came periodically to pick them up. By the end of a long day, the 135-pound Cohen was bone-weary.

Tired but not disillusioned, Harry was continually inspired by the news accounts he heard of military crisis. These would get his adrenaline pumping and enable him to handle the weight of his bed frames with ease. Cohen's sense of outrage at the Arab attack was so strong that he found release in the simple work and comfort in the motley crew with whom he worked. They were a mixed bag of idealists and rogues, mostly Jewish but not all. One was a Frenchman, ex–Foreign Legion, who had come to fight because Algeria was opposed to Israel and he sought revenge for his friends who had been killed fighting in Algeria. There was a Scot from the University of Edinburgh and a retired Danish soldier who never tired of saying that "the only things I hate are Arabs and intolerance." There were even two drifters, caught in Israel by the outbreak of war, who were volubly and ill-advisedly pro-Arab.

Cohen's work partner was a middle-aged man from Romania whose name Harry could never pronounce. The Romanian's English was poor, and the sole topic of his conversation was how bad off the Romanian Jews were. Harry drew strength and inspiration from him as well—if the Romanian could handle the job, no matter how tedious or how tiring it was, Harry could, too. Always indifferent to food, the teetotaling Cohen did not object to the rough fare and crude accommodations of the boardinghouse where he and his factory group were assigned to live. Muscles aching, he would sit at night with the family who owned the boardinghouse, watching the war in nearly real time on Israeli television.

The Israeli media was ruthless in its censorship but also rigorous in telling the truth; only information of possible tactical aid to the enemy was omitted. In the boardinghouse there were those who had family members fighting both in the Golan and in the Sinai, and reports from those areas brought a hush to the room. The quiet and tense, measured breathing of those huddled around the TV set taught Cohen more about the war than the scenes of soldiers fighting only a few hours away. Despite his cot-after-cot life, Harry felt a part of a united Israel, committed to independence or death.

General Carlton, still seeking support from the Civil Reserve Air Fleet, put in a call on October 10 to Brigadier General Paul F. Patch, who was Director of Transportation, Strategic Mobility, at the Pentagon. Carlton's message was brief and to the point: "Paul, I would hang my head in shame if there were a big airlift with no U.S. carriers involved."[11]

Patch pointed out that finding a foreign base where commercial or U.S. military carriers could land was going to be difficult. The foreign countries, most of them allies in NATO, were afraid of offending the Arabs. The U.S. air carriers were themselves afraid that the Arabs, if offended, would raise their oil prices, driving jet fuel prices sky-high. In the end these fears were realized, even though these countries all declined to transport Israeli supplies.

Meanwhile, the Israelis had muddied the waters by going directly to U.S. commercial carriers to contract for 130 loads of cargo to Israel. The U.S. carriers refused, upset by the Israelis violating procedure by not going through MAC and determined, in any event, not to fly into a combat area or offend the Arab world.

Carlton now began a search to find out where his aircraft could land. The C-5s could fly nonstop from the United States to Israel, but only with such reduced loads that it made the task far more difficult. Of the two strategic airlift aircraft, the C-141 Starlifter and the C-5 Galaxy, only the latter had been designed with an in-flight refueling capability.[12] MAC had decided not to use in-flight refueling for ordinary operations because of concerns about the fatigue life of the C-5's wing. Now there were no MAC crews qualified in the demanding task, and even though crews could be borrowed from experimental facilities and even from SAC, in-flight refueling was not a viable option. Carlton had to find a stop on the ground or there would be no airlift, no matter what happened to Israel.

Most of us, like Kissinger and Schlesinger, do not realize that an airlift is not simply a bunch of aircraft carrying freight. It is instead a massive operation involving intense logistical coordination to create what Major General William Tunner, the architect of the Berlin Airlift, called an airborne conveyor belt.

Airlifts had a checkered history. The Germans used one with great success in January 1942 in Russia at Demyansk, where the Luftwaffe kept the six divisions alive for three months, averaging 276 tons per day. It was a costly miracle, for no fewer than 265 Junkers transport planes crashed, most due to weather.

The success at Demyansk would be followed by the travesty of Stalingrad beginning in November 1942. There the entire German 6th Army had been trapped by the Soviets, with some 250,000 men requiring support to the tune of 600 tons a day. Reichsmarschall Hermann Göring, the corpulent leader of the Luftwaffe, assured Hitler that the miracle of Demyansk would be repeated. It was not, and the 6th Army died of cold and starvation as a result.

In contrast, U.S. airlifts had been far more successful, beginning with Major General Tunner's first triumphs over the Himalayas in World War II. Immortalized as "flying the Hump," the system Tunner created moved matériel on a mammoth scale. His crews carried as much as 70,000 tons to the Chinese and U.S. forces in a single month and had carried a total of 650,000 tons by the time the airlift ended in November 1945. The cost in lives had been high, with 155 accidents and 168 deaths, but the supplies got through.[13]

Tunner would repeat his success in the Berlin Blockade of 1948. The Soviets had cut off all access by road, rail, and canal to Berlin, and the 2 million inhabitants required 4,500 tons of supplies a day to subsist and 5,620 tons to live at a level of minimal health and comfort. Of this amount about two-thirds of the tonnage was required for coal, with the remainder devoted to food, medicine, and other essential items.

The operation began on June 26, 1948, when eighty tons of supplies were ferried in by a pickup unit of C-47s. Within the month, Major General Tunner had arrived and set up his "conveyor belt" of aircraft for Operation Vittles, as it was called. Tunner had standardized on four-engine Douglas C-54 transports, landing and taking them off at three-minute intervals, regardless of the weather, bringing in a total of 1,783,000 tons over the duration of the airlift. In April 1949, there was a record one-day total of 12,941 tons, an incredible amount that represented more than one and one-half times the total amount that the Luftwaffe had flown into Stalingrad during the entire seventy-five-day siege. The cost had been high, with twelve accidents and thirty-one lives lost, yet the airlift represented a stunning triumph of diplomacy and compassion over brute force, and the humiliated Soviet Union canceled its blockade on May 12, 1949.

The difficulty now was that everyone from Nixon down to the general public expected MAC to pull a full-fledged airlift from its hip pocket, without any recognition of the immense effort that would be required. At MAC Headquarters, everyone knew precisely what had to be done. The problem was finding the assets, particularly the people, to do it. Since the Vietnam War, a comfortable "operations tempo" had been established that allowed MAC to run its far-flung routes with a minimum number of crew members. There was provision for rest and even time to be spent with families between flights. The Israeli airlift requirements would change all that dramatically, as the ops tempo was rapidly accelerated. Certain skilled folk, such as navigators, load masters, and Aerial Port personnel, were critical but already in short supply.

The Aerial Port personnel acted as organizers, administrators, and facilitators of the airlift, arranging for the necessary supplies and equipment to be positioned for loading on the aircraft, allocating the aircraft and crews to the routes, then monitoring in-flight progress. They arranged for refueling and off-loading, as well as for the living arrangements of transient crews at foreign airports. The key to the airlift operation would be the establishment of Airlift Control Elements (ALCEs) at the en route and terminal airports. MAC did not have enough people to man the ALCEs that would be required. All of this meant an eighty-hour-or-more workweek until the airlift was over.

Flying the supplies and equipment was only part of the problem. Other Air Force commands had to be involved, particularly Air Force Logistics Command (AFLC), headquartered at Wright Patterson Air Force Base (WPAFB), Ohio. General Brown, the Air Force Chief of Staff, had alerted AFLC the previous day to begin preparing for the movement of supplies from warehouses, factories, and *operational units* to distribution points where the matériel could be picked up for transport to Israel. The term *operational units* is emphasized in the previous sentence because it was such a departure from standard practice, a violation of all theories of Cold War preparedness. Ever since the Korean War, the stocks of equipment, spare parts, and munitions for active duty units were kept at wartime levels. It was a complete reversal of practice to take equipment away from an active duty squadron and send it overseas, even to an ally like Israel.

AFLC was ordered to have people available twenty-four hours a day to meet requirements specified by the Departments of State and Defense. Cost data were to be accumulated, but more important, the impact on Air Force stocks of key matériel had to be carefully tallied. This was particularly necessary in regard to McDonnell F-4 Phantom and Douglas A-4 parts, which the Israelis needed in huge quantities. Both types had incurred heavy losses during close air support operations, and few of those that returned to base did so without damage from enemy antiaircraft or missiles. The urgency of the situation demanded that parts be replaced, for there was no time to repair them.

The delay in getting the U.S. airlift under way had, by default, left the transport of supplies to the ill-suited El Al civilian transports. Since October 7, they had been loading up and flying out of Pease Air Force Base, New Hampshire. It was too little—but it would not be too late.

Kissinger had spent the morning as he customarily did, moving from phone call to phone call, keeping diplomatic events moving as a juggler keeps plates spinning, with a deft touch always just in time. His main task was stalling Dobrynin and urging Israel to gain the upper hand militarily as soon as possible. Once the Israelis had either ousted the Egyptians from the east bank of the Suez Canal or made their position there untenable, Kissinger felt confident about proceeding with a "cease-fire in-place" resolution in the United Nations. The situation in the Golan Heights, by his office's estimate, was apparently already sufficiently in hand for such a move.

That afternoon Kissinger had an unprecedented but constitutionally required task: accepting the resignation of Vice President Spiro Agnew. Agnew had become a laughable Republican attack dog, spitting out long, amusing strings of alliterative insults that no one took seriously. Now, rather than face a criminal trial in a federal court, Agnew chose to resign. The resignation was an embarrassment but not a loss; Nixon would replace Agnew two months later with the Republican leader of the House, Congressman Gerald Ford. Ford was an honest, likable man who was respected by both Republicans and Democrats. One wonders if Kissinger ever dreamed that within a year's time he would exercise the saddest duty of his tenure as Secretary of State: accepting the resignation of a President.

In the meantime, Kissinger inherited a vexing problem from Carlton at MAC Headquarters: finding a place for the airlift planes to land and refuel.

5 Pushing the Red Line

WORKING ROUND-THE-CLOCK was now standard procedure for Israeli generals. Dado Elazar's iron constitution enabled him to do so, but it was wearing and he began an uncustomary process of making a decision and then very carefully rechecking his thought processes to make sure he was not making a critical error. It was a difficult time. On October 11 his staff had estimated that the IAF would reach the dreaded red-line status in four or five days.[1] Now on Friday, October 12, that time was reduced to forty-eight hours—the same time remaining before the cease-fire was expected. The red-line gap was closing fast because of continued heavy losses and the extraordinary rate at which munitions were being used. There was a general dearth of replacement aircraft and supplies, particularly bombs (500- and 750-pound) and air-to-air missiles, all of which had to come from the United States. The first airlift had been expected yesterday, yet there was still no sign of their coming, an ominous development.

Elazar had also made the fateful decision on actions to be taken against Syria. While the attack had not gone as well as hoped and the Syrians had not dropped their arms and fled as they had in 1967, the results were still satisfactory, and with some tough fighting it should be possible within twenty-four hours to drop Israeli 175mm long-range artillery shells on the outskirts of Damascus—the sort of message Assad understood.

Now, as so often during this murderous, violent war, the center of gravity had shifted once again to the Southern Front, where an even more important decision had to be made. There were two unpalatable alternatives. If the IDF stayed in place, it would have to fight a war of attrition in which just "ordinary wastage" would destroy Israel's ability to defend itself. If the IDF attacked across the canal, it risked tremendous losses and even a crushing defeat—but there was at least a chance of a dramatic victory.

If it came, the victory would be the result of a reversal of the usual Israeli battle tactics. Instead of the IAF clearing a way for the armor, this time the armor would rampage over the Arab SAM sites, clearing the way for the air force.

Either alternative was as much political as military, and the top defense leaders met to brief Prime Minister Meir and her cabinet. Elazar, Dayan, Bar-Lev, Zamir, Tal, and the others listened to the Chief of Intelligence, Zeira, hold forth on the possibilities available to the IDF if it elected to go on the offensive. In a manner much more subdued than his usual practice, a chastened Zeira outlined three separate plans but advocated an attack across the canal at the "soft seam" Sharon had discovered. In this preferred plan, the first objective would be to stamp out the SAM sites and AAA installations to give the IAF the freedom it needed. Then the armor could go on in a wide flanking movement to surround the Arab forces still on the west bank and isolate those on the east bank. After that, a cease-fire would not only be welcome; it would be absolutely necessary if the U.S. airlift had not arrived. Left to its own resources, the IDF would not have the strength or the munitions to continue operations. There would be a difficult and costly retreat back across the canal, one that the Egyptians might exploit by an attack with their forces on the west bank. If the Egyptians fought as well in this situation as they had on the first three days of the war, the results could be catastrophic.

The IDF was most vulnerable in its bridging capacity. Much depended on a new massive roller bridge that resembled nothing more than a gigantic millipede. The design had been conceived under Bar-Lev's tenure as Chief of Staff and was stored out of sight behind the lines. Moving these millipede bridges was a slow, tedious job, but in place each bridge would be the vital artery for a crossing. However, if the bridges were destroyed or did not make it to the canal, the IDF would have to depend upon captured Egyptian bridges. (Israeli information on the Egyptian bridges was wrong and potentially disastrous. The Egyptian bridges were not strong enough to handle Israeli tanks.)

The biggest question hanging over this plan was what actions the Egyptians might take. In the best of all scenarios, they would soon attempt the breakout from the east bank in an effort to retake the Mitla and Gidi passes. Two benefits would derive from this. First, once the Egyptians moved, they would be out from under the shelter of their SAM sites and the IAF could attack with impunity. The assumption was that the Egyptians realized this and that was why they had not attacked. Second, if the Egyptians attacked it meant that they were not going to ask for a cease-fire and this gave Israel another day or two to prepare its own offensive—and another day or two for the U.S. airlift to arrive.

Dayan and Elazar continued their bitter standoff, unable to mask their mutual dislike even in the company of others. The Defense Minister acquiesced under protest when Bar-Lev and Elazar combined to advocate the attack across the canal. In his position as former Chief of Staff and now politician/ Defense Minister, Dayan had adopted the practice of ultimately approving Elazar's recommendations even while signaling that he did not agree. It was an absurd posture, for it did him no service and impeded whatever Elazar wished to attempt.

In the ongoing struggle between Elazar and Dayan, Golda Meir acted equitably as an arbitrator and as a friend to them both. She valued Dayan's service and had a soft spot in her heart for Elazar. Such was the strength of her personality that both men looked to her first as Prime Minister and then as a woman and a friend. She valued their advice—even when it was contradictory—and factored elements of it into the final decision, which was always her own.

As the meeting drew to a close, word came that the Egyptians were obviously preparing an offensive to break out of their pocket on the west bank. The welcome news allowed the meeting to end on an almost amicable note.

The interpersonal and philosophic problems of Elazar and Dayan were an order of magnitude less than the corresponding problems on the Egyptian side. Sadat was being pressed by Syria's President Assad to make a counterattack that would relieve pressure on the Golan Front. Sadat, while not in any way sympathetic with Assad or the Syrians, whom he believed had systematically betrayed him, was very receptive to the idea. He had been trying for days to force the Egyptian Chief of Staff, Major General Shazli, to use his enormous forces on the east bank to race eastward to capture the vital Mitla and Gidi passes.[2]

To Shazli, a highly competent—and very proud—professional, the plan was madness. They had spent a year planning their goals. They had just achieved those goals in two days of the most able Arab military operations since 1948. Sadat's plans had been fully realized. The Israeli myth of invincibility had been shattered, and Egyptian forces had reclaimed part of the east bank of the canal. The past four days had been spent in building a virtually impregnable defensive position, one that had blunted all Israeli counterattacks. All this had been possible because the massive strength of the SAM system had effectively countered the IAF while antitank defenses mauled Israeli armor. To deliberately move away from the SAM shield now seemed suicidal to Shazli.

As revealed in Victor Israelyan's brilliant book *Inside the Kremlin During the Yom Kippur War,* Friday, October 12, was the gloomiest day of the war in the Kremlin. There the chief of the KGB, Yuri Andropov, ranted that the Americans were not only providing "secret supplies" to the Israelis; they were also now moving the Sixth Fleet aircraft carriers toward the

Suez Canal. That morning, the Israelis sank the Soviet mer-
chant ship *Ilya Mechnikov* in the Syrian port of Tartūs. This
was an event akin to the 1898 sinking of the battleship *Maine*
in Havana and one into which the Soviet press could sink
their teeth. Members of the Presidium gave heated talks about
the sinking, and the crew members of the *Ilya Mechnikov* were
given a heroes' welcome upon their return to Odessa. At
Brezhnev's direction, Andropov worked with Gromyko to
prepare a stern communiqué to the United States stating that
the Soviet Union was aware that the United States was supplying Israel with fighters, tanks, missiles, and bombs and,
further, that 150 American pilots were going to Israel disguised as tourists. (The latter was a fantasy that echoed the
days in 1937 when Germany sent its "volunteer" members of
the Condor Legion to Spain dressed as tourists. Yet, as we
shall see, there is a distinct possibility that some American
pilots flew missions later in the war.) The two notes were
submitted to Brezhnev for approval and signature; within
hours, Dobrynin would relay them to the White House.

A decision was then made to inform the Soviet media about
the extent of U.S. support of Israel, to offset any disapproval
of the high level of Soviet expenditures on the Arab nations.
The Soviet public, always patriotic but worn under the continual deprivations of the wasteful economic system, might
well resent money going to the wealthy Arab oil states when
it was increasingly difficult to find basic food or clothing in
the stores in Moscow and almost impossible to do so in the
rest of the country.

October 12 also started badly for Henry Kissinger, for word
had been received that Soviet airborne divisions were being
readied to go on alert.[3] If these were employed, a U.S. counterstroke was mandatory. A suitable ground response was virtually impossible. The American public had just heaved a
collective sigh of relief at the end of the war in Vietnam, and

they were certainly not going to embrace another ground conflict in a foreign land, 3,600 miles from home, and this time fighting not Soviet surrogates but the Soviets themselves. Further, the U.S. Army was in a military funk and desperately needed time to rebuild its spirit and modernize its equipment. A war on the ground was out of the question.

Congress, reacting to the American people, would that day pass the War Powers Act, severely limiting the President's powers in the employment of armed forces. Kissinger knew that this development would immediately be factored into Soviet planning.

Despite the stress of his deep concerns, Kissinger worked the media well. He conducted a very evenhanded news conference on the situation on the morning of October 12, soft-pedaling the importance of the Soviet actions by insisting that the actions, though not "helpful," still did not threaten détente. He emphasized that the Soviet airlift was significant—preparing the way for the inevitable American airlift in response—and reaffirmed the American policy of supporting Israel.

It is significant to note that the press conference had preceded a full day of Kissinger jousting with Ambassador Dobrynin, who was continually relaying Brezhnev's anger over the developments in the war. As a first step, Dobrynin hand-delivered an unsigned note to Kissinger at a luncheon, cataloging Moscow's complaints. The note protested American actions and statements in support of Israel, even though the Soviet Union was doing exactly the same, and more, for the Arabs. Despite his irritation at the almost frivolous nature of the Soviet complaints, Kissinger's response was, to say the least, diplomatic. He admired the ambassador personally even when Dobrynin was bringing problems and now assured him that he would give the note his fullest personal attention.

But Brezhnev did not allow Dobrynin and, in turn, Kissinger any peace. At 7:00 P.M. the Soviet Chargé d'Affaires, Yuli Vorontsov, requested an immediate personal meeting by

Dobrynin with Kissinger. The timing was bad, for there was a White House reception at 9:00 P.M. to announce Nixon's selection of Gerald Ford to be Vice President. Kissinger reluctantly agreed to a meeting fifteen minutes before the ceremony.

That night, Dobrynin delivered a very unfriendly message stating Brezhnev's concerns over the Israeli bombing of civilian targets in the Arab states and, most especially, the sinking of the *Ilya Mechnikov*. Then, to add insult to the Soviet airlift injury, the message sharply protested the airlift being carried on from the United States by El Al aircraft.

Dobrynin's position puzzled and troubled Kissinger, who was unable to determine whether his hostile tone heralded a new level of Soviet involvement or was merely masking concern about the Arabs' ultimate failure. The latter seemed more probable, given that there was a bright spot buried in the text of the message, a statement indicating that Moscow was still willing to take steps toward a cease-fire. There was nothing to learn from Dobrynin's demeanor, for despite the tenor of the messages, he was jovial as ever. So, as professional diplomats, Dobrynin and Kissinger went to the ceremony for Ford, both wearing smiles.

As they talked and nodded and pressed the flesh of the celebrants, Kissinger realized that the timing of the cease-fire had now become the strategic focus on both sides. Israel wanted it after another forty-eight hours of successful action. Syria wanted it at once. Egypt was divided: Sadat did not want a cease-fire until the next offensive was concluded; Shazli wanted one immediately. The Soviet Union wanted one as soon as possible but only in association with the United States and, if possible, Great Britain. All of this played into Kissinger's hands. He would determine when a cease-fire would yield the optimum advantage for the United States, then press for it.

The advice Moscow sent President Hafiz al-Assad on October 12 was unwelcome. The last thing he wished to hear from Soviet ambassador Mukhitdinov was the benefits of coordinating joint attacks with Egypt against the Israelis. The advice was obvious and the opportunity for taking it long past. Assad knew that the Syrian thrust to eject Israel from the Golan Heights had failed and that it would not be long before Israeli shells began falling on Damascus. The capture of the capital was a distinct possibility, and quiet preparations were already being made for Assad's evacuation.

Assad boiled with a double sense of betrayal. Sadat had lied to him first when he concealed his intention to merely grab a foothold on the east bank and then stop. Had the Egyptians pressed on, the Syrians might well have swept down from the heights over the Jordan to join them in a dance on Israel's dead body. Then Moscow had betrayed him by not bringing about the cease-fire after the first two days of the war.[4] Had they done so, Syria would now be ensconced in the Golan Heights. Instead the Soviets had sought to involve the United States in the cease-fire—a critical error from Assad's point of view. He knew full well that the United States would support a cease-fire only when it would help Israel.

Moscow's betrayal was hardly a surprise. It had always supported Assad's opponents in Syria, not recognizing him or his Baath socialist political party until he seized power in 1970. Despite massive Soviet support, he felt that Moscow had been far more generous with the Egyptians. In his view, Moscow had always favored Egypt over all the Arab nations since Nasser's time.

Assad wanted no more advice from Moscow. What he wanted was two or three Soviet airborne divisions in place on the line in front of Damascus. If they were not provided, the Israelis might indeed take the capital.

Simcha Dinitz, the peripatetic Israeli ambassador to the United States, had taken on the challenge of a U.S. airlift as a personal crusade. He knew all the arguments against an airlift of arms to Israel better than many of his American colleagues. He knew that there were strong opponents in both the Pentagon and the Congress to allowing U.S. aircraft to land in a foreign battle zone. He was also aware that the threat of an Arab oil embargo sent shivers of fear into the heart of every government in the world and that this fear would induce Japan, NATO allies, and especially third world countries to put enormous pressure on the United States to refuse an airlift. Even a minor airlift would not just threaten détente; it would probably end it, at a time when President Nixon's position was already dangerously threatened by the Watergate crisis. Dinitz was equally aware that the U.S. military services were critically short of modern weapons as a result of the post-Vietnam drawdown and that the amount of supplies Israel had to have would reduce U.S. ordnance stocks to critically low levels. Furthermore, the unkindest cut of all, he knew that there existed within the State Department, and to a lesser extent within the DOD, a pro-Arab sentiment. One symptom of this had surfaced when an order came down that all El Al aircraft carrying munitions would have to have the Star of David on their tail painted over. Dinitz also knew of the complex game that was being played by Kissinger and Schlesinger. Both would claim to wish to send aircraft to Israel, and each would blame the other for the airplanes' not being sent.

None of this mattered to Dinitz. His purpose was to raise enough diplomatic hell to see that an abundant flow of arms and supplies would stream to Israel via U.S. military aircraft. Anything short of this would indeed be the death knell for the Third Temple.

Dinitiz had received word on October 10 that the United States would replace all Israel stocks of war matériel, and since then the fleet of eight El Al 707s and 747s had made thirty trips from Wright Patterson AFB and other aerial ports, carrying munitions for the most part. It was immediately apparent that El Al's passenger aircraft were not efficient cargo transports. They took far too long to load and unload through the passenger-size doors and could not accept large pieces of ordnance.

Unflagging persistence in seeking a meeting with the Secretary of Defense finally paid off for Dinitiz. Realizing that he could not put the ambassador off indefinitely, Schlesinger agreed to see Dinitz on Friday at 6:00 P.M. Schlesinger's remarks were disquieting. The promised flow of F-4 Phantoms turned out to be a trickle of sixteen, to be supplied at the rate of two a day—much smaller than the rate the Israelis were losing them. Then Schlesinger admitted that the DOD was "experiencing great difficulty in mobilizing charter planes" to carry munitions to Israel.

Schlesinger was in a very difficult position. According to his later writings, he believed that both Nixon and Kissinger were against using MAC aircraft in an airlift to Israel and that the DOD's attempts to get charter aircraft were in clear conformance with their wishes. He also maintained that the only way to supply Israel as required was to commit the full resources of MAC to it and that this meant flying directly into the war zone. Yet domestic politics prevented his stating this openly to Dinitz.

Thus Schlesinger's remarks were insulting to the Israeli ambassador, who saw them as annoying power plays with Kissinger.[5] Dinitz heatedly responded that the Secretary's remarks were outrageous and left. Shortly before midnight Dinitz met again with Kissinger. His loud and vociferous complaints about Schlesinger were music to Kissinger's ears. He expressed his shock to Dinitz, emphasizing that he had heard Nixon give Schlesinger direct instructions to "get things moving."

Having won a point—however meaningless—over Schlesinger, Kissinger moved swiftly, calling in National Security

Adviser Brent Scowcroft to discuss the airlift and telephoning Schlesinger to say that U.S. diplomatic policy required Israel to go on the offensive and regain the initiative prior to any cease-fire. It was mandatory, therefore, that the airlift should begin. Kissinger next called General Alexander Haig, Nixon's Chief of Staff, and relayed the situation to him. Haig promised to get things started.

Kissinger made his last call of the night to Dinitz, assuring him that everything was in hand and that supplies would be flown to Israel shortly. While true in spirit, this was not accurate, for one more meeting had to be held before the official orders to start the airlift would be given.

It was quitting time when the newly promoted Colonel Donald Strobaugh got the phone call that would pull him from the pleasant office routine at McGuire Air Force Base, New Jersey, and plunge him once again into the heart of a combat zone. Strobaugh was a type-A personality who devoted himself to his job, but tonight he was ready to go home to a cocktail party he and his wife were throwing. As he stood to leave, he was called by Major Don Justice at 21st Air Force, telling him to alert about thirty men and prepare for a special mission.

Cheerful and businesslike as always, Strobaugh made the initial contacts and then went home to enjoy at least a few minutes of the party. Just under six feet tall and weighing 175 pounds, he stayed fit not only because his job running a Combat Control Team required it but also because he had to be fit to practice his hobby—his folly, some called it—of parachuting out of airplanes. He'd been jumping for more than twenty years and tried to make a parachute leap in every country he visited.

Long familiar with the way these special missions escalated and accelerated, Strobaugh knew that in the next few hours he would be engaged in a stream of telephone conversations that would set the time and date of the deployment. The call came within the hour. Strobaugh was ordered to be prepared to deploy with an Airlift Control Element (ALCE) within the next eighteen hours. (An ALCE is a compact organization that handles all the functions of a major airport terminal, including maintenance, Aerial Port functions [loading, unloading, and transshipping cargo and personnel], and command and control. It is able to operate on its own but fits, like a gear within a transmission, in the MAC organization.) Twenty minutes later, he was advised that he would be leaving for the Azores at 11:00 P.M. Things were accelerating fast for the Air Force Chief of Staff, General George S. Brown, as well. Brown called General Carlton at MAC Headquarters, saying, "Get a package ready to augment your terminal in the Azores. You'll be getting a written execute within an hour—but do not wait; get ready."[6]

Carlton knew that this meant he could begin assembling and loading aircraft, but that none could leave the country until the orders came. Carlton immediately sent word to his numbered Air Force commanders, Major General Lester T. Kearny of the 21st Air Force and Major General John F. Gonge of the 22nd Air Force, telling them that the airlift was imminent. As currently planned, MAC planes would fly the matériel to the Azores, where the State Department had negotiated an agreement to permit airlift operations. There the supplies would be picked up by El Al aircraft. The airlift would probably consist of at least 250 MAC planeloads. Carlton urged both of his commanders to "move fast and plan on using lots of cargo handling equipment." This meant that the majority of the matériel to be moved was crated and palletized, unable to drive off on its own power as tanks or trucks might have done.

The next steps were automatic. MAC Headquarters activated its Contingency Support Staff, and all C-141 and C-5 aircrews were placed on alert. All training and leave was canceled. The first utilization plan called for the C-141s to fly eight hours per day and the C-5s five.

Lajes, in the Azores, remained the key to the whole airlift. C-5s, with loads of a mere twenty tons, could fly from the United States to Israel nonstop, but the return trip was questionable because of prevailing head winds.

All around the world, the effect of General Brown's phone call was already being felt on MAC units to the loneliest Aerial Ports. Colonel Strobaugh was already back at McGuire, where he would spend the night waiting for his airplane to arrive. The airlift would start, as most military events do, with a series of "hurry-ups and waits."

Presidents and Secretaries of State can decree airlifts—but they cannot predict bad weather or prohibit mechanical malfunctions. The airlift would start with both.

While both sides prepared for major actions on the Sinai Front, the war went on in Syria in small, savage battles. Instead of long armored sweeps, encircling thousands of prisoners, the Israelis now had to fight for every inch of ground, contested all the way. Despite their retreat, and notwithstanding Assad's fears, the Syrians were far from beaten. Now instead of exposing themselves in armored attacks against dug-in Israeli positions, the situation was reversed. Well-camouflaged and -emplaced Syrian armor and artillery now focused on chewing up the advancing Israeli units, blocking every road and village with barrage fire. Although the Israelis maintained a general air superiority, Syrian MiG and Sukhoi fighter-bombers would still appear to strike the probing Israeli armored units, causing many casualties.

Some of the Syrian spine stiffening had come about as a result of draconian disciplinary tactics handed down from above. When the commander of the Syrian 68th Brigade, Colonel Rafiq Hilawi, permitted a retreat on October 11, he was court-martialed.[7] His punishment echoed the French heritage of the Syrian army. After having his badges of rank torn off, Hilawi was paraded around an army camp on the outskirts of Damascus and publicly executed by a firing squad. Assad's message was clear: no retreats; Damascus was to be defended at all costs

On the previous day, the Israeli Lieutenant Colonel Avigdor Kahalani's 7th Battalion, already exhausted by four days of intense fighting, had been tasked to move forward through Syrian lines and capture two key points, Hader and Mazrat Beit Jan. The men of the 7th Battalion had to battle through strong Syrian opposition and across dense minefields. It was not until the afternoon of October 12 that they stood outside Mazrat Beit Jan, ready to make one last lunge at their objective.

Kahalani, who would emerge from the war as Israel's most famous armored commander, found himself in a strange situation. Most of his tanks were deployed on a ridge that ran around the southern perimeter of the village, taking advantage of whatever cover was available—small groves of trees, farm buildings, folds in the terrain. One battalion was actually inside the village, fighting street by street and taking losses from antitank guns in ambush.[8] Opposing him were an unknown number of Syrian tanks, some deployed in the village itself but others hidden in the same sort of natural cover. For the moment, the battle was a standoff, and the Syrians seemed emboldened, pushing a column of five tanks to a point that threatened to cut off the road to the village.

Kahalani countered by directing a recently arrived company of Israeli tanks to move to the south and attack. The Israeli tanks moved against the Syrian armor, destroying three tanks. The commander of the Israeli tank company had been in New York when the war broke out; he had flown back to Israel and immediately been assigned to a scratch unit being outfitted with repaired tanks. In classic style, he had driven to the sound of the guns and tipped the balance in the battle.

Help sometimes comes from unexpected sources. Kissinger was feeling pressure from the Soviet Union to go forward with a cease-fire resolution in the UN Security Council, and he had just about exhausted his stock of stalling tactics. Now, however, reconnaissance photos confirmed the fact that the Egyptians were making preparations for a large-scale offensive in the Sinai, and he saw at once that it ended the possibility of a cease-fire. Still, he needed a gracious way out.

This came when Great Britain's Foreign Secretary, Sir Alec Douglas Home, counseled him that with an offensive under way, Sadat would never agree to a cease-fire. Without Great Britain's support for the resolution, it was easier for Kissinger to keep stalling and convince the Soviet Union to wait.

Even more important was the fact that one element of the great Kissinger-Schlesinger guessing game was drawing to a close, thanks to resolute action by President Nixon. The President first reassured Schlesinger about the use of MAC aircraft in the airlift, stating unequivocally that he took full responsibility for any adverse reaction by the Arabs. Later, his anger aroused because there appeared to be lingering arguments in the Pentagon and the airlift still had not started, he told Kissinger, "Goddamn it, use every one [i.e., C-5] we have. Tell them to send everything that can fly."[9] The reason for Nixon's vehemence was simple: it had been three days since the promise of an airlift had apparently induced Israel to back away from the use of nuclear weapons. No one knew what the effect of the pending Arab offensive would be. If the Egyptians were as successful as they had been on the first three days of the war, Israel might reach again for "the Sampson Option."

The simple order, so typical of Nixon with its use of the invective, was all that was needed. Like a racehorse released from the gate, the USAF began to assemble all the manifold bits and pieces that would be required to funnel supplies from depots all over the world to . . . where? The Department of State, for all of its concerns about the airlift, had not yet secured permission for it to go anywhere except nonstop to Tel Aviv. At the moment, the tentative landing area was Lajes, but the permission requested on October 12 had not yet been received. The government of Portugal was in turmoil. The longtime strongman Antonio Salazar had died of a stroke in 1970, and his successor as Prime Minister, Marcelo Caetano, was preoccupied with movements for independence in Mozambique and Angola.

Given that all of the other NATO allies of the United States had absolutely refused permission to use their bases or airspace for an airlift, Portugal sought to gain an advantage from allowing the use of the Azores. Like the other nations, Portugal did not wish to antagonize the Arab countries, but it desperately needed arms to conduct operations in its African colonies. Perhaps relieved to have a nation he could bully, after the rebuffs from France, Germany, Great Britain, Italy, and Spain, Kissinger later wrote that he had come down hard on Caetano, flatly refusing the request for military assistance and threatening to abandon Portugal to its fate.

The facts were somewhat different. Portugal was assured that the Nixon administration would attempt to get an amendment further tightening exports to Portugal removed from a pending congressional foreign aid bill. And of all the NATO countries, Portugal was least affected by the threat of an Arab oil embargo, because Angola was capable of supplying Portugal's total petroleum needs. So in the end, Portugal acquiesced, granting unlimited transit rights, and then steadfastly looked the other way for the remainder of the war as Lajes was turned from a sleepy terminal with perhaps an average of thirty to sixty flights per month to a beehive of round-the-clock activity, with aircraft arriving and departing every fifteen minutes.

The Azores, which were acquired by Portugal by virtue of

discovery in 1427, consist of nine major volcanic islands located about eight hundred miles from the motherland. The island chain first came to prominence in American aviation in 1919, when the Navy's Curtiss NC-4 landed there en route on the epic first trip across the Atlantic. Lajes, on the island of Terceira, became an important sea, air, and communications facility during World War II, after Portugal, despite being a supporter of Franco's pro-Axis Spain, allowed Great Britain to begin operations there in 1943. U.S. operations began in Lajes in 1946, and in 1951 Portugal allowed the United States to establish an air base for NATO operations. It became a popular stop, not least because of the good food and good wine that aircrews found there.

As a major hub for an airlift operation, however, Lajes had little to recommend it besides a 10,865-foot-long runway. Parking space was limited, as there were only two fuel hydrants available. Local messing and billeting facilities were totally inadequate: This would not be an "island vacation" for anyone. Initially, both air and ground crews were sleeping in the airplanes, on cots in the operations area, and in showers of abandoned barracks, and a few were sleeping in the psychiatric ward of the nearby hospital. In time more than fifteen hundred people would be stationed in Lajes for the airlift, but in typical Air Force fashion, austere but comfortable quarters soon sprang up as old abandoned barracks were reopened and renovated.[10]

Almost from the day the airlift started, fuel and fueling would be of critical concern. The initial daily requirements for 660,000 gallons of fuel soon rose to 1,155,000 gallons, and additional Navy tankers had to be diverted to meet the demand.[11] Fueling was hazardous because aircraft had to be parked closer together than standard safety practice allowed, but there was no alternative.

Given the preparations General Carlton had made and given the general awareness in MAC of what was going to be required, it might be imagined that the airlift would now proceed smoothly. It did not quite work out that way.

Back at Scott AFB in Illinois, General Carlton received word that Lajes was "a go." Relieved, Carlton informed Major General Maurice F. "Moe" Casey of the Joint Chiefs of Staff that "we are going to have three C-141s every two hours and one C-5 every four hours on the way." It was an innocuous statement, but Casey knew that at 25 tons per C-141 and 80 tons per C-5 it represented a total of 1,380 tons of supplies a day. Both Casey and Carlton knew that the Israelis did not have the capability to transship such huge quantities of goods and this almost certainly spelled further involvement for MAC.

Carlton and Casey got along well together, which was fortunate, for, amazingly enough, given that the Vietnam War had just ended, there was still no central point of control at the Joint Chiefs of Staff for coordination of the separate services in transportation matters. Working together, Carlton and Casey in effect created that central point for the airlift and removed much confusion and duplication.

And as they had expected, the entire operation now received both a shot in the arm and a kick in the pants on October 12, as the decision came down from the Chief of Staff, General Brown, that El Al would not be picking the supplies up at Lajes for transshipment. This eliminated a huge problem, for it was obvious that the C-141s and C-5s could bring matériel in many times faster than the converted El Al airliners could take it out. However, it also meant that Lajes was now going to be merely a staging base for refueling, changing crews, and performing minor maintenance, with the cargo planes now flying directly to Lod Airport in Tel Aviv. Another ALCE would have to be established at Lod, equipped with the 40K loaders designed especially to unload and load the C-5s. (The 40K loaders were part of the total 463L materials handling equipment that was an integral part of the C-5 weapon system.) The returning loads would prove to be of tremendous value, for they consisted of examples of the latest Soviet tanks, missiles, radar, and so on, that had been captured by the Israelis.

Speed was of the essence—the C-5s were an expensive asset, and they would make a prime propaganda target for any Arabs who would try to destroy them in the air or on the ground. Protection in the air would come from careful routing to avoid danger areas, the aid of aircraft escorts of the Sixth Fleet, and, when close to Israel, the protection of the IAF. On the ground, however, the cargo planes were vulnerable to attack from bombers, Kelt missiles, and even handheld rocket weapons like those used to destroy tanks.

At MAC Headquarters, Carlton was generally pleased with the way the pieces of the airlift were beginning to come into play. The change from Lajes to Lod provided a whole series of additional problems, particularly in navigation, where his planes had to avoid all Arab and NATO airspace. MAC was short on navigators but could resort to the standard Air Force solution: everybody works harder for longer hours.

The single greatest threat to the Israelis in Syria was the Iraqi 3rd Armored Division. It had been sent to Syria immediately upon the outbreak of war, but the 310 tanks had not begun off-loading from the transporters until the morning of October 12. Later that day, they had their initial brush with Israeli forces and were beaten back, with a loss of seventeen tanks.

Facing the Iraqis was a scratch division commanded by Major General Dan Laner and consisting of four brigades—the 17th, 19th, 20th, and 69th—and miscellaneous units that had gravitated together in the earlier fighting.[12] Laner's unit was nearly exhausted and short on ammunition. To avoid the stress and casualties inevitable in an armored assault, Laner decided instead to use the terrain to create a perfect tank Cannae. He disposed his forces along three sides of a box, leaving a four-and-one-half-mile wide opening through which the still-inexperienced Iraqi forces were invited to come.

And come they did, the 3rd Armored Brigade marching in impeccable open order into the square area dominated by Israeli tanks and artillery. The Iraqi forces then stopped, waiting for reinforcements from their 6th Armored Brigade.

When the 6th Armored Brigade arrived, the Iraqis moved to attack. Laner allowed them to reach within two hundred yards of Israeli lines before opening fire. Within minutes, the Iraqis were in full retreat, with more than eighty tanks destroyed. The Israeli tanks reportedly did not receive a single hit. The Iraqi attack had been blunted, and while the threat had not vanished, the front was once more secure. Laner's forces mopped up the area, then set up defensive positions. They were desperately short of 105mm ammunition—and of sleep.

Golda Meir's addresses were always matter-of-fact, especially when she was speaking to the Knesset. However, when she addressed the public Meir could rise to almost Churchillian eloquence on occasion. On October 13 she sought to boost morale with the following:

> We will win because we must live. Our neighbors are not fighting for their lives, nor for their sovereignty; they are fighting to destroy us. We will not be destroyed. We dare not be destroyed. Therefore, the spirit of our men on the front, the spirit of our people in every home, in every city, in every village, is a spirit of a people that hates war but knows that in order to live it must win the war that had been thrust upon it.

Harry Cohen had not heard the speech, but he read it in the *Jersualem Post*. His own morale needed a boost. His hands were sore from where the stretched springs had pinched them, and heaving metal beds was a far cry from flying a courier plane as he had hoped to do. After less than a week the work was starting to get old, and despite the old soldier's maxim about never volunteering, Cohen jumped at the chance of a new job when his supervisor stuck his head in the door and asked, "Who wants to unload Yank airplanes at Lod?"

6 *Airlift and Breakout*

TWO EVENTS WOULD OCCUR on October 14 to make it the decisive day of the war. The first of these was the ill-fated Egyptian offensive. The second, but equally important, was the arrival of the first airlift aircraft from the United States.

The Egyptian offensive came only after a bitter internal fight. Dissension in the top ranks of Egyptian military leaders was widespread. Sadat had reversed his original stand against holding a strip of the Sinai because he felt an obligation to Syria, now facing utter defeat by the Israelis. He could not refuse Assad's appeal for help, brought to him by a special emissary on October 11.[1] If he did, he risked facing the disapproval of the entire Arab world—one simply did not abandon one's ally in time of need. Ironically, Sadat was now aligned with his field commanders, who had been straining at the leash. Having tasted victory, they wanted more. Yet his Minister of War, General Ahmed Ismail Ali, and Chief of Staff, Lieutenant General Saad el Din Shazli, disagreed with him and, within the very limited confines of Egyptian military protocol, tried to make their point.

Ismail and Shazli were unlikely allies. In the past they had rarely been in agreement, being completely opposite in personality and character. Ismail was older at fifty-six and valued more for his loyalty to Sadat and his soldierly qualities than his intellect. In contrast, the fifty-one-year-old Shazli had the fiery toughness of a paratrooper, his first duty in the Egyptian military.

However, despite people and politics, something had to give. After eight days of war, the Egyptians had packed 1,200 tanks and 190,000 men with all their equipment into a ten-to-fifteen-kilometer slice of land that ran the length of the east bank of the Suez Canal. Even though the Egyptian armies did not consume the same amount of matériel per man as did their opponents, sustaining them across the canal was a daunting logistic operation. The two armies were separated by the natural twenty-three-mile-long barrier of the Great Bitter Lake and were unable to assist each other tactically.

Sadat realized that he was in a difficult position and that the arguments of Ali and Shazli were not without merit. There was another factor. Sadat had seized the territory he wanted but still had not inflicted the massive losses he felt were needed to establish at the bargaining table the credibility of Arab fighting power. The issue of attrition was important; he knew that Egypt would suffer losses, perhaps even massive losses, in a breakout battle from the canal. Yet Egypt could sustain such losses and Israel could not. It was an awful choice, but one he felt he had to make. Sadat insisted that his Minister of War and Chief of Staff carry out his orders, which were quite explicit. In contrast to the opening days of the war, when the Egyptians had pressed forward on a broad front along the length of the canal without a central focus for the attack, Sadat now ordered an advance at six points. Then, in one of the major mistakes of the war, he ordered the 4th and 21st Armored Divisions across the canal.

Sadat's plan called for three of the six thrusts to come in the northern part of the front, under Major General Saad Mamoun's 90,000-man Second Army. (The night before the attack, and perhaps in reaction to the orders, Mamoun suffered a massive heart attack and had to be replaced by Major General Abd al-Munim Halil.) Three more advances were to be made in the south, delivered by Major General Abd al-Munim Wassel's 100,000-man Third Army.

Six separate thrusts was still a broad front, but unlike the original offensive, the desired depth of the attack had changed. On the first days of the war, the plan had been to seize a strip twelve to fifteen kilometers in depth. This kept the Egyptian army concentrated. Now the six thrusts were to extend far beyond enemy lines, leaving each thrust with two vulnerable flanks and reducing the concentration of infantry.

Each army had specific objectives. In the north, the Second Army was to capture the crucial junction at the Tasa and Lateral roads. A second force would move on to Romani, well beyond Israeli lines. In the center, the newly arrived Egyptian 21st Armored Division was to plow directly into Ariel Sharon's defenses, with the intent of smashing through and supporting both the northern and southern thrusts. In the south, two tank brigades were thrust against Brigadier General Kalman Magen, with the aim of taking the fabled Mitla and Gida passes, the prize Sadat's field commanders had wanted for so long. Finally, another force would drive south along the canal toward Ras Sudar. Generals Ali and Shazli attempted to carry out Sadat's plan to the letter. They were good soldiers, obeying orders. And if things went wrong, they wanted to be able to place the blame on Sadat.

At 6:20 A.M. the battle commenced with a thirty-minute artillery barrage by the endless array of Egyptian guns. There followed a general offensive, with an armored brigade spearheading each of six thrusts. Five infantry divisions would remain behind to guard the bridgeheads. The EAF put up surprisingly few sorties, focused as it was on defending strategic targets against the Israeli Phantoms.

As Ali and Shazli well knew, the execution of Sadat's plan would deprive the Egyptians of the main reason for their great success so far, the mass use of infantry well armed with antitank weapons. Had the six attacks been reduced to two major thrusts, there might have been adequate infantry for the task. As it was, the effort thinned out Egyptian strength.

Elazar had hoped for and anticipated the attack, basing his plans on a reprise of the battles of the Golan Heights. He wanted to let the Egyptians advance, inflict heavy losses on them, then counterattack.[2] On October 14 the entire IAF was concentrated in the Sinai, for it was eager to come to grips with Egyptian armor out from under its SAM umbrella. The

Israeli army had now been able to fully mobilize, and it had 750 tanks spotted in defensive positions. The scene was set for the greatest tank engagement since the German-Soviet battle at Kursk in 1943.

Each prong of the Egyptian attack ran into immediate trouble. In the north, Sukhoi Su-7 fighter-bombers strafed targets as the Egyptian 15th Armored Brigade advanced. The Israeli defenders allowed the tanks to approach within three thousand yards before opening fire. Then the accuracy of the Israeli gunners prevailed, as it had done in the Golan. Before 9:00 A.M. more than forty Egyptian tanks had been destroyed, at a cost of three Israeli tanks. Bren Adan then sent his division forward, pushing the Egyptians back and destroying another fifty tanks.

In the center, Sharon's tanks were sited on the high ground. Many of them were TI-67s (rebuilt T-55s), retrofitted with the deadly 105mm gun and a U.S. fire-control system. Sharon's armor was under the command of Colonel Yoel Gonen, the ill-starred Major General Gonen's brother. When the battle began, the shooting distance was sometimes reduced to one hundred yards, virtually point-blank range. The most important element of the battle, however, was the introduction of new Israeli tactics. They now employed armored personnel carriers along with the tanks to engage the Egyptian Sagger and RPG teams. The APCs, with their better visibility and firepower, laid down a massive suppressing fire. The brave Egyptian Sagger teams would poke their heads up to shoot and either were shot or forced to duck. When they ducked, they lost sight of the target and were unable to control the flight of the wire-guided missile to its target. The tactics worked well, especially since the Egyptian teams were now reduced in number. When more than forty tanks had been destroyed, the attack faltered and the Egyptians fell back with the Israelis in hot pursuit. By the time the fight was over, the IDF had destroyed 110 tanks and virtually wiped out an Egyptian armored formation.

In the south, Magen deliberately gave up ground, allowing the Egyptians to come forward before counterattacking and destroying sixty tanks. A flanking effort to the south by the Egyptian 3rd Armored Brigade of the 4th Armored Division moved them out of the protection of their SAM sites. In an incredible tactical blunder, the Egyptians funneled a mass of tanks through a wadi, a dry riverbed, in the hope of flanking the Mitla Pass. Almost 100 tanks, along with the two battalions of 122mm artillery and a mechanized infantry unit, were trapped in the wadi and set upon by small groups of Israeli Patton tanks and the IAF. Virtually all the Egyptian tanks were destroyed, cremating their crews as they sat trapped. The same havoc was wreaked on artillery and APCs. The hapless Egyptians were then sniped at as they retreated.

All day, Egypt's official radio sent out optimistic reports of successes on all fronts, in the propagandist style for which it was notorious. By evening, however, all of General Shazli's doomsday forecasts had been fulfilled and all Egyptian forces were ordered back to their original lines. The Israelis had lost 10 tanks, most to Saggers. The Egyptians had left more than 260 tanks burning in the Sinai—10 more than they had lost all combined since October 6. The most bitter, hard-fought battle of the war marked the demise of the Egyptian effort to retake the Sinai.

A key component of the Israeli victory was the first tangible fruit of the airlift, the new Hughes BGM-71 TOW. The acronym TOW stands for "Tube-launched, Optically tracked, Wire-guided." It carried an eight-pound warhead and could penetrate almost twenty-four inches of armor. The TOWs had been brought into Israel on El Al aircraft on October 10. They were followed by a team of Israeli instructors who had received training from U.S. specialists on October 11. The instructors quickly taught the antitank crews to use the TOW with deadly effect when the Egyptians attacked.

General Shazli found no satisfaction in having his strategic views validated. The Egyptian tank losses had been so great that the Israelis now had the dominant force in the region. In the battles past, the Egyptian superiority in the antitank missiles employed by the infantry had been decisive. That advantage was now offset by comparable Israeli tank-killing teams. Shazli now began to consider the prospect of consolidating his forces and pulling them back to the west bank of the canal to await the Israeli counterattack. He knew it could not be long in coming.

It was not until early afternoon that the Israeli commanders permitted themselves to think that the war's momentum had at last shifted in their favor. In a quick message to Prime Minister Meir, Dado Elazar summed it up saying: "Golda, it will be all right. We are back to ourselves and they [the Egyptians] are back to themselves." (Sharon had a quote attributed to him that made the same point but in a rougher fashion. He told Bar-Lev, "It was the same as 1967. The Egyptians came. We killed them. They left."

Elazar was being optimistic, as events would prove, but he was essentially correct. Sadat's acquiescence to Assad's wishes had resulted in an avoidable defeat. The Israeli casualties had been far less than Sadat had wished for. Now his hopes centered on blocking the inevitable Israeli offensive and inflicting casualties on the IDF on an unprecedented scale. Only then could he be taken seriously at the peace conference that would follow the cease-fire.

Elazar was happy at the scope of the victory and happier still that Israeli losses were so light. Now he had two things foremost in his mind. First, on October 15 Israeli forces must break through Arab lines and carry the war to enemy territory—where, according to all Israeli doctrine, it belonged. Second, on October 16 would begin the crucial battle to defeat the Egyptians in the field and cut off their forces on the east bank of the canal.

Tactically, the situation was very favorable. Elazar knew that of the approximately 2,000 tanks that Egypt had at the beginning of the war some 1,300 had been transferred to the east bank and many of these had been destroyed. This meant that in all of Egypt there were no more than 700 tanks spread about the country and beyond the Suez.

Unlike the Egyptians, with their six axes of attack, the Israelis would focus on a single point of attack—a *Schwerpunkt*. They would establish a fairly large bridgehead, secure it with artillery, then funnel the tanks across. When the armor was ready, it would fan out, striking first at the SAM sites before moving to surround Suez City. This would cut off the Egyptian Third Army on the east bank from their supply depots on the west side and, with a further thrust, essentially surround it.

The single point of attack was also dictated by the weakest link in the Israeli plans: bridging equipment. Everything depended upon a strange device, unique to this war.[3] It was the huge *gesher baglilim*—a roller bridge. The design of the roller bridge resulted from the collaboration of Major General Tal, Elazar's sometimes-difficult deputy, with Colonel David Laskov of the Engineering Corps. The seventy-year-old Laskov conceived of the idea of the roller bridge and oversaw its construction and test. Three of these huge structures were built. Each bridge consisted of more than one hundred Styrofoam-filled iron rollers. When the sections were connected, they formed a 180-meter-long bridge weighing about four hundred tons. When pushed into the canal, the bridge floated and could be pushed across to touch the opposite bank.

The roller bridges were, to say the least, cumbersome. It took sixteen tanks to move them into place, using specially trained crews moving over ruler-straight roads built in carefully selected terrain. Each bridge had to be tugged, pulled, pushed, and rolled laboriously into place, then shoved through an opening in the ramparts into the canal and across to the opposite side. The Israelis had also created rafts for moving tanks, sixty-six feet long and thirty-three feet wide and weighing sixty tons when assembled. Tanks towed the preassembled rafts to the shoreline, pushed them in, then clanked aboard to be ferried across. Once the first waves of tanks were landed, the rafts were hooked together to form another bridge. These could be used in combination with more conventional self-propelled Gilois-type bridging equipment purchased in Europe. For the first twenty-four hours of the attack, however, the roller bridges were vital, and the IAF was tasked to protect them at all costs.

Sharon and his 143rd Armored Division were given the mission he wanted: leading the attack with a brigade of tank-reinforced paratroopers across the canal at Deversoir, on the north tip of the Great Bitter Lake. With his left flank protected by the lake, he was to move three miles inland to protect the precious covered bridge from mortar and antitank missile attack. This was far less than normal Israeli tactical doctrine, which called for the bridgehead to be large enough to prevent enemy artillery from shelling the bridges. Such a task was beyond Sharon's means, for he was also expected to open the territory on the east bank wide enough to permit the rapid transport of the follow-up divisions. Adan's division, the 162nd, would come next, followed by the 252nd Armored Division, newly commanded by Brigadier General Kalman Magen. The 252nd would relieve Sharon on the west bank for mobile operations.

When Adan's division was across, both the 162nd and 143rd armored divisions would sweep south, with Adan on the eastern flank, crushing as many SAM sites as could be found. The 162nd would then move south to capture Suez City. Sharon was allocated the less glamorous task of protecting Adan's flank. The subordinate assignment was just another flick of the Israeli political/military whip.

The code name for the attack, Stouthearted Men, was almost whimsically chosen from an old Victor Herbert song. It seemed fitting, given the losses of the past week, and particularly so for Elazar, who had continued functioning in an outstanding manner, despite the many bruises his ego had suffered since October 6 and given his certain postwar fate. With his optimism slowly reviving, Elazar knew that his decision was now backed by Bar-Lev, Sharon, and Adan. Even Dayan had come on board, despite the boldness of the gamble, and the Prime Minister had approved, as she did so often, the plans of her Chief of Staff.

Yet Elazar believed that the battle could be concluded in forty-eight hours, and the schedule he laid down was absurdly optimistic, one that ran counter to all the experience of the current war. Elazar should have known better than anyone the risks involved and the danger Israel would face if Arab resistance was as fierce as it had been in the first few days of the war. Looming over every decision was the question of the U.S. airlift. Where was it and when would it arrive? If it did not arrive soon, an aborted offensive across the canal might truly backfire and leave the Israelis defenseless.

The news of the Egyptian offensive in the Sinai made Washington and the world realize that cease-fire resolutions were unlikely for the next few days. Neither Kissinger nor Nixon believed that the offensive could go on for long—the scale of the fighting and the long distances involved meant that both sides would soon exhaust their supplies, no matter how large the respective airlifts were.

Awaiting word of the outcome, Kissinger turned his attention to other matters. Whatever his contributions to getting the airlift going may—or may not—have been, Kissinger now expressed his anger by demanding a formal investigation of why the airlift was delayed by the DOD. This was of course a slam at Schlesinger. When the investigation was later concluded, it reported only that the airlift had got under way as soon as it was authorized and that any delays were due to the reasons previously given: high winds at Lajes and the requirement for crew rest. It also showed that only nine hours after the decision to begin the airlift was finally made MAC had the first of the C-5s and C-141s ready to depart, complete with crews and Aerial Port personnel.

In the meantime, Kissinger had fences to mend, for the Soviets were sure to take umbrage about the size of the U.S. airlift, which would be equally offensive to the Arab world. Kissinger notified Dobrynin that the airlift would be of "considerable magnitude," a fact the Soviets were already well aware of from their intelligence sources.

Kissinger then notified his "secret correspondent" in Cairo, Hafiz Ismail, that the airlift was under way in response to the Soviet airlift to Egypt and Syria.[4] However, he assured Ismail that the United States was prepared to stop its airlift efforts as soon as a cease-fire was established. Further, Kissinger promised that the United States would help to bring about a peace in the Middle East that was acceptable to Egypt. Ismail's reaction was predictable, given that he was courting Kissinger: he agreed with everything that was said.

Next were the all-important Saudis. The U.S. friendship with Saudi Arabia called for a more delicate approach—letters to King Faisal from both Nixon and Kissinger. The message was that the United States was neither pro-Israel nor pro-Arab; it was pro-peace. And, finally, it was necessary to reassure the Shah of Iran that U.S. efforts to strengthen Israel were intended to forestall Soviet influence in the Middle East. This was language the Shah understood, however much his sympathies might lie with the Arab nations. And, despite that, the Shah had already shown his mettle by refusing to allow Soviet airlift aircraft to fly over Iran. With the internal vendetta with Schlesinger and Middle Eastern diplomacy taken care of, Kissinger now awaited two things: Soviet reaction to the airlift and the outcome of the Egyptian offensive.

A sleepy Don Strobaugh rolled off his airplane at three o'clock in the morning, Azores time, after a strangely comfortable five-hour flight in the semiluxurious flight deck lounge of C-5A #69006. So far everything had gone wrong; his airplane had been delayed first for maintenance and then by high winds at Lajes, where his assignment had been changed. He was now going to be detachment commander for a twelve-man unit working at Lod Airport. The broad brush of his instructions said only that he was to wear civilian clothes and be prepared to handle four C-5s and twelve C-141s a day.

Strobaugh wanted to get there at once, before any of the U.S. airlifters landed, and get the ground-handling equipment set up and procedures established. At 8:45 A.M. he departed Lajes for Tel Aviv—only to return two hours later when the C-5 developed engine trouble. Strobaugh immediately sought out a replacement aircraft and began transferring the heavy specialized materials handling equipment to a new C-5.[5]

While Strobaugh fought the odds to get to his destination, the rest of MAC had swung into action to plan the airlift operation. The traditional route across the Atlantic, using optional stops in Iceland, Greenland, Scotland, and Spain, was not available. A southern route was chosen that took aircraft from major MAC bases in the United States directly to Lajes. From there the route to Lod Airport in Tel Aviv had to be flown with extreme precision through the Strait of Gibraltar and then on a precise path that kept the aircraft outside of the Air Traffic Control Flight Information Regions controlled by Arab states on the North African coast. This path took them to a point near the vicinity of Crete, where a turn southeast was made to reach Tel Aviv.

The routes of the Soviet and the U.S. aircraft actually intersected at the eastern end of the Mediterranean. Fortunately, the Soviets were operating turboprop transports while the United States was using jets, so that their operational altitudes were separated by a difference of several thousand feet. It was here that one MAC aircraft was unable to raise Cyprus radio to get clearance for the region. And then at that moment an Aeroflot pilot, speaking perfect English, said, "MAC aircraft, this is Aeroflot Twelve-thirty-four; I'll relay your message to Cyprus." He did and then came back and asked, "What's your destination?" The MAC pilot replied, "Tel Aviv," to which the Aeroflot pilot rejoined, "That figures. I'm going to Damascus."

The need for tightrope precision was obvious to the crews. They had to fly within a few miles of Morocco, whose troops were fighting and dying in the Golan. They had to skirt Algeria and Libya, both of which had strong anti-U.S governments. Libya was the more aggressive, monitoring the MAC aircraft on radar and keeping its MiG interceptors conspicuously on alert. Egypt was of course belligerent, with a strong air force and both air-to-surface and surface-to-surface missiles that posed a threat to MAC on the ground. Syria posed a similar threat.

Shooting down a MAC transport would have been a risky business for any of the Arab nations, but in the white heat of the Middle East war anything was possible. The U.S. Sixth Fleet provided two carrier task groups for the necessary air cover. The USS *Independence* and the USS *Franklin Delano Roosevelt* had ninety-eight aircraft, including thirty-nine F-4 Phantoms, available to support the airlift. In the final leg of the route into Tel Aviv, the IAF was tasked to meet the transports 190 miles out and escort them in.

Although no attacks materialized, the MAC transports were shadowed on several occasions by unidentified fighters and often experienced very strong radar jamming. On one occasion a death threat was radioed.

The requirement to use the southern route and the extended center-line journey through the Mediterranean added several hundred miles to the trip, making the one-way distance an average 6,450 nautical miles. The round-trip of 12,900 miles was too much for one crew to handle. As a result, supplemental "stage" crews were positioned at three bases in the United States and at Lajes to handle the planned flow of seventy-two C-141s and twelve C-5s. (The numbers had jumped while Strobaugh was en route.) Aircraft were sequenced into Lajes according to a tight schedule with little time to spare for landing, refueling, and taking off.

Congestion increased when SAC deployed thirteen Boeing KC-135 tankers and 141 personnel to Lajes without informing MAC Headquarters. Initially, billeting was so bad that a sleeping bag on board the airplane became the preferred housing.

In the words of the official report on the operation: "The airlift could have started better." As previously noted, the first C-5 dispatched from Lajes for Lod took off at 8:45 A.M. and returned a little over two hours later with engine trouble. There were eleven C-141s ready to go—but they were delayed for eight hours so their crews could rest. The C-141 did not have augmented crews, and after the long flight to Lajes an eighteen-hour round-trip to Lod would have exhausted them. Understandably enough, the White House did not want to hear about crew rest—they wanted to hear about aircraft landing at Lod. After Nixon's order to go ahead, Henry Kissinger was demanding action from the DOD and Schelsinger was demanding action from the Joint Chiefs of Staff.

At 8:45 A.M. the same time the C-5 had departed from Lajes, General Carlton received a call from Admiral Thomas A. Moorer, the hard-nosed chairman of the Joint Chiefs of Staff. Moorer wanted to know why the planes were not taking off, what the crew rest problem was, and what the wind problem had been, telling Carlton, ". . . get this thing going because it is getting pretty exciting over here at the highest level—I mean the highest."

After Carlton had explained the situation, Moorer went on, saying, "We just want you to keep on going. In other words, a continual flow until it stops with the average of effort. You are not limited to three C-5s and the first twelve C-141s. There is no limit now. You just keep going."

Once again Carlton explained the crew rest situation, but he added that he would waive the crew rest requirements as necessary to get things started.

Moorer's response was terse! "We'll have to get them moving or we'll lose our jobs."[6]

Carlton followed up the conversation with directions that the C-141 crews would have to get by with six hours of sleep. In a follow-up report to the Air Force Vice Chief of Staff, General Horace M. Wade, Carlton stated that the first loaded C-5 would arrive in Lod at 1:01 A.M., Tel Aviv time. Carlton's native optimism came out in the report, as he stated: "We are just about to get going on a good operation. Once this flow starts, it's going to come like a bushel basket of oranges just being dumped."

Carlton was exactly on the mark. The first C-5A (#00461 of the 60th Military Airlift Wing at Travis Air Force Base, California, but flown by a crew from Dover AFB) had touched down at 1:01 A.M., after a 32.5-hour mission from its home station. The last leg of the trip, the 3,163 miles from Lajes, had taken 6.7 hours. On board were 93.1 tons of munitions, mostly 105mm shells. (The cavernous interior of the C-5 looked empty even when carrying a maximum load of the 105 shells. The ammunition was so heavy that it had to be palletized and placed near the center of gravity, a small heap in the center of an otherwise empty airplane.)

Though few perceived it at the time, the arrival of the first C-5A was as important as the battle being won in the Sinai. The appearance of a U.S. cargo plane in the combat zone gave the world notice of American resolve and commitment. To Israel it meant that all concerns about diminishing ammunition and other supplies were over.

The waiting crowd cheered wildly as the plane taxied up and its cavernous doors were opened. Keenly aware that the

IDF was down to about a one-week supply of ammunition, the Israeli workers off-loaded the twenty-two pallets of munitions in just over three hours without any special handling equipment. The ammunition reached the Syrian Front in about three hours, the Sinai in eight.

By October 14, seven days had passed since the Kremlin had made its first efforts to obtain a cease-fire at the United Nations and absolutely nothing had happened. The loss of face was bad, but even worse was the sense of uncertainty. The peace process had not only been foiled by the United States and Great Britain—it had also been foiled by Sadat himself.

This was cause for suspicion, compounded by the belated discovery that Sadat's national security adviser, Hafiz Ismail, was secretly communicating with Kissinger. The information was annoying, both because it exposed Sadat's double-dealing and because Soviet intelligence had been so late in picking it up. When Ambassador Vinogradov made a discrete inquiry about this, Sadat flew into a rage, denying the connection and stating flatly that he had kept no secrets from his "Soviet friends."

Even as Kissinger tried to assuage the interests and sensitivities of Egypt and its allies, the Arab world now came to Moscow in the person of Algerian president Houari Boumedienne, the very man who had enraged Brezhnev by his release of secret agreements to the press. Boumedienne had not been invited, but as a head of state and the leader of the Non-Aligned Movement (NAM) he received every courtesy, including a marathon ten-and-one-half-hour meeting with Brezhnev and the other top leaders of the Kremlin. Boumedienne stressed the importance of the recent Arab victories and the absolute requirement for Moscow to both speed up and increase its shipments of arms to Egypt and Syria. Brezhnev was coldly tolerant, pointing out the considerable effort

Moscow was already making and underlining that it was at least in part the high quality of Soviet weapons that had made the victories possible.

As Boumedienne droned on, word began filtering into the Kremlin of the drubbing that Israel was administering to the Egyptian forces in the Sinai. In the course of the long meeting, Brezhnev's manner became more and more reserved, but in the end he agreed to Boumedienne's offer to have Algeria pay for additional weapons for both the Arab combatants and Algeria itself. The Soviet leaders realized that a $200 million arms sale is a $200 million arms sale, even if one has to listen to a boring political pitch to boot.[7]

The redoubtable Chief of Staff, Elazar, had one item to clear up on his agenda before proceeding on a whirlwind tour of the Sinai Front. Elazar needed assurance that the coming offensive in the Sinai would not be hampered in any way by untoward developments in the Golan. Elazar summoned the commander of the Northern Front, Major General Yitzhak Hofi for a meeting in the Pit. The two men agreed that no attempts to take further Syrian territory were to be made and that Dan Laner's division would continue to contain the Iraqi armored forces as economically as possible, giving the troops as much rest as they could possibly get. They also agreed that as soon as possible Mount Hermon should be recaptured to wipe out the indignity Syria had imposed on the first day of the war.

The next agenda item was more delicate. During the tough early days of the war Moshe Dayan had frequently absented himself from headquarters and made a practice of offering only "ministerial opinions" rather than orders. Now Dayan had instructed his liaison officer, Major General Meir Amit, to tell Elazar that he was to submit each day's plans for Dayan's personal approval, especially any raids deep behind enemy lines. Elazar, who ordinarily could control his temper, went

Perhaps the most unusual aspect of the October War was the clandestine diplomatic relations that were sustained by Egypt's President Anwar Sadat (*left*) and American Secretary of State Henry Kissinger. What is even more unusual is that Sadat selected Kissinger to be his contact when the latter was President Nixon's National Security Adviser, before he became Secretary of State. (NATIONAL ARCHIVES PHOTO)

Much has been made of the infighting between Secretary of Defense James Schlesinger and Henry Kissinger over the aid to be supplied to Israel, and the method by which that aid would be supplied. Though it is clear from contemporary evidence, and from Kissinger's memoirs, that the rivalry existed, it had little effect upon the delivery of weaponry. Once President Nixon ordered the materiel to be delivered, the United States Air Force's Military Airlift Command moved into action and soon established an incredibly effective airlift. (NATIONAL ARCHIVES PHOTO)

The world grew used to photos of Kremlin strongmen surveying Soviet might. This one is symbolic of the impression the Soviet leaders wished to give: a unified block of experienced leaders who were firmly behind their chosen spokesman, Leonid Brezhnev. The truth was far different, of course, for Brezhnev did not consolidate his power completely until 1977. From the left , the 6-foot-6-inch Minister of Defense Andrei Grechko, a tough commander who authorized the launching of the Scuds; Chairman of the Presidium of the Supreme Soviet, Nikolai Podgorny, a would-be rival to Brezhnev who called on the Arab world to break with capitalism; General Secretary Leonid Brezhnev, who loved fast cars and pretty women; Prime Minister Aleksei Kosygin, who fell further from grace during the October War, and Secretary of the Central Committee Mikhail Suslov, whose lack of knowledge of the Middle East did not keep him from aligning with the more radical views of Podgorny. (NATIONAL ARCHIVES PHOTO)

Strangely enough, it was this scene that dominated Brezhnev's thinking all through the October War, for he felt his greatest achievement was not just furthering détente, but doing so by gaining a personally friendly relationship with Richard Nixon. (NATIONAL ARCHIVES PHOTO)

The serious business of agreement ratified by the signatures of Leonid Brezhnev and Richard Nixon. This was the high point of Brezhnev's work in foreign relations, and greatly strengthened him in his struggle for power within the Kremlin. (NATIONAL ARCHIVES PHOTO)

The October War caused such a revolution in politics that the Kremlin leaders were forced to look to the U.S. Secretary of State to end the conflict. This meeting between an informally attired Brezhnev (no tie, but wearing decorations) and Kissinger took place on October 20, 1973, in what was undoubtedly the most important of the literally thousands of meetings that took place during the war. The two men settled in four hours the fate of several nations. (NATIONAL ARCHIVES PHOTO)

The word charisma is often overused but it undoubtedly applies to the colorful Moshe Dayan, shown here in a formal portrait done in 1957. Like so many of the Jewish leaders, Dayan loomed large for decades, and had an informal influence that sometimes overshadowed his formal positions. (NATIONAL PHOTO COLLECTION OF THE STATE OF ISRAEL)

Another indication of the longtime ties of Israeli leadership is the photograph taken on October 9, 1955, some twenty-eight years before the October War. The importance of David Ben-Gurion (center), the Father of the Nation of Israel, in both political and military matters cannot be overstated. Israel's first Prime Minister and first Defense Minister, he established the Israel Defense Force and his relations with senior officers was important until the time of his death in December 1973. At his right is Chaim Herzog and on his left is the indomitable Dayan. (NATIONAL PHOTO COLLECTION OF THE STATE OF ISRAEL)

Another picture from the past, this 1965 photo is a striking example of why the Israeli forces worked together so well: their commanders led from the front, not the rear. At left is the great aviator and head of the Israeli air force at the time, Ezer Weizman. To his right is Israel Tal, later Deputy Chief of Staff to David Elazar, but at the time commander of the Israeli armored forces. The two men knew how to coordinate their forces in harmony. (NATIONAL PHOTO COLLECTION OF THE STATE OF ISRAEL)

A solemn and moving moment as the retiring Chief of Staff Chaim Bar-Lev reads his farewell address. Prime Minister Golda Meir listens with head bowed, while the new Chief of Staff, David Elazar stares into the distance. All three would undergo great trials during the Yom Kippur War and its aftermath. (NATIONAL PHOTO COLLECTION OF THE STATE OF ISRAEL)

Chief of Staff David Elazar looks up attentively, his hands folded at a briefing of the absolutely desperate situation that existed on October 8, when the Israeli counterattacks failed up and down the line and the outcome of the war was suddenly in doubt. This is the infamous "Pit," the war room that eventually became so choked with people and cigarette smoke that it was almost unbearable. (NATIONAL PHOTO COLLECTION OF THE STATE OF ISRAEL)

Defense Minister Dayan is briefed by who can only be called the Golden Boy of the IDF, Major General Avraham "Bren" Adan. Dayan was constantly in the field, contravening the normally rigorous Israeli chain of command. To outside observers Dayan always seemed happiest when he was under enemy fire. Adan, despite some mishaps, conducted brilliant armored operations. (NATIONAL PHOTO COLLECTION OF THE STATE OF ISRAEL)

General Bar-Lev in an unusual situation: discussing mercy for Arab troops. The Israeli officers shown here on October 28, 1973, are determining how relief supplies will be given to the surrounded Egyptian Third Army. The decision to aid the enemy army was a political one, forced on them by the superpowers, but was in their own long-term interest. (NATIONAL PHOTO COLLECTION OF THE STATE OF ISRAEL)

It was almost unendurable for the Egyptian soldiers to accept Israeli aid, but there was no alternative. Here Bar-Lev returns the salute of Egyptian Brigadier General Bashir Sharif as the transfer of relief supplies is about to begin. (NATIONAL PHOTO COLLECTION OF THE STATE OF ISRAEL)

Creature comforts were few in the desert. General Adan is giving a situation report to Prime Minister Golda Meir, Dayan, and others on October 29, 1973. The situation was still fraught with anxiety, for no one knew what the Arab forces might yet be capable of, and Israel was strained to the very limits. (NATIONAL PHOTO COLLECTION OF THE STATE OF ISRAEL)

Golda Meir never spared herself and visited with her officers and troops as often as possible. Here, on October 29, she is escorted by Major General Shmuel Gonen as they step down past the debris of battle. Note the dirty and tired Israeli troops in the background—the battle has obviously been hard-fought. (NATIONAL PHOTO COLLECTION OF THE STATE OF ISRAEL)

Prime Minister Golda Meir did not stand on ceremony. She dropped in to see "the giant planes" and meet the crew members without regard to protocol. At her left is Colonel Robert Strobaugh, commander of the MAC ALCE detachment at LOD. (PHOTO COURTESY OF ROBERT STROBAUGH)

Colonel Robert Strobaugh in the ALCE headquarters at Lod International Airport. The aircraft movement board at the rear was crucial to timing the arrival of the various cargoes. Strobaugh's detailed journal was vital for this book. (PHOTO COURTESY OF ROBERT STROBAUGH)

Secretary of State Henry Kissinger arrives directly from Moscow. Lod Airport was in the war zone and there were concerns about Kissinger's security. There need not have been—he was as important to the Arab world as he was to the Israelis. (PHOTO COURTESY OF AIR MOBILITY COMMAND MUSEUM, VIA HARRY HEIST)

The Lockheed C-5 Galaxy proved itself beyond any doubt during Operation Nickel Glass. The size of the aircraft can be estimated from the people standing near the front entrance hatch. (PHOTO COURTESY OF AIR MOBILITY COMMAND MUSEUM, VIA HARRY HEIST)

The Lockheed C-5 lifts off over a line of McDonnell F-4 Phantoms; both aircraft were vital to Israel. (PHOTO COURTESY OF AIR MOBILITY COMMAND MUSEUM, VIA HARRY HEIST)

There was no attempt made to deliver a significant number of tanks to Israel, for other equipment was more vitally needed. However, some tanks were delivered to show that it could be done. (PHOTO COURTESY OF AIR MOBILITY COMMAND MUSEUM, VIA HARRY HEIST)

The El Al refreshment truck pulls up alongside a C-5A, while Israeli soldiers stand guard. (PHOTO COURTESY OF AIR MOBILITY COMMAND MUSEUM, VIA HARRY HEIST)

Kenneth Smith, a C-5 Aircraft Commander, prepares to leave the cockpit of the giant aircraft. (PHOTO COURTESY OF AIR MOBILITY COMMAND MUSEUM, VIA HARRY HEIST AND KENNETH SMITH)

A comforting sight, a friendly McDonnell F-4 off the wing. Other aircraft were sighted, including MiGs, but no actual attack was made on any of the airlift aircraft. (PHOTO COURTESY OF AIR MOBILITY COMMAND MUSEUM, VIA HARRY HEIST)

Aircraft are only part of the airlift equation. Ground handling is equally important, and the crews at Lod excelled at off-loading the aircraft. (PHOTO COURTESY OF AIR MOBILITY COMMAND MUSEUM, VIA HARRY HEIST)

Two MiG-21F fighters of the United Arab Republic Air Force escort a Tupolev Tu-16 bomber carrying stand-off missiles. The Tu-16s fired Kelt missiles against Israeli targets. (PHOTO COURTESY OF LON O. NORDEEN)

One of the most underrated fighters in the Western press, the Soviet MiG-17 was in fact a superb airplane and proved itself in numerous wars over the last forty years. The Egyptian Air Force camouflage seems more suitable for temperate than desert regions. (PHOTO COURTESY OF LON O. NORDEEN)

The Egyptians made excellent use of the MiG-21, which was the preeminent fighter of the Soviet era. Although totally different in concept than its principal opponent, the McDonnell F-4, it was always a dangerous opponent. (PHOTO COURTESY OF LON O. NORDEEN)

Perhaps more than in any other war, bridges were the ground lifeline of the October War. Bombing attacks like this one rarely completely destroyed a bridge, and most were quickly repaired. (PHOTO COURTESY OF LON O. NORDEEN)

The F-4 Phantoms, with their long range, were used against the deepest targets. Here they attack the Tanta air base on October 19, 1973. (PHOTO COURTESY OF LON O. NORDEEN)

The Libyan Arab Republic Air Force supplied Dassault Mirage 5E fighters for the October War. (PHOTO COURTESY OF LON O. NORDEEN)

The Tupolev Tu-16 was a rough equivalent of the Boeing B-47, and was always a primary target for Israeli fighters, especially when they could catch them on the ground. (PHOTO COURTESY OF LON O. NORDEEN)

The efficiency of the Israeli ground crews matched that of the aircrews. Here a 750-pound bomb is being manhandled to a Phantom for loading. (PHOTO COURTESY OF LON O. NORDEEN)

A posed shot, beloved of public information officers, shows the McDonnell Douglas A-4 Skyhawk with a representative selection of the ordnance it could carry. (PHOTO COURTESY OF LON O. NORDEEN)

The deadly effective SA-6 missiles were mounted on a modified PT-76 chassis and were air transportable, mobile and amphibious. A fire unit consists of three vehicles each with three launchers, a loading vehicle, and a "Straight Flush" radar vehicle. (PHOTO COURTESY OF LON O. NORDEEN)

Ariel Sharon as he loved to be, in the midst of his adoring, approving troops. Sharon took pride in leading at the front, and often used his firsthand information to argue with his superiors. A less popular general probably would have been sacked for what appeared to the Israeli high command as insubordination. Sharon's conduct was approved in postwar reviews of the situation, and he went on to become first and important political influence, and eventually, Prime Minister of Israel. (NATIONAL PHOTO COLLECTION OF THE STATE OF ISRAEL)

The war is over, but its political outcome is still being decided on December 31, 1973. Sharon is shown here leaving the polling tent after having voted in the 8th Knesset election. The faces of the surrounding Israeli troops reflect his popularity. (NATIONAL PHOTO COLLECTION OF THE STATE OF ISRAEL)

through the roof, absolutely refusing, shouting that he "would not have it" and that "this is a war."[8] Amit backed off, knowing that Dayan and Elazar were scheduled to meet that evening in the Sinai at Southern Command Headquarters.

Having defeated the Egyptians in the desert, the Israeli forces were now to plunge themselves into the very problem they had sought to avoid: an assault on well-dug-in Egyptian troops. Recent successes had created an optimistic frame of mind, but Elazar's schedule failed to reckon with the new breed of Arab soldiers that they were fighting. On the eve of October 15, an IDF attack would bring about exactly what Sadat wanted: Arab armies inflicting serious damage on Israeli forces.

Problems began immediately. The Egyptians had dug themselves in at two vital positions, "Missouri," south of Ismailia, and the "Chinese Farm," southeast of the junction of the Akavish and Lexicon roads. The Chinese Farm had been a Japanese experimental farm prior to the 1967 war, and the Israeli soldiers had given it that name when they mistook Japanese characters for Chinese writing. Both positions were located in a small area, no more than fifteen kilometers long and twelve kilometers wide, but the entire 180 square kilometers now bristled with defensive positions.[9]

Reflecting the serious training they had been given, the Egyptians had turned the desert into a miniature version of World War I's Western Front. The farm had been crisscrossed with irrigation ditches edged with the mounds of dirt thrown up when each had been dug. These became natural defensive sites for machine guns and antitank weapons. Tanks were emplaced to back up the defenses. The Egyptian 16th Infantry and 21st Armored Divisions, rested and well armed, defended the area.

Sharon's mission on the night of October 15 was to secure a bridgehead that reached out to three miles beyond the area comprising Missouri and the Chinese Farm. The Tirtur road, which was designed for the passage of the roller bridge, ran through the center of the Chinese Farm. Once the bridgehead was secure, the crossing could begin. By 5:00 the following morning, both Adan's and Sharon's divisions were to be across the canal.

Instead, the Egyptians resisted valiantly, pinning down the Israeli forces for forty-eight hours and exacting heavy casualties. All the things that could go wrong for the IDF did. Traffic jams clogged roads; bridge parts were mistakenly sent to other rendezvous points; a roller bridge broke loose from its tanks to roll down a hill and was damaged. Artillery fire from the Missouri position rained down constantly on the Israeli troops. But more than anything else, it was the well-dug-in Egyptian infantry, with their Saggers and RPG-7s, which took their toll of Israeli armor. In a barrel-to-barrel tank fight for the key road junction in the Chinese Farm, where Lexicon intersected with Tirtur, the Israelis lost sixty tanks—and failed to take the position.

Yet in the Sinai war of stroke and counterstroke this time it was an Israeli deception that misled the Egyptians. A feint in the north and attacks in the south led the Egyptian leadership to believe that the Israelis were engaged in a general frontal assault to retake the Bar-Lev line and not attempting to cross the canal. This belief would offset the delays the IDF had encountered for a precious twenty-four hours—until Golda Meir would let the cat out of the bag.

Back at the Kremlin, Brezhnev had a serious meeting with the Politburo. The first matter to be discussed was a cease-fire to be put before the UN Security Council. The second was the dispatch of Premier Kosygin to Cairo for face-to-face talks with Sadat. The draft Soviet resolution was short and to the point. The first paragraph called for an immediate cease-fire, with the hostile forces to remain in the positions that they currently held. Paragraph 2 called for a "staged with-drawal of Israeli troops from the occupied Arab territories in accordance with Security Council Resolution 242, completing the withdrawal within a three-week period." Brezhnev and his colleagues in the Politburo did not expect the proposed resolution to be accepted, but it was a useful political maneuver to show that the Soviet Union was seeking peace in the Middle East.

UN Security Council Resolution 242 was signed on November 22, 1967, and had been hotly debated ever since. In essence, the resolution called for the establishment of a just and lasting peace, the withdrawal of Israeli forces from territories conquered in the recent conflict (the Six-Day War), the termination of all states of belligerency, and the right of states to live within secure and recognized boundaries free from threats and acts of force. It further stipulated freedom of navigation of international waterways in the area, a settlement of the refugee problem, and the guarantee of territorial inviolability for every state in the area.

Resolution 242 was never implemented, for many reasons. One was a minute difference between the French translation, which called for "evacuation from the territories," and the English translation, which called for "evacuation from territories." Thus the innocuous word *the* became a principal sticking point upon which thousands of hours of debate were lavished. Despite the arguments, the United States had clung to Resolution 242 for years, fighting off both Soviet and Arab pressures to jettison it, because it believed that the resolution was the only legal basis for future negotiations. Now the Soviet reference to Resolution 242 was interpreted as a gracious gesture to the United States, signaling that it was still interested in détente.

The choice of Kosygin to go to Cairo instead of Foreign Minister Gromyko surprised some. Brezhnev and Kosygin nominally worked with Nikolai Podgorny in their system of "collective leadership," but Brezhnev was gradually increasing his power at the expense of his two colleagues.[10] Kosygin hated to travel, especially by plane, and held the Arabs in open contempt. Sadat disliked Kosygin intensely, terming him "stubborn and vicious." Insiders saw the trip as a move by Brezhnev to diminish Kosygin by giving him a task that a subordinate could have handled and one that held little prospect for success. The feeling was amplified by the detailed instructions that Brezhnev gave Kosygin. He instructed his premier to remind Sadat that although the Soviet Union had warned him against going to war, it would continue to support him regardless of outcome. In a patronizing tone, Brezhnev told Kosygin to "conduct the negotiations in a calm, comradely way. Give him our regards and best wishes, our congratulations on the military victories. Tell him that a friend in need is a friend indeed." For Kosygin, a veteran communist since 1919 and a man who had negotiated with the top leaders of the world, including U.S. President Lyndon Johnson, the assignment was insulting.

If Brezhnev wanted results in the Arab world, Kosygin was the last man he should have chosen. The veteran Andrei Gromyko would have been a far better choice. Yet, even in the midst of a war, the Kremlin's internal politics were overriding.

The oranges were not yet tumbling out of their baskets. As of October 15, MAC had a fleet of 65 C-5As and 255 C-141s. However, 112 of the C-141s were already on missions elsewhere and 75 were "not operationally ready." The C-5s were in even worse shape, with 32 down for maintenance or parts. Twenty-six C-5s were away on missions, and only 3 were immediately available.

On October 14 General Carlton had taken steps to get more aircraft into commission, cutting down on maintenance inspections and delaying new entries into modification programs. The order went out to "button them up" (i.e., get the aircraft operational and into the air as soon as possible). All C-5s in the Pacific area were ordered to return to the United

States immediately. Though he knew it to be risky to the long-term life of the fleet, Carlton also ordered the utilization rate to be increased for both the C-5 and the C-141. He knew full well that using the aircraft at a higher rate would result in increased maintenance and possible shortages downstream, but he was willing to take the chance. Then, as an added measure, he asked that the current weight limitations on the C-5 be increased. For the past year, the normal maximum cabin load had been reduced to 100,000 pounds, to lessen the stress on the C-5's wing. At this weight limit, the C-5s would have been precluded from carrying the M-60 tanks. Carlton now asked and received permission to operate the aircraft at its maximum capacity of 265,000 pounds. The C-5 was being tasked to flex its airlift muscles.[11]

By 7:00 on the morning of October 15, Colonel Don Strobaugh was taking the first of his twelve-hour shifts as commander of the MAC ALCE at Lod Airport. His first job was to locate walkie-talkies so that he could utilize the 150-odd Israeli volunteers who had been assigned to move cargo. Strobaugh organized them into ten- or fifteen-man groups, appointed a leader for each, and gave him a walkie-talkie. Equipment was very short—only two forklifts and a lot of pallet trailers—but under Strobaugh's direction they were soon off-loading a C-141 in about forty minutes. His mind was put at ease when a C-5 arrived carrying an essential piece of equipment, the 40K loader, which, as its name implied, could handle 40,000-pound loads.

At the end of the first day, Strobaugh had the main elements of an ALCE running. Refueling operations were proceeding swiftly, and he had arranged for automatic clearance of U.S. planes with the Israeli air traffic control. By 7:15 P.M., he was relieved by his second-shift deputy and went back to the Avia Hotel at Savyon, skipping dinner and going to bed for the first time in forty-eight hours. Strobaugh would have many more sleepless days and nights in the weeks to come.

7 Back Across the Canal

AT 1:35 A.M. ON OCTOBER 16, one of Sharon's favorite soldiers, Colonel Danny Matt, began paddling across the canal at the head of six hundred paratroopers. Matt had distinguished himself in previous wars as a specialist in behind-the-scenes operations, dropping out of the blue to storm Arab artillery positions, fortifications, and headquarters areas. One of his triumphs had been the capture of the Old City of Jerusalem during the Six-Day War. A tall and handsome figure, Matt might well have carved out a successful career in politics; instead, he stayed with the army, rising later to the rank of Major General.[1]

Once across the canal, Matt encountered no opposition from the Egyptians, who had been totally unaware of his presence. It was a sneak assault that Elazar later called the golden opportunity of the war—all it needed was a rapid follow-up by Adan's division to break the back of Egyptian defenses.

Seven hours after Matt crossed, the first thirty Israeli tanks were in place in Africa, as Ariel Sharon called the west bank of the canal. Matt deployed his tank force to establish a bridgehead five kilometers deep, then waited for the rush of armor reinforcements to follow.

Unfortunately, the first armor Matt met was Egyptian—the 116th Mechanized Infantry Brigade, which he managed to rebuff. Across the canal, Matt's reinforcements were cut off. In tough hand-to-hand fighting, the Egyptian 16th Infantry Brigade had first sealed off the road behind Matt, then hunkered down to hold off the advance of the desperately needed Israeli bridging equipment. The 16th was soon backed up by the first major Egyptian counterattack. Thirty-nine tanks of the 1st Armored Brigade and thirty-one tanks

of the 18th Mechanized Infantry Brigade came in to consolidate the position. What Sharon had seen as a quick mopping-
up operation had turned into a charnel house. Within
twenty-four hours, the Israelis would lose fifty tanks and two
hundred men. The standoff would result in a change of plans,
seasoned as always by the mutual distrust among the Israeli
leaders.

The rest of October 16 was spent in bitter fighting, trying
to eradicate the Egyptian stranglehold on the roads that led
to the embarkation point for the cross-canal operation. The
bloody effort would gradually expand the Israeli perimeter
and allow a moderate flow of reinforcements but would not
succeed in removing the Egyptian presence for more than
twenty-four hours. The one bright spot in the battle came
late in the day when columns of Israeli tanks—all captured
Soviet equipment and disguised in Egyptian camouflage—
broke out from Matt's bridgehead to begin the process of
raiding SAM sites and destroying ammunition dumps. This
maneuver would serve as a model for the next two days'
fighting.

While the Egyptian and Israeli warriors were battling it
out with skill and bravery for the crossing point, their respective efforts were being nullified by mistakes at the very
top, in the second-guessing style that had come to characterize the war.

In Cairo, President Anwar Sadat had made a fiery speech
before the People's Assembly, threatening Israeli cities with
Scud missiles. He demanded that any cease-fire be linked to
total Israeli withdrawal to the June 4, 1967, borders. In doing
so, he ignored the defeat the Egyptian army had just suffered,
the probable shift of Israeli forces from the now-quiescent
Syrian Front to the Sinai, and the roadblock the speech threw
in the path of Moscow's cease-fire efforts. The speech even ran
counter to his own plans, because a cease-fire in place, with
tens of thousands of his soldiers in "liberated" territory, would
have been a tremendous political victory for him. Yet Sadat

chose to antagonize not only his enemy but also his friends, and his speech alienated the Soviet Union and the United States. Moscow was particularly offended that he had made no mention of Soviet aid, Soviet equipment, or the Soviet airlift.[2]

One can only speculate on the motivation for Sadat's choice of words, but they were probably chosen to placate his domestic political opponents. An intuitive politician, he may have felt comfortable with the way his relationship with the United States was developing and reasoned that the Soviet Union was going to continue to support him no matter what he said. One can be sure only that the words were deliberately chosen. Sadat sometimes chose to give the appearance of being hotheaded, but he was always in command, harnessing his mercurial personality to his political advantage.

With all the bitter fighting, the one essential advantage that had remained with the Israelis attempting to cross the Canal was the fact that Egypt had not yet recognized that this was more than a "television operation," as Sadat would characterize it.[3] In an address to the Israeli Knesset, Golda Meir responded defiantly to Sadat's speech, terming his condition of a withdrawal to the pre–1967 war borders as ridiculous. Then, to the utter dismay of her military advisers, she boasted, "Right now, as we convene in the Knesset, an IDF task force is operating on the west bank of the Suez Canal."[4]

The remark was not a calculated slip; it probably simply erupted from Meir in her desire to offer some good news to a country that needed it desperately. However, the cat was out of the bag, and the Egyptian high command responded almost immediately, bringing in heavy artillery fire that would continuously increase over the next several days. Worse, Meir had removed the option of pulling Danny Matt's force back and cutting the losses. To do so would provide Egypt with a propaganda coup of the first order—the Arabs had crossed the canal and were still there; the Israelis had crossed the canal but had been thrown back.

The combination of the bitter fighting at the Chinese Farm and the Israeli incursion across the canal caused yet another fight at Center Ten, the Egyptian headquarters that corresponded to Israel's Pit. General Shazli wanted to pull the 4th Armored Division and the 25th Armored Brigade back from the east bank to strike northeast at the Israeli bridgehead. His recommendation threw Sadat into a fury, and he threatened Shazli with a court-martial if he mentioned moving troops back from the east bank to the west once more. This screaming match signaled the end of the road for Shazli, who was relieved of command just three days later.

The earlier successes of October had led Sadat to adopt a less militant pose. Instead of going in uniform to Center Ten, he began to receive visitors in Cairo, maintaining an outward calm, sipping tea and sometimes going so far as to wear comfortable, pajama-style clothing. As the tide of battle shifted, however, he donned his uniform again, becoming intensely involved and in no mood to have a four-day visit from Premier Aleksey Kosygin.

Nonetheless, Kosygin was greeted with full military honors at the Cairo International Airport (which had become a full-time military airfield and remained so for the duration of the war). Sadat did not meet Kosygin personally, sending his National Security Adviser, Hafiz Ismail. There was more than a little irony in this, and perhaps a gentle snub, for Ismail was also Sadat's contact with the United States—and Kosygin knew it.[5]

The state visit was trumpeted by all the world's media—except in the Soviet Union, where it remained, for internal reasons, a state secret. Brezhnev wanted Kosygin to have the inner-circle humiliation of going but not the attendant prestige that the unknowing Soviet public might have attached to it. Soon after his arrival, Kosygin received a special briefing on the details of the Israeli breakthrough across the canal from the Soviet military attaché who had just returned from the front. The news was not good, and Kosygin's ordinarily dour manner became even glummer.

But in diplomacy protocol is everything. In their first private meeting, Kosygin and Sadat exchanged fulsome wishes and the customary kisses that their cultures demanded. Then they immediately got down to business, with Kosygin heartily recommending that Sadat accept a cease-fire and Sadat responding that he would do so gladly—*if* the Israelis would withdraw to their pre-1967 borders. Sadat explained in a very straightforward fashion that his aims were simple: he wanted to get the Middle East peace settlement under way and demonstrate the new efficiency of the Arab military. He also acknowledged that he did not expect to defeat Israel because the United States would not allow it.

The first talks ended with the same formal cordiality but with no genuine results. In the next few days, the Israeli offensive would completely undermine Sadat's position, but by then Kosygin would have returned with his visit a complete failure. So far, things were working out well for only one person: Brezhnev.

The Soviets' progress made in space since *Sputnik* now proved vital, as their satellites were able to detect the Israeli buildup for the cross-canal operation. The satellite operations were soon supplemented by MiG-25 Foxbat supersonic reconnaissance planes. Other intelligence sources revealed that the U.S. airlift was, as Kissinger had warned, indeed "substantial." More disturbing were reports of panic among Egypt's military and civil leaders as the knowledge of Israelis crossing became generally known. It was said that plans were being made to withdraw the government from Cairo to Asyût and to begin (as Dayan had suggested for Israel in the early dark days of the war) the organization of a popular resistance movement, that is, guerrilla warfare.

Kosygin's lack of progress and Sadat's adamant refusal to consider the Soviet cease-fire led Brezhnev to prepare a very straightforward letter to Nixon. In it Brezhnev openly acknowledged the differences between U.S. and USSR goals and sympathies in the Middle East. Then, unfortunately, instead of new ideas, he put forth the hope that Israel could be persuaded to relinquish her hold on all the occupied lands in exchange for the border integrity of the lands of all nations in the region, guaranteed by either the United Nations or a joint agreement among the "great powers," which were not specified in the message but implied to be China, France, the United Kingdom, the United States, and the Soviet Union.

This was in fact not a bad proposal and indeed forecast a trend of events over the next two decades. But Brezhnev's most important message was contained in the last paragraphs, in which he urged restraint by both the United States and the USSR so that "the edifice that we have started" (détente) could continue to build. The letter had an almost poignant quality, differing markedly from the usual gruff and often threatening official communications from the Soviet Union. But his position was difficult: He distrusted his Arab clients and would not benefit from their victory. He was hostile to Israel (despite his protests to the contrary) and would lose face if they won the war. He placed his hopes on a negotiated settlement, one that might be achieved in large part because of his personal relationship with Nixon.

Unfortunately for Brezhnev, Nixon was too preoccupied with his political problems to give thought to this letter. The conduct of Middle Eastern affairs was now almost solely in the hands of Henry Kissinger, who dismissed the letter as "the usual rhetoric." It was not. It represented Brezhnev's best effort at solving the problem. Three days later Brezhnev would get a dismissive response from Nixon. From that point on, misunderstandings would abound and relations between the two countries would deteriorate to a potentially catastrophic nuclear level.

Jordan had been severely mauled in the Six-Day War and forced to cede the West Bank to Israeli occupation. It wanted no more wars with Israel. To avoid trouble, it tried to prevent Palestinian guerrilla groups from attacking Israel from Jordan. The years 1970 and 1971 were marked by bitter infighting that resulted in Jordan expelling the Palestinian forces. One untoward result was an armed conflict with Syria (which encouraged Palestinian terrorist activity). The Syrians launched an armored division against the Jordanians, whose crack 40th Armored Brigade, trained by the British, managed to contain the Syrians until they were advised by the Soviet Union to stop their offensive.

In September 1970 the Egyptian leader Gamal Abdel Nasser attempted to mediate between King Hussein and Yasir Arafat but collapsed and died shortly after the meetings had begun. Two months later, Hafiz al-Assad came to power in Syria and saw to it that relations with Jordan remained extremely tense.

King Hussein had done what he could to alert Israel to the October 6 attack, but his warnings had gone unheeded in the general malfunction of the Israeli intelligence system.[6] Now, however, with Syria in desperate straits, he had to make at least a token gesture to his Arab colleagues. In another twist of irony, Hussein sent the 40th Armored Brigade to Syria's aid. The 40th fell into line between Syrian and Iraqi forces on the southernmost part of the front.[7] It was an unlikely coalition, and the inter-Arab cooperation was so faulty that Syrian planes shot down their Iraqi comrades. Nor could the Arab forces coordinate their ground attacks, allowing the Israelis to deal with them in turn.

The Jordanians were equipped with Centurion tanks, but an earlier model than the Israeli version. At Tel El-Mal on October 16 the 40th faced the Israeli 17th Armored Brigade, under Colonel Ran Sarig. Badly wounded only six days before, Sarig had "discharged himself" from the hospital and now appeared, bandaged and bleeding, to command his unit again.

As with other Israeli units in the heights, the 17th had a severe shortage of ammunition, particularly the indispensable 105mm shells.

The Israeli tanks were once again bunkered on a ridge, and once again their superior gunfire demolished the enemy— twenty-eight tanks were destroyed, and the Jordanian brigade withdrew from the battle. Arab honor was satisfied and a costly lesson learned.

Don Strobaugh found that this war was going to be a little more pleasant than the last one. El Al opened a special MAC Lounge in the building where he worked, installing first-class seats from a Boeing 707 and filling the tables and refrigerators with sandwiches, pastries, fruit, and soft drinks. Even more delightful, it was staffed with El Al stewardesses. When a plane arrived, an El Al Volkswagen bus picked the officers up and took them to the lounge to relax while their aircraft was unloaded and refueled. A mobile lounge, with similar refreshments, came to each aircraft for the benefit of enlisted personnel who were servicing it.

The Israelis had improvised off-loading equipment, including a "rollerized" semitrailer that worked perfectly for off-loading crates of ammunition. A long consecutive series of rollers had been installed in the semitrailer bed, and the device worked as well as far more expensive specialized equipment.

A system quickly evolved in which the special U.S. K loader would pull two pallets off the aircraft and deliver it to the rollerized trailer. There the Israeli crews broke down the pallets and loaded waiting trucks with the shells and equipment. When loaded, the trucks took off directly for the front lines. It was a streamlined process, not burdened by excessive paperwork on the Israeli side.

Strobaugh's priority enabled him to "press" technicians from the aircraft passing through, and by the end of his shift he had acquired four more specialists to beef up his maintenance operation. His position at Lod was turning out to be exactly the kind he liked: plenty of responsibility, plenty of authority, and plenty of results. Within a few days his staff would grow to more than fifty.

By day's end on October 16, the oranges had truly begun to tumble out of the basket, for in that one day his crews had off-loaded 753,337 pounds of matériel from five C-5s and 499,352 pounds from ten C-141s. It was the start of what would become a torrential flow. Included were the first two M-60 tanks, sent as a symbol of what could be done if necessary. For the most part, however, the loads would consist of a combination of the most basic and most vital matériel: 105mm shells, air-to-air missiles, and electronic countermeasures equipment.

The air war, which had begun in such a markedly different fashion from the glory days of the Six-Day War, was now beginning to assume a more familiar pattern than that of the shocking first days when Arab missiles were slaughtering Israeli fighters. While the two opposing air forces had very similar missions—close air support, strategic bombing, and air defense—their tactics differed greatly. The Arab air forces began the war with a series of strikes on airfields, headquarters, and supply centers. They next concentrated on close air support, using cannons and rockets rather than bombs as the weapon of choice. Both the Syrian and Egyptian air forces employed Sukhoi Su-7B and the elderly but effective MiG-17 in the close support role, supplemented by Iraqi Hawker Hunters and Libyan Dassault Mirages. As Israel began its counterattack, the Arab emphasis then shifted to air defense, deploying their forces—primarily MiG-21s—to counter the Israeli raids deep behind the line.

In contrast, the Israelis had counted on their air force to substitute for artillery and to be the sword by which Arab defenses would be cut apart. Douglas A-4 Skyhawks were the primary aircraft, using rockets, guns, and bombs. It was soon realized that the Israelis were sadly deficient in electronic countermeasure equipment and in the tactics of missile suppression, and requests for such equipment went to the top of the list of matériel sought from the United States. The A-4s, used in desperation to halt the Syrian advance despite the ferocious missile environment, suffered heavy losses, with fifty-four being downed. One of the great assets of the Lockheed C-5 transport was that it was able to move very large replacement sections for the A-4s, including entire rear fuselages and wing sections, and these soon became priority airlift items as well.[8]

The Israelis had started the war with 150 of the redoubtable McDonnell Phantoms, and these were assigned the task of strategic interdiction, flying long distances to hit enemy airfields, convoys, and headquarters. The Phantoms were also used as required for close air support and keeping the skies clear of Arab planes. The Phantoms suffered heavy losses in the ground assault mission, with 35 being shot down. (The United States would supply 48 additional Phantoms.) As with the A-4s, the loss of aircraft was serious, but the loss of seasoned aircrew verged upon the catastrophic. In the Phantom's stead, IAF Nesher and Dassault Mirage aircraft were given the majority of the air superiority missions.

Postwar claims by both combatants varied widely. The Israelis claimed to have shot down as many as 351 Arab aircraft while losing 115. Of the 351, 43 were shot down by missiles or antiaircraft fire, while the rest were downed by fighters. In natural contrast, the Arabs claimed that several hundred Israeli aircraft were shot down, while admitting to the loss of about the same number. Most of the Israeli aircraft were lost to ground fire, and the Israelis claimed that it had lost only four fighters in air combat. Egyptian fliers scoff at this number, claiming that it is far short of the actual total.[9]

The Arabs fired more than twenty-one hundred SAMs at

Israeli aircraft, downing at least 40, a kill rate of one in every fifty-five launches. During the war in Southeast Asia, North Vietnamese gunners averaged one kill for every sixty launches, indicating the relative gains in Arab offensive and defensive capability.

The Israeli intrusion across the canal triggered a violent reaction by the EAF, which began putting up hundreds of sorties against the bridgehead. In the late afternoon of October 16, a force of MiG-17s strafed Danny Matt's forces on the east bank. The IAF responded, shooting down 10 of the MiGs without any losses. Another 10 Egyptian aircraft were shot down in the course of the day. Egypt claimed 11 Israeli aircraft destroyed, but the actual figure was disputed.

More important than the losses, and conforming exactly to Sadat's wishes, the EAF continued to fight and fight well. Some of the largest dogfights in the history of the jet age took place that October, with as many as 60 aircraft involved.

Major General Izz al-Din Mukhtar stated in a press conference in Cairo that the Israelis had lost five times as many aircraft as the Egyptians. It was, like most such claims are in wartime, an exaggeration, but Sadat could well be proud of both his air force and his air defense system. Both had functioned exactly as planned so far—now both were beginning to weaken.[10] Egyptian losses had not been light, with more than 100 aircraft destroyed, most in air combat. Yet the loss of the aircraft was far less important than the loss of skilled pilots, who were already in short supply. Of the 4,000 sorties flown so far, about one-sixth of them had been flown by Iraqi and Algerian pilots, who had suffered a dozen losses in the process. In addition, a North Korean MiG-21 squadron was also flying missions out of the El-Minya air base. The Egyptians had supplied aircraft, ground crew, and support for thirty North Korean pilots whose specialty was flying combat air patrol missions.

One interesting aspect of the war was the purported participation by Soviet and U.S. fliers. Soviet fliers had been a significant presence in Egypt in the past and, acting as instructors, had been dismissive of the skill and aggressiveness of Egyptian pilots. On July 30, 1970, a squadron of MiG 21s, flown by Soviet pilots, engaged in battle with a mixed bag of Israeli Mirage and Phantom fighters. When the dogfight was over, five MiG 21s had been shot down, without any Israeli losses. That night, EAF officers' clubs had tremendous parties, celebrating—for once—the Israeli victory.[11] Soviet personnel did not attend.

In his press conference, Major General Mukhtar also noted a significant change in Israeli tactics, reinforcing the belief that U.S. pilots had entered combat. *Aviation Week and Space Technology* (*Aviation Leak,* as it is known) quoted an Egyptian air defense commander as saying, "These Phantom pilots we met . . . had a much different style to their combat tactics than we ever encountered with the Israelis. Whether they were volunteers, reservists, or regular U.S. military pilots we do not know, but they were certainly not Israelis."

Foreign fliers fighting in the Middle East was not new. There had been volunteer American pilots flying for Israel in the War of Independence and French pilots in 1956. The possible participation of U.S. fliers in the October War is far less definite and, of course, officially denied. Rumors persist, however, that veteran U.S. Phantom pilots did engage in combat and score victories. One very well known personality, who scored several victories in Vietnam, has admitted this in informal conversations but will not permit his name to be used. There is one compelling reason to believe that U.S. pilots might have participated. As previously noted, Israel was desperately short of electronic countermeasures equipment, particularly the highly specialized equipment needed for the "Wild Weasel" role, the suppression of enemy SAM defenses. The Wild Weasel equipment requires a great deal of training and a high degree of expertise to use successfully, and there was no time for Israeli pilots to acquire either. If

U.S. pilots were used, it is logical in one sense that they would have been used in the electronic warfare role. However, the Wild Weasel mission is the most dangerous of all, and if any aircraft had been shot down, they would have landed in Arab territory, exposing the use of U.S. pilots.

In summary, the IAF, though handicapped by its lack of sophisticated electronic equipment, flew valiantly into the face of Arab missile defenses, accepting losses at a higher level than anticipated but getting the job done. In air combat, the IAF maintained its dominance, as it did in strategic bombing. The Arab air forces, for their part, did remarkably well in the ground attack role and in general demonstrated a level of proficiency far in excess of any shown in the past.

Meanwhile the Pentagon had scoured its resources and now had at least twenty-five Phantoms and about twice that many Skyhawks on the way to make up for Israeli losses. More would follow. And, even more important, regular shipments of air-to-air missiles and electronic countermeasures pods were now arriving. If the sea of combat had not yet parted for the IAF, the tide had at least shifted finally in its favor.

Both the Egyptian and Israeli air forces directed their fighters from the ground. The Israeli system of command and control was far more sophisticated, however, and was directed by a single commander who could immediately send his forces to meet any new threat. The biggest difference between the two air forces unquestionably was in training. The Israeli pilots routinely flew three to four times as many flying hours per year as their Egyptian counterparts. As a result, they were far more confident and naturally far more aggressive. But the IAF had some technical advantages as well. Its main air superiority fighters, the Dassault Mirage III and the Israeli adaptation of that aircraft, the Nesher, carried two 30mm cannons and two heat-seeking missiles, either the AIM-9 Sidewinder or the Israeli-built Shafrir. Both were excellent and were matched to the fighters so that they performed well in a high-G dogfight. The Israeli fighters typically used their missiles first, at longer range, then closed to short range to use their cannons.

The opposing Egyptian MiG-21 fighters were fast and agile, but their armament was inferior, particularly their lead-computing gun sight, which tended to tumble in a dogfight. Their missiles, either the K-13 Atoll, a heat seeker, or the radar-guided K-5 Alkali, were difficult to fire in a dog fight because of their G-limitations. Egyptian fighter pilots were often frustrated when they had closed to a sure kill position, twisting and turning on the tail of an Israeli plane only to find that they could not fire their weapons.

As an instructor-navigator, Lieutenant Colonel Harry Heist felt a little uncomfortable on this, his first trip along the tightrope route to Tel Aviv. He would have far preferred to be doing the navigation, rather than constantly looking over the new guy's shoulder with nervous concern about any mistake that would result in an interception by Arab fighters. Heist was not a worrier, but he knew from past experience just how dangerous their position was. There had already been reports of unidentified fighters closely shadowing inbound transports.

The Arab air forces were all schooled in Soviet tactics, and these included the fast hit-and-run approach of MiG-21 fighters. In Vietnam the tactic had developed of the MiGs, operating under ground control, sneaking in low, at heights where they could not be acquired by radar. When they neared their target, they would pop up, fire their heat-seeking Atoll missiles, and turn back to safety. The aircraft of the 6th Fleet were on hand to prevent attacks, but there was no way they could contain a determined enemy from Libya or Egypt. They might be able to catch such enemies and shoot them down, but not before the MiGs had launched their missiles. And Heist knew that an Atoll would turn a fuel-laden C-5 into an enormous fireball, with no chance of escape. After surviving the hazards of Korea and Vietnam, Heist had no wish to be shot down over the Mediterranean.

On the plus side, the C-5 was better equipped than any other aircraft he had ever flown. He'd spent seven thousand hours in the old Douglas C-124 and another one thousand in the trouble-prone Douglas C-133 turboprop, sloshing through every thunderhead in the sky. At the end of a trip Heist would be dead tired from the flight and the ceaseless shaking of the aircraft. But the C-5 was one of the new generation of jet aircraft, able to clip smoothly along at a high speed well above the weather. The airplane was a dream to work in, being well equipped with radar, Loran, Doppler, a periscopic sextant, and a single Inertial Measurement Unit that almost made navigators surplus. When it was working, the IMU was terrific, keeping them exactly on course, but it had some maintenance problems. The IMU was mounted in the huge visor that rose up, opening like a gigantic mouth, to receive freight through the front of the aircraft. If the visor was raised while the IMU's gyros were initializing, it would tumble and have to receive maintenance.

After one last check of the course, Heist left the cockpit to give the navigator receiving the route checkout a little breathing room. Besides, it was a pleasure to walk back through the big relief crew area (it could accommodate fifteen men), grab a cup of coffee, and stroll through the airplane, just for the exercise. Heist kept in shape with lots of hard work when he was home, and it showed in his wiry build. Just over five feet, eleven inches tall, he had weighed 170 pounds for years, never gaining or losing. Years ago, he had thought nothing of staying crouched over a tiny table, doing the calculations necessary for dead-reckoning or celestial navigation. He'd move only when he had to take a celestial observation. Now Heist was older and wiser and took the time to stretch his legs and limber up.

Holding his coffee in one hand, Heist steadied himself with the other as he eased down the polished metal stairway to the lower deck for a walk in the cavernous hold. It was pressurized and heated but felt colder than the crew area above. Striding down to the center of the airplane, he examined the neat row of pallets full of 105mm shells the Israelis needed so desperately. Against the side of the fuselage were the long cases that held Maverick missiles, another crucial need.

Standing inside the lower cargo deck was like being inside a subway tube. The rounded walls were clad in green insulated padding and brightly lit by the overhead lights. In the rear, the loading ramps were folded to form part of the pressurized compartment. There was no impression of speed or of height or of flying in a pitch-black sky above a pitch-black ocean. It was calm, efficient, almost serene in the cargo hold. He hoped it would stay that way.

Heist glanced at his watch. Four hours to go. They would off-load and fly to Lajes to rest, then back to Dover. There'd be a day or two off when he might get some work done on his house; then he'd be right back, doing the same thing, guiding close to 700,000 pounds of airplane, people, and cargo through the air at 500 mph—and loving it.

The long day had gone very well for Henry Kissinger, which in his mind meant that it had gone well for the United States. The airlift was running so beautifully that he had been able to insert the needle into Schlesinger's ego with the remark "I must say when you want to work you are terrific. You are equally awe-inspiring when you don't."[12] Schlesinger of course was not the author of the airlift's success, for MAC was simply functioning as it always did—efficiently and with great energy. It pleased Kissinger that the vital, perhaps war-winning matériel was arriving at the rate of fifty tons per hour. MAC had already exceeded the total tonnage that the Soviet Union had airlifted to the Arab world, despite the latter's earlier start.

All the same, Kissinger sent out word that the triumph of

the airlift was not to be boasted about. He did not want to annoy the Soviet Union any more than necessary and certainly did not wish to goad them into outright airlift competition. Nor did he wish to make the Arab nations any more resentful or apprehensive about the airlift than they already were. Fortunately, the responses to his letters to the Arab leaders on the airlift were now coming in and were much more moderate than expected. The response from the Shah of Iran was sympathetic but noncommittal. Saudi Arabia's King Faisal's message was equally temperate, simply restating the old formula of Israel withdrawing to its pre-1967 borders as a prerequisite for beginning talks. While the letter was innocuous, other Saudi diplomatic actions were not. The Saudi Deputy Foreign Minister, Ibrahim Masuud, unmasked another battery: the oil weapon. In an address to the ambassadors of the European Community, Saudi Arabia warned that it would reduce oil production, a clear foreshadowing of the results of the meeting of OPEC nations in Kuwait. The European countries were already so petrified with fear of an oil embargo that they had written off aid to Israel in any form, and the Saudi warning shook them to their roots.

To Kissinger's surprise, Sadat had not attempted to rally the Arab world against the United States in a religious holy war. To the contrary, he sent a secret message through Ismail, deploring the airlift in a pro forma manner—and then inviting Kissinger to Cairo so that he might be able to link a political settlement of the war to a military settlement. The request was totally unprecedented and even implausible.

Kissinger composed a thoughtful message to Ismail, stroking the Egyptian's ego by praising their military successes, but still hinting that under the current circumstances (i.e., the resurgence of the Israeli forces) the time was not right to demand Israel to retreat to its pre-1967 war borders. He urged that a cease-fire be accepted and conditioned any visit by him upon such an agreement.

It was a pleasure to work with dignified and cultured Ismail. Tall, with a military bearing, the balding Ismail gave the impression of a genial, gray-fringed Yul Brynner, a smile always on his lips. Kissinger found that Ismail's agreeable personality concealed a brilliant mind and a tough, disciplined working style. Heir to five thousand years of Egyptian diplomacy, Ismail was a proud man and was quoted as saying, "We Egyptians are Arab, and don't ever forget this—but we are not like those other Arabs."

The satisfactory passage of the day's events was capped by an Associated Press bulletin announcing that Vietnamese Special Adviser Le Duc Tho and Secretary of State Henry Kissinger had jointly been awarded the Nobel Peace Prize for their efforts in ending the Vietnam War. The sweetness of the prize was heightened by Nixon's obvious pique that Kissinger was being rewarded for an action that had cost him dearly in prestige and public confidence. Nor was it diminished in any way when Le Duc Tho, with the insolence that had characterized his negotiating technique, declined to accept the prize.

All of the knife fights between State and Defense disappeared like dew with the morning sun as the MAC airlift operation swung into top gear on October 17. For the time being, none of MAC's other commitments was being given short shrift, although the future would hold a new turn of events that might severely restrain resources.

For the present, however, everything functioned normally. The airlift to remove supplies from Vietnam and return the massive infrastructure of B-52 operations from Thailand and Guam to the United States continued unabated. The return of personnel and equipment from the massive annual RE-FORGER (Return of Forces to Germany) maneuvers in Europe would go on uninterrupted, and all the many other missions within the United States and around the world were flown as planned. The extra effort for what was now officially termed Operation Nickel Grass was taken, as usual, from the hides of the crews and support personnel involved. No one objected and few even noticed, for such was life in MAC: the mission came first and would be accomplished, in spite of all difficulties.

For Don Strobaugh, October 17 was an important day for many reasons, despite a bad start. The newly arrived 40K loader had been loaded with five pallets of Class A explosives and was backing away from a C-141 when the front suspension collapsed. There were no spare parts on hand, but the El Al mechanics took the part into their machine shop for repairs. Nine hours later, they had it back on the K loader, in a tangible expression of the synergistic atmosphere that permeated the Lod operation.

At 2:30, a security team showed up surrounding Prime Minister Golda Meir, who had come for a briefing on the airlift. Strobaugh escorted her around the ramp and explained the intricacies of unloading a C-5 Galaxy. In Strobaugh's words at the time, "She is a quiet, plainly-dressed woman who gives you the feeling that you have just given her a miracle." At one point she was overcome with emotion and said, "For generations to come, all will be told of the miracle of the immense planes from the United States." A few days later, Meir would visit again, this time for semipersonal reasons.

Strobaugh remarked in his journal that he must have caught the Israeli spirit, for he felt fresher and more eager to work after four hours of sleep here than he did anywhere else after ten hours. Some of this came from the scope of the task. By the end of the day, five C-5s had delivered 761,601 pounds of cargo and nineteen C-141s had off-loaded 872,410 pounds. There had flowed a steady stream of ammunition, Maverick and TOW missiles, parts for damaged F-4s and A-4s, 175mm cannons, 155 mm cannons, and even M-60 and M-48 tanks. It was a cornucopia of military wealth that freed Israeli planners from any concerns about exhausting their supplies. Within the steady flow of bulky arms were tucked more ordinary household items, including medical supplies, rations, and clothing for the cold desert nights, things that made life at the front a little more livable.

Almost as amazing as the abundance of matériel was the manner in which it was absorbed instantly into the very fabric of the Israeli armed forces. Cannon shells still cold from the long flight over were slammed into the hot breeches of 105mm guns. Douglas A-4s stood with their aft ends already removed, ready to have completely new tail sections bolted into place. The paint was sometimes mismatched but not the parts. TOW missiles completed their journey from stateside depots to the breeched hull of an Arab tank within a thirty-hour period.

It was later revealed that a far different situation had occurred with the Soviet airlift to the Arabs. Some critical supplies were quickly identified and used, but much of the matériel was lost track of as it was trundled into warehouses. Other equipment, particularly tanks, arrived ready to drive but not ready to go to war, for vital equipment was lacking. The Soviets and the Arabs had worked together for a long time but had never overcome their inherent antagonisms and distrust. Where the Americans and the Israelis had worked hand in glove, the Arabs and Soviets were like mismatched gear wheels, meshing only occasionally and often stripping. Only the Yugoslavians seemed to be able to send functioning equipment, including tanks fully equipped with fuel and ammunition.

Israeli bases were rocked with cheers as the first fourteen of the vitally needed F-4 Phantoms touched down. The planes were quickly prepared for combat. Another eleven Phantoms were promised for October 18, along with twenty-six A-4 Skyhawks. The Egyptian Air Force noted their arrival—and also noted a suspicious change in the style with which the Israelis fought.

With the fighting intensifying on both banks of the Suez Canal the battle had become so convoluted that a major Egyptian mistake worked first in their favor—then against them.

Despite Meir's remarks to the Knesset on the Israeli operation on the west bank, the Egyptian forces in the area of Chinese Farm and Missouri believed that the Israeli attack was intended only to recapture ground on the east bank, rather than as a prelude to a cross-channel crossing. In turn, the Egyptians rushed reinforcements to the already-formidable defenses and fought well.

There was confusion on all sides, from the soldiers, fighting courageously in the desert trenches, to the command posts in Tel Aviv and Cairo. No one could control the fighting, for there were three battles going on at once in the Sinai. Matt's forces, on the west bank, had made some progress in securing the western element of the bridgehead but had run into increasingly tough Egyptian resistance.[13] Sharon's division was in the thick of the fight to destroy the Egyptian strongholds in the Chinese Farm and Missouri positions, while Adan's division was moving in three directions—north to secure access to the canal road, south to stop Egyptian 3rd Army reinforcements arriving to confront Sharon, and west in an attempt to link up with Sharon's embattled forces.

The parachute battalion that had been flown to the Sinai to "clean up" the Chinese Farm had gone into action at 10:30 P.M. on October 16. The Egyptian defenses were formidable, with their artillery firing over open sights at clumps of Israeli soldiers trying to come to grips with Egyptian infantry. The Israelis were unable to find a weak point to puncture and were forced to overcome the resistance pocket by pocket. The fighting turned into a sandy Stalingrad, where hand-to-hand combat bought only a few square feet of territory at a time and where an entrenching tool became more valuable than a Sagger or an RPG.

Even when the Israelis had captured the entire front line of defenses, the volume of Egyptian fire from positions in the rear continued to exact casualties at a fearsome rate. The two sides fought all night, both taking heavy losses. By 4:30 A.M. on October 17, the paratroopers were in a desperate situation, pinned down in small groups by hordes of Egyptian infantry backed up by armor.

Sharon, viewed as a superb field commander but also as a publicity seeker by Dayan, Bar-Lev, Gonen, and others, had been given new orders that same day at 9:00 A.M. Now, instead of leading the main force across the canal, Sharon was limited to cleaning up the bridgehead area so that his archrival Adan could cross. Later, when Sharon had concluded his task on the east bank, he could follow Adan. Sharon naturally resented the change and assumed it was politically inspired.

In his memoirs Sharon waxes eloquent on the misinformation flowing from Gonen's headquarters, including the news that he was surrounded and cut off. His view was just the opposite: he felt he had the Egyptians surrounded and needed only time to get a full division across the canal. Sharon was in the front lines, in the marshaling yard he had created for the cross-canal attack; he pleaded for someone from Southern Command Headquarters to visit him and see the battle as he saw it—but no one came. From this point on, to the intense annoyance of his superiors, Sharon would wave the flag of "I was there and you were not" on all occasions.[14]

No matter how bitter Sharon was, he never forgot about his troops. He now ordered that the paratroopers be rescued by an armored column. The tanks ground in, crushing the Egyptian infantry in their sand trenches. APCs followed to pick up the wounded paratroopers. The Egyptians responded vigorously, using the Sagger and RPG weapons with success, knocking out five Israeli tanks and a number of APCs.

The Israelis had made a fighting retreat, leaving the Egyptians in control of the battlefield. It was an Israeli defeat— yet because the Egyptians had focused their attention first on repelling the paratroopers' attack and then on opposing the rescue effort they had made a serious mistake. The Israelis had used the time to reach the embarking point for the cross-canal operations.

Sharon would later call the paratroopers' fight a suicide mission, protesting bitterly that they had been sent in without armor to be slaughtered by the well-entrenched Egyptians.[15] Sadat was getting the battle of attrition that he wanted, and the Egyptian troops had proved their valor for all time. At one point, Israeli reserves were so low that Sharon personally led a group of APCs into battle against Egyptian tanks to stop an incursion that threatened the Israeli position.

When reports of the road opening reached Moshe Dayan, he called for an Israeli council of war for noon the next day. Sharon, his head bandaged from a shrapnel wound, reluctantly returned from the front lines for a meeting with the senior commanders. His mood was bitter; in the battle some of his companies had lost their commanders twice, and the cost in junior officers was devastating.

Dayan, Bar-Lev, and Elazar had flown in by helicopter to the desolate spot on the hills near Kishuf, mere coordinates in the sandy dunes but out of range of Egyptian artillery, while Adan had come in his APC. Sharon's wounds won him no sympathy. Instead, Bar-Lev dressed him down for failing to clear the eastern approaches as he'd promised to do. In his memoirs Sharon contrasts his bloody, bedraggled appearance with that of the men from headquarters in their neatly pressed uniforms and expresses amazement that he did not strike Bar-Lev in the face.[16] But for all his bluster and bravado, Sharon was above all a soldier. He could take a chewing out as well as the next man, deserved or not. His staunch fighting qualities, his outspoken nature, and his willingness to take chances had served him well in the IDF. They would serve him better still in politics over the next thirty years.

At least the orders Sharon got relieved some of the pain of his perceived failure. Part of his division would continue to hold the corridor he had opened, but as soon as he had cleaned up the rest of the east bank he could cross the canal and sweep north toward Ismailia and then lunge west toward Cairo. Adan and Magen would take their divisions south around the Great Bitter Lake to surround the Egyptian 3rd Army. First, however, Adan was tasked with stopping a new Egyptian threat, the advance of the Egyptians' 25th Armored Brigade.

Prior to Sharon's arrival, Bar-Lev had again advised Elazar to relieve Sharon of command, citing that, as usual, Sharon wanted to plunge ahead with or without the bridges, using the Gilois rafts and pontoons to ferry more tanks across to the west bank. Adan, dismayed because Sharon had not yet cleared the road that blocked the roller bridge, violently disagreed. But even Elazar did not dare to relieve Sharon; he was far too popular with the public—and far too fine a field commander to lose.

On the other side of the canal, while his leaders were arguing, Danny Matt, a soldier's soldier, had finished a rapid round-robin inspection of his perimeter. As soon as he had learned that the roads his reinforcements were supposed to travel were cut off, he had sent out orders to his troops to begin conserving both fuel and ammunition. Twenty of his tanks formed the basis for perimeter defense. He kept seven back with him at his headquarters, in case he had to make a last stand.

By now the Egyptians were determined to wipe out the bridgehead by throwing their toughest troops, including the commandos usually reserved for special attacks, into the fray. Although Egyptian Sukhoi fighter-bombers had a tough time penetrating the screen thrown up by Israeli fighters, nothing prevented the continuous pounding by guns, mortars, rockets, and FROG surface-to-surface missiles that rocked the tiny bridgehead with thousands of explosions. Even the Egyptian helicopters, despite their losses early in the war, got into the act, lumbering over to drop barrels of napalm. One of the barrels, which failed to explode, almost struck no less a dignitary than Moshe Dayan on the head as he was walking through the bridgehead "scratching at the sand for ancient shards of pottery," according to Bren Adan's account. Dayan was always cool under fire—and lucky, too.

Matt and his men held on, hoping that the bridge would get built and still unaware that the battalion of his paratrooper colleagues had almost been wiped out the night before.

In the midst of the fire and the arguments, the Engineering Corps had to build a bridge, despite constant artillery fire from more than 150 cannons, not counting mortars and the awe-inspiring Katyusha rocket batteries concentrating fire on the east bank jumping-off area. Following Soviet doctrine, the Egyptian artillery never rested; when guns grew too hot or tubes wore out, replacements were brought quickly in to continue the barrage. The men of the Engineering Corps pressed on despite continuous losses and finally got a bridge across in the late afternoon. The only problem: no armor had arrived to cross it. It would be seven hours before the first tanks crossed and the next morning before they would begin their offensive sweep.

Meanwhile, Egyptian resistance had stiffened. In making their first major counterattack against the Israeli cross-canal threat, the Egyptian high command had ordered the 21st Armored Division, with one hundred tanks, and the 16th Infantry Division to attack to the south at the Deversoir crossing point. Tenacious Israeli resistance blunted this attack, but at heavy cost to both sides.

Then, as the Israelis already knew, the Egyptian 25th Armored Brigade was ordered to attack to the north and link up with the 21st Armored Division. The commander of the Egyptian 3rd Army, Major General Wassel, protested the plan, stating that it would lead them into a trap. Overruled, Wassel said that he would carry out his orders, but with the knowledge that his brigade would be destroyed.

The 25th's route covered a distance of eighteen miles and led them, just as Wassel had predicted, directly into an ambush personally laid by Adan.[17] This battle began at 2:45 P.M. on October 17, with preliminary fire exchanged between the slowly moving Egyptian advanced units and a small unit from Sharon's division that happened to be in the area. Adan called for Sharon's tanks to withdraw and also ordered Israeli artillery to hold their fire for a while.

The first major attack was by an Israeli armored brigade, charging head-on into the flank of the Egyptian column. The result was chaos, with the Egyptian tanks milling about, some blowing up when they wandered into a huge Israeli minefield that had been laid two years before. The Egyptians regrouped, then mounted a charge straight into the mouth of Adan's trap, where Israeli tanks lay concealed in the higher ground. By 4:00 P.M. most of the Egyptian tanks were left burning in the sands.

Adan's "jump-out" ambush once again proved that operating without aerial reconnaissance was fatal. Egypt had lost control of the sky, and it could not conduct reconnaissance.

Moving along the desert floor, the Egyptians were unable to see the Israeli tanks, which, as always, used the terrain to mask their positions. The 25th Armored Brigade was ripped apart. Eighty-six of its T-62 tanks were blown up, and only ten tanks escaped to safety. Many APCs, fuel tankers, and ammunition trucks were also destroyed. Major General Wassel's prediction had been exactly right. The Israelis lost only four tanks that had run into a minefield. At other sections of the front, a further twenty Egyptian tanks were destroyed.

The victory caused sufficient rejoicing at headquarters for some kind words to be uttered, a rare occurrence. Bren Adan was the beneficiary. Elazar remarked, "He's worth gold, that Bren," and Bar-Lev responded, "No excuses, no problems, he quietly does whatever he has to do. A real pro." In the back of their minds was the thought: *If only Sharon would behave the same way.*

Adan was not there to hear the compliments, as he was too busy moving his division across the canal.

On October 17, the soon-to-be Nobel Laureate Henry Kissinger looked on that Wednesday as a time for patience and preventive maintenance. Things were developing swiftly and well for the Israelis, and now his task was to convince the more moderate Arab states not to increase their level of help to Egypt and Syria and at the same time keep U.S.-Arab relations moderately friendly.

In many ways it was a difficult negotiating position, for the Arabs were well aware of the full extent of the airlift and were more and more convinced that the oil weapon should be invoked. However, things were not harmonious among the Arab states themselves—witness Syria and Jordan—and the United States offered a shield and a means of mediation to both internal and external threats. And of the two superpowers, the United States offered an increasingly more agreeable alternative than the Soviet Union.

Surprisingly, it was the beleaguered Richard Nixon who mollified the representatives of Saudi Arabia, Morocco, Algeria, and Kuwait. At a late-morning meeting in the Oval Office, Nixon put aside his Watergate cares to soothe the Arab ministers. He promised them no more than Kissinger had done—to work toward a cease-fire on the basis of the UN Security Council Resolution 242. In essence, he stated again what Kissinger had already told them, that the Israelis were not ready to accept Arab demands and that the United States would be necessary to influence Israel in any future negotiations. These were not promising words, but Nixon's manner was so convincing that it induced the Saudi Minister of State for Foreign Affairs, Omar Saqqaf, to state to the press that "the man who could solve the Vietnam War, the man who could have settled the peace all over the world, can easily play a good role in settling and having peace in our area of the

Middle East."[18] Nixon deeply appreciated Saqqaf's comment. For weeks the President had seen nothing in the press but critical investigative reporting, blistering editorials, and nasty editorial cartoons.

The general good feeling of the morning evaporated in the afternoon, when word was received that OPEC had announced an immediate reduction in oil production of 5 percent, with a promise of a further 5 percent cutback each month until Israel withdrew to its 1967 borders. At the same time, an announcement was made that oil prices were increased from $3.01 to $5.12 a barrel

This was the oil weapon pointed at the world, and the reaction, particularly in Europe, was predictable. There were demands for an immediate cease-fire to be followed by negotiations leading to a Middle East peace. Unfortunately, wars, once started, are not so easy to stop.

Armed with the latest information on the continuing successes of Israeli forces, Premier Kosygin felt better prepared for his second meeting with Anwar Sadat. After perfunctory formalities, Kosygin delivered his message. It was time for the Arabs to accept a cease-fire.

Sadat once again insisted that the Israelis had gained only a minor tactical success on the west bank of the canal and that most of the infiltrating tanks had been destroyed. He used this as a platform to launch into a complaint about the failure of the Soviet Union to deliver additional tanks and SAMs. Within moments the two men had reached the same stalemate on which the previous meeting had terminated. Kosygin pointed out that the Soviet Union had already airlifted 1,600 tons of supplies, admitting that much of this had gone to Syria, where they had considered the danger greatest. There was no further progress, and the two parted, again with protestations of mutual regard. Kosygin's mood was muted because he had to report the results to Brezhnev over the creaky telephone system that operated between the Soviet embassy and Moscow.

The strained conversation between the two old rivals was described as being a "dialogue of the deaf and the dumb" by a KGB representative in Moscow. Kosygin had a hearing impediment and had to ask Brezhnev to repeat every remark over the crackling of the telephone line. For his part, Brezhnev was disgusted that Kosygin had been unable to carry out his "persuasive and convincing" instructions.

The third meeting took place on October 18, and once again Kosygin was well prepared, this time with photographs taken by a MiG-25 reconnaissance plane. The photos showed just how far the Israelis had progressed and how dangerous the situation had become. Further, the Soviet military attaché briefed Kosygin that not only were the main elements of the Egyptian 2nd and 3rd Armies liable to be surrounded and cut off from their supply trains, but it was entirely possible that Israeli armor could capture Cairo, too.

Sadat once again refused to accept Kosygin's view of the military situation, restating that Egypt would not accept a cease-fire that did not guarantee Israel's withdrawal to the pre-1967 borders. He added a new verse to the old song, however, stating that there also had to be a joint Soviet-U.S. agreement to police the cease-fire and guarantee the borders of all countries in the Middle East. The meeting ended as the other two had, with outward protestations of eternal friendship and internal contempt and derision. Kosygin left to return to Moscow, but not before one final humiliating phone call to report the stalemate.[19]

That night in the Kremlin, Brezhnev met with members of the Politburo to discuss Kosygin's final report, which left them mystified. They could not determine whether or not Sadat had agreed to a cease-fire or what Assad's views were on the subject. The only hard facts that they knew were gained from the photographs taken by the MiG-25 of the improved Israeli positions and the knowledge that Hafiz Ismail was again in contact with Henry Kissinger.

In times past, the Kremlin would have reacted with anger and force to such a development. By October 18, however, they saw the Ismail/Kissinger connection as a ray of hope. If Kosygin could not get the Egyptians to agree to a cease-fire, perhaps Kissinger could. The irony of seeking salvation through the efforts of the Secretary of State of their most formidable enemy was not lost on them. That they now depended upon Kissinger to further their own goals made the Kremlin even more suspicious than ever. It was a key factor in the chain of events that was now building toward the possibility of a nuclear war.

8 *The Kremlin Turns to Kissinger*

SHORTLY AFTER MIDNIGHT on October 18, Dado Elazar began modifying the "Stouthearted Men" plan upon which the offensive across the canal had been based. Golda Meir's revelation of the Israeli presence had so stiffened Egyptian resistance that Adan's orders were changed.[1] His men were now to move directly west to a region of hills where the Egyptians had many depots, in the hopes of destroying enemy resistance by cutting off their fuel and ammunition supplies. After Adan's division was across, Sharon was—at last—to cross the canal and advance another two miles to the north. There he was to seize an Egyptian bridge and cut off the water and fuel pipelines that had been so swiftly and expertly put in place across the canal. Finally, a major effort had to be made by Sharon to capture the strong point Missouri, described by Bar-Lev as "a thorn stuck in the northern side of the crossing zone." Eliminating Missouri as a threat would allow the Israelis to expand the bridgehead to a meaningful size.

Sharon opposed the Missouri mission passionately, for he felt the Egyptians were no longer a threat and that ejecting them from the formidable defenses would cost too many casualties. Elazar insisted on it, fearing that a sudden Egyptian breakout from Missouri might close off the bridgehead on the east bank and do to the IDF what he was proposing to do to the enemy—cut them off from their supplies and surround them.

Up to this Thursday, the thirteenth day of the war, Elazar had been fighting for Israel's survival. The improved situation in the Golan and the opportunities that seemed to beckon in the Sinai now caused him to think in longer-range strategic terms.

The heavy Israeli losses sickened him—906 killed, 266 missing, 77 captured, and 4,204 wounded. This total of 5,453 casualties was an unacceptable number, one that threatened the future ability of the IDF to function. There had been massive losses in World War I—60,000 on the first day on the Somme and hundreds of thousands at Verdun. In World War II, the Soviets had lost as many as 600,000 in the early battles, while the Germans lost more than 250,000 at Stalingrad. The difference was in the relative size of the countries. "Only" 5,453 casualties might seem relatively small—until contrasted against Israel's 3 million population. To put it in perspective, the United States, with a population at the time of roughly 210,000,000, would have to incur 381,000 casualties in less than two weeks to have suffered proportionately.

The computation confirmed an obvious fact that Elazar had known all along—a war of attrition was out of the question. What was needed was a decisive victory, one that would force the Arabs to the negotiating table and would give Israel breathing room in which to recover. The Egyptians were heavily entrenched on the east bank of the canal and had defended their gains with tough, effective fighting. The only place that a truly decisive victory could be won was on the west bank, where the Israeli armor could operate freely as soon as the SAM sites were destroyed. Elazar realized that he was now in a race to get armor on the west bank to surround and then destroy the Egyptian armies.

Ironically, Elazar's opposite number, General Shazli, had for days been advocating the biggest threat to an Israeli victory, that is, a massive withdrawal of Egyptian forces back across the canal, with a forced march to the Israeli bridgehead to follow. It was Israel's good fortune that Shazli was not in good standing with Sadat and his recommendations had been rejected.

After a long day of pondering, Elazar finally had a clear vision of what must happen if Israel was to prevail. At 4:56 P.M. he took an unusual step. For the first time since the war began, he went home, took a shower, and changed his clothes. He was back in the Pit in eighty-five minutes.

Elazar's plan went into action, and the same men who had praised Adan for his ambush of the Egyptian 25th Armored Brigade were now chastising him for not moving his forces more rapidly across the canal. Without offering the obvious explanation that his tanks needed to be refueled and rearmed after the ambush, Adan stolidly accepted the criticism and began sending forces only partially refueled across on rafts or the pontoon bridge, hoping to complete their replenishment when tankers were able to cross to the other side.[2]

Initially, there had been no Egyptian resistance to his crossing, but that changed rapidly, and Adan's forces had to repel a series of counterattacks. The EAF reentered the fray, losing heavily in attempts to take out the Israeli pontoon bridge and the rafts, a more difficult target because of their smaller size and movement. The EAF flew with desperate courage, sometimes attacking with twenty aircraft at a time. But when Egyptian planes flew in the combat zone, their SAM sites had to shut down. Happy to be free of the SAM threat, the Israeli fighters slammed into the Egyptians, shooting down sixteen planes and seven helicopters. It was not without cost—six Israeli planes were lost.

The unceasing attack by both artillery and aircraft was almost—but not quite—enough to stop the Israeli attack. Adan was reduced to ferrying his tanks across in driblets, instead of setting up a massive stream that the plans had called for. For the IDF men involved, no effort was too great, and the deeply laden Israeli rafts plowed repeatedly through waters cluttered with the floating dead bodies of both friends and enemies.

The accurate Egyptian artillery lay down barrage fire that succeeded in reversing the manner in which Israeli tank crews died. Instead of being incinerated by a jet of molten metal, some were drowned, trapped inside a tank sunk when the raft was destroyed. Sometimes the shelling broke up the pontoon bridge itself, forcing the Engineers to move another pontoon into place to ready the bridge for traffic again. Despite the obstacles, the Israeli strength continued to flow across the canal, with tankers, supply trucks, and artillery joining the procession of tanks and APCs. In the Israeli army, the logisticians and the supply clerks did not stay in the back lines; they grabbed rifles and went forward to fight alongside the troops as they were supplying them at the front.

While Adan continued to force-feed his division by rafts and the pontoon bridge, the epic journey of the roller bridge was nearing completion. It was like a feat of biblical proportions, with the Israelis straining every fiber to achieve an impossible task. For thirty-six hours the roller bridge had been dragged forward by sixteen tanks, their belabored engines roaring as they inched and bumped along the straight road that led through the Chinese Farm toward the preplanned jumping-off point. As the bridge lurched forward, bulldozers were brought in to clear the battle debris of wrecked tanks and APCs from its path. The Herculean effort had been subjected to unrelenting Egyptian artillery fire and fighter-bomber attacks all the way, and more than a hundred men had been killed, forty-one in a single night. Late in the evening of October 18, the roller bridge was finally levered into position, ready to be pushed into the canal about one kilometer from the pontoon bridge. By midnight, it had touched the opposite bank, but at a slant. A few more frantic hours were spent getting it ready to take traffic across the canal.

When dawn broke, Adan had 170 tanks across. It was forty-eight hours after the planned time and 170 was not all he wanted, for he knew that the Egyptians had at least 500 tanks. But his armor was concentrated, while the Egyptian tanks were spread out on the west bank rear areas. Furthermore, Adan now held the initiative and could decide where the battles would be fought.

Fate conspired against the choices he made, as it had already done so often in this war. The Sweet Water Canal was positioned about a mile west of the Suez Canal, bringing freshwater from the Nile to irrigate the fertile farms and orchards spotted at close intervals along its length. Adan planned to sweep through this area quickly, then break out through the surrounding desert to hit the Geneifa Hills, where many SAM sites were located. When these were destroyed, the IAF would be free both to cover his further advance to the south and to attack the Egyptian 3rd Army, now caught between the east and west banks.

Instead of a quick sweep, progress was slow, for the Egyptians, heavily reinforced, used the green fields as the Germans had used the hedgerows of Normandy, forcing the Israelis to fight their way forward inch by inch. Adan called for air strikes to soften the Egyptian defensive positions in the jungle, as the IDF was calling it, but was told that they were impossible because of two SAM batteries that had been brought forward for air defense. The response brought the familiar mutters of "where is the air force when you need it?"

Adan countered with a risky proposal to send one battalion from each of his two brigades out deep in enemy territory to attack the missile sites.[3] Southern Command Headquarters agreed at once. He slipped the battalions, composed mainly of tanks and APCs, past the dug-in Egyptian infantry to move out from the fertile green belt for more than eight kilometers, fighting off Egyptian counterattacks all the way. Then, from a distance of four kilometers, they shelled the two missile sites and destroyed them.

There were two results from these forays, one totally unexpected. The IAF could now provide close air support—and the Egyptians began pulling back SAM sites from other areas of the front, to prevent their being overrun as well. Adan's attacks proved to be the thin edge of the wedge that would help decide the war in Israel's favor.

Back in Cairo, Kosygin's insistence that the war was going badly had its effect upon Sadat, all diplomatic formalities notwithstanding. Early in the afternoon, Sadat visited Center Ten and had the good grace to acknowledge that Egyptian forces on the east bank would have to be withdrawn across the canal to counter the Israeli incursion. He now ordered Shazli to withdraw the 3rd Armored Brigade from the east bank. And, in a "return with your shield or on it" move, Sadat ordered Shazli to take personal command of the 2nd Army. Shazli was to go to Ismailia and defeat the Israeli armor.[4]

One can only imagine Shazli's mental state. After days of having his suggestions receive nothing but bitter scorn and threats of court-martial, he was now given the task of defeating the Israelis just as they had seized the initiative and were breaking down his missile defenses. It was, he knew, a setup. If he succeeded, the credit would go to Sadat for his wisdom in choosing the new commander and sending him to the crucial battle. If the battle was lost, Shazli's head would be on the block.

A good soldier, Shazli fought his armies well on both sides of the canal for most of the next two days. And while he could not stop the Israeli advance entirely, he did keep Ismailia from falling to Sharon and maintained a tenacious hold on most of the Missouri position.

In battles that raged without interruption, night and day, the Arab soldiers continued to give a good account of themselves, but their performance was hampered by the inflexible Egyptian system of command. The Egyptians favored meticulously preplanned operations, which were kept under close central control. The opening days of the war had demonstrated their skill for this sort of warfare.

But now things were different, and it was necessary for commanders to interpret orders to meet the actual situation they were facing at the front, a task they were reluctant to perform. The lack of flexibility was shown at the very top by the War Minister, Ahmed Ismail. He had committed all of the forces still at his disposal—the 4th Armored Division, the Republican Guard Tank Division, and the 113th Mechanized Tank Brigade—to halt the Israeli advance toward Suez City. Unfortunately for him, he had done so in piecemeal fashion and the units were never coordinated enough to gather the mass necessary to stop the IDF.

Like water slowly enlarging a breach in a dam, the Israeli forces squeezed across the canal and began systematically expanding their bridgehead. In contrast to the Egyptians, the IDF prided itself on its flexibility in new situations and ability to take advantage of any opportunity. The early years of service under the British had instilled a Nelsonian touch in the Israeli commanders, who were always more than willing to use their own initiative to bring their guns to bear on the enemy.

Sadat listened stolidly to the reports coming on the difficulties both Shazli and Ismail were having, for they confirmed the bad news of the MiG-25 photo-reconnaissance photos. It was now apparent that Kosygin was correct and that a cease-fire in place was absolutely necessary. The question Sadat faced was how to get the cease-fire and not lose face in the Arab world.

The oil weapon began to have its full effect in Washington and around the world when Saudi Arabia announced that it was doubling its cut in production to a full 10 percent. Then King Faisal underlined the act with a mild threat by sending a message to President Nixon that U.S.-Saudi relations would "risk being diminished" if the war went on.[5]

Henry Kissinger felt that things had gone far enough, and he told Ambassador Dinitz that Israel should speed up its military actions as much as possible in the next forty-eight hours, for a cease-fire was now absolutely necessary.

Distressed by Kosygin's reports and by their military intelligence reports on the progress of the Israeli armor, the Soviet Union was now also determined to have action. Ambassador Dobrynin delivered a three-part message requesting a cease-fire in place, tied to Israeli withdrawal in accordance with Resolution 242, and negotiations leading to peace. It was not an acceptable proposal but a workable one, and once again Kissinger elected to stall, realizing that time was on his—and the Israeli—side if he could somehow placate Sadat and the OPEC nations for a few more days.

Stalling, however, was problematic. Kissinger knew that Yugoslavia had been preparing a cease-fire resolution and some other nation might introduce one as well. If entered, it would almost certainly pass, and the United States would not be able to veto it on any plausible grounds. Playing for time, Kissinger sent off a stream of messages to Arab leaders, each one emphasizing how much he admired the Arab military successes and how solidly he supported Sadat. It was transparent, but it worked—for another twenty-four hours. In the meantime, Kissinger was plying Dobrynin with attention, suggesting that he would welcome an invitation to come to the Soviet Union. If the Soviets accepted the idea, he would gain even more time for the Israelis.

Meanwhile, at Lod, Don Strobaugh was getting by with three or four hours' sleep a night, his energy still buoyed by the enthusiasm with which the Israeli ground personnel supported the airlift. Four days into the process, everyone was still learning.

The first aircraft had seen some two hundred Israelis swarm into the cargo hold to unload the aircraft in a pell-mell fashion onto the ramp. It was patriotic but dangerous, and it was only good luck that had prevented someone from injuring himself. Now Strobaugh had them shaped up into teams of ten to fifteen, each supervised by an Israeli with a walkie-talkie, with the supervisor working under the direct instructions of a MAC loadmaster.

Other Israelis were assigned to the pallet-breakdown area, where the matériel was loaded into long lines of trucks. The combination of the MAC cargo planes and the long lines of trucks was a tempting target, and Strobaugh often wondered why the Arabs had not hit them with aircraft or missiles. Certainly there was no problem in finding the airport. Tel Aviv, with a metropolitan population of almost 1 million, had a nearly perfect blackout. When the sun went down, there was scarcely any movement, by foot or vehicle, because the streets were pitch-black. At Lod, in contrast, there were hundreds of high-intensity lamps mounted on poles at least one hundred feet high. These were supplemented by thousands of smaller lights that kept the ramp area fully lit to speed unloading cargo. From the air, the airport looked like a glistening diamond against a pitch-black velvet background and was visible for at least fifty miles.

The Arabs had done so well with their Sagger missiles that there was concern about teams targeting MAC aircraft. As in Vietnam, a policy was established that there would be only one C-5 on the ground at a time, and the schedule was arranged accordingly.

Within the unloading procedures, three minor difficulties had surfaced. The manifests showing the cargo aboard incoming aircraft were not arriving in time to assemble the proper crews or equipment. If the aircraft was carrying tanks or APCs, qualified crews had to be on hand to drive them off. A series of messages got the problem straightened out, but not before some C-5s had been delayed on the ground.

The next problem was resolved on the spot. When each of the K loaders was loaded to its maximum capacity with pallets, it had to be driven to the pallet-breakdown area to be off-loaded itself. The unloading area became a bottleneck. Strobaugh suggested that semitrailers fitted with rollers be built and used as the off-loading area by the K loaders. The simple, inexpensive solution saved hundreds of hours of unloading time. Eight of these trailers were subsequently built.

Finally, the masses of containers that had been emptied now needed to be placed on pallets and returned—and there was no pallet-buildup area. In short order, the Israelis had assembled a production line, made up of rollers installed on nonmovable barrels, and were soon creating pallets and installing the containers on them.[6]

These changes were the last touch necessary to make the airlift function like the gigantic conveyor belt that the legendary Major General Tunner had always advocated. On this Thursday, six C-5s had landed, off-loading 871,435 pounds, while ten C-141s had brought 549,471 pounds—710 tons of supplies in a single day. This was about three times the average load handled by an Aerial Port in the United States.

Performance had picked up across-the-board. It now took the ground crews only fifty-five minutes to unload and refuel a C-141 and less than two hours to do the same for a C-5. There was a rousing spirit of competition, with records being set for unloading aircraft—forty-six minutes for a C-141 and an hour and one-half for a C-5. It was break-back work at breakneck speed, but the U.S./Israeli teams loved to compete.

The one flaw in the scenario was the lack of a suitable alternate airport in the event of bad weather. The IAF made facilities available for landing at the Hatzor and Ramat David Air Force Bases, but these lacked the unloading gear and meant a long delay. Nonetheless, on one occasion four C-141s and one C-5 had to be diverted to Ramat David when bad weather shut down Lod. The airplanes just waited there until the weather cleared before flying back to Lod to unload.

Strobaugh was weary, having now to supervise more than fifty people, plus acting as guest, boss, and diplomat to the Israelis who ran Lod so well. Late in the afternoon, he felt inclined to sneak back to the hotel for a nap when he was picked up by one of his Israeli counterparts and given dinner and a quick tour of the local battlefields. These ranged in time from the site of Joshua's biblical victory over the Amorites, to a Crusaders' fort, to the trenches used by the Arabs in 1948. More than anything else, the little trip showed Strobaugh just how many centuries the Israels had been defending their country. Charged up again, his nap forgotten, he went back to the office to make sure the airlift was working.

Across the hangar at Lod, things had not worked out quite as he had planned, but Harry Cohen did not care. He'd come over to fly liaison planes, then wound up making iron military beds. When he'd volunteered to unload aircraft, he hoped to be working on the big C-5s or C-141s and at least getting into an airplane, even if it was on the ground.

Instead, he was now hammering pallets together and helping manhandle the big containers into position so they could be shipped back. He briefly considered talking to the American airmen he saw running the operation and asking for a better job, then thought better of it. He was a volunteer; he would do what he was told, just like the soldiers at the front. And, in a way, he felt he was at the third front of the war, and was amazed that the Egyptians had not fired some missiles at Lod Airport or at least sent in some fighter-bombers to strafe. When doing the more mundane chores, he almost wished they would.

And, almost for the first time in the war, the news from the front was good. Rumor had it that both Damascus and Cairo were threatened by Israeli armored columns and that the Egyptian armies, north and south, were about to be surrounded. When that happened, his job would not mean much anymore, and he could go back to Detroit in good conscience.

Kosygin returned to Moscow bitterly disappointed with the results of his meetings with Sadat and properly apprehensive about the effect his failure would have upon his standing in the Kremlin. His opinion of Sadat as a stubborn, inflexible fanatic had only grown stronger.

Brezhnev made no pretense of concealing his disapproval

of the way Kosygin had conducted the meeting. He was particularly voluble over the fact that Kosygin had not definitely stated to Sadat that the Soviet Union was not going to become involved in the war. The premier claimed that he had done so, privately, with Sadat, but Brezhnev had wanted the statement made for consumption in the United States. The omission was indeed a critical one, as events of the next week would reveal.

The media coverage of Kosygin's return was muted in both Moscow and Cairo. In the Soviet Union, a simple one-sentence bulletin announced—for the first time—that Kosygin had visited Cairo to meet with Sadat. In Cairo, the coverage was more conventional, citing the useful nature of the talks but not going so far as to say that they indicated a prospect for a cease-fire. The simple absence of a joint Soviet-Egyptian communiqué on the meeting spoke volumes: everyone knew that if something worthwhile had taken place, there certainly would have been a joint statement highlighting the positive aspects of the meetings.[7]

The trip was the beginning of a long slide for Kosygin, highlighted by his omission from the imminent peace negotiations and culminating in his retirement for "reasons of health" on October 24, 1980. He did emerge with one unusual distinction, however: he was the last high-level Soviet official ever to visit Cairo.

To this point in the war, the Iraqi armored forces had not achieved the successes they had hoped for. On Friday, October 19, they struck again, this time with a battalion of commandos, moving against Tel Antar and Tel El-Alakieh in the southeastern corner of the Golan Front. Following the commando raid, an Iraqi armored division rolled forward with 130 tanks and more than 100 APCs, driving against the 19th and 20th Brigades of Major General Moshe "Musso" Peled's 146th Armored Division.

Peled could muster only about one-third the armor that the Iraqis possessed and the latter's timing was perfect, for the IAF was fully committed to the battles raging in the Sinai. The Iraqi performance was much steadier than in previous battles, and for seven hours they attempted to wrest away the two key hill positions held by Peled's forces.

The first of three heavy Iraqi thrusts came early in the morning and succeeded in overrunning parts of the 19th Brigade. The 19th, which had blunted the deepest Syrian armored penetration on October 7, managed to extricate itself by sending its armor in a sweeping movement that caught the Iraqi forces in their left flank.

The next major Iraqi effort came three hours later, aided by the crack Jordanian 40th Armored Brigade, which sought to envelop Peled's position. Once again, the Iraqi and Jordanian forces lacked coordination, with the 40th advancing slowly and not in good order. Assessing the situation, "Musso" Peled ordered an armored unit to take the Jordanians in the flank just as they reached their objective, a small force of Israeli troops holding Tel Maschara. In the intense firefight that followed, twenty Jordanian tanks were destroyed, and the 40th withdrew from the battlefield. In the meantime, the Israelis had taken advantage of the Jordanian delay to concentrate all of their artillery on the advancing Iraqi forces, keeping the second Iraqi push at bay.

Undaunted, the Iraqis began a third attack, sending continuous waves of armor that thrust their way directly into the 20th Brigade's positions, with tanks exchanging fire at gun-to-gun distances. Peled had built up a tiny reserve force of three tanks, which were sent in a wide sweep so that they appeared in the north, the clouds of dust disguising their small number. The Iraqis, stressed to the limits after seven hours of heated battle, withdrew just at the point where they might have triumphed. More than one hundred Arab tanks and APCs were left behind, most of them burning, in what proved to be the last major armored battle on the Golan Front.

The air within the Pit was so choked with tobacco smoke that even the hardiest smokers themselves had to bolt outside periodically to gather in some oxygen. The prevailing mood was running hot and cold. There persisted the almost wistful hope that the Egyptian resistance would suddenly collapse as it had done in past wars, allowing swift columns of Israeli armor to wrap up the war. Against this, and despite the growing conviction that the war had less than forty-eight hours to run before a cease-fire would be imposed by the United Nations, the general attitude was defensive. Even Elazar, so convinced of a need for a striking victory, said, "I'm more worried about Asia than Africa," meaning that he was still concerned about the bridgehead being cut off. Dayan agreed with him but insisted that in the next two days Israel must seize possession of both banks of the canal.

Both men were worried that the men and equipment of the Israeli army were exhausted. Yet as the hours unfolded it was impossible not to sense a new and rejuvenating spirit as word came in of swift advances in all directions. Adan's division had first reported moving another nine miles to the west, destroying a missile site and bypassing the Fayid airfield. It then expanded its attack, moving both west and south, to overrun another ten missile bases. The foray into the Geneifa Hills had yielded a tremendous amount of equipment, including badly needed fuel to keep the armor moving. It also allowed time for Fayid to be refurbished for use as an advanced base for the IAF.

Israeli generals were consistent, for they bickered in good times as well as bad, and the rapidly expanding advance of the Israeli forces did nothing to solve the endemic interpersonal squabbles. Gonen, still smarting from his position having been downgraded by Bar-Lev's arrival, was again demanding that Sharon be relieved for not following orders. Later in the day, Elazar visited Sharon at the front and came away convinced that he was doing all that he could do and more. Despite all hopes, the Egyptians were still fighting fiercely, and, in Elazar's eyes if not Sharon's, Missouri remained a threat to the east-bank bridgehead.

The long series of pitched battles fought since October 14 had cost the Egyptians some seven hundred tanks, and more were being lost during the movement of Egyptian forces from the east bank to the west. Despite this, there still was no sign of the imminent collapse of the Egyptian forces.

By 10:00 P.M. on October 19, the minor lift that had allowed Elazar to go home for a few minutes had long since passed. He was faced with new information and the need for an agonizing decision. Word had been received that President Nixon had sent a request to Congress for $2.2 billion in aid to be sent to Israel, in addition to the $825 million that had already been sent in less than two weeks of war. His message also contained a message of vital import: "The United States is making every effort to bring this conflict to a swift conclusion, measured in days, not weeks."

The concept was heartening, but the reality was not. Despite the airlift, the Israeli cross-canal effort had resulted in an expenditure of munitions on a scale beyond anything yet conceived of in the Middle Eastern war. Elazar was presented figures that showed that the vital 105mm ammunition, used primarily by the tanks, would be exhausted in two days. Events would show that the figures were not accurate, for the airlift had provided ammunition in such quantity that many depot stores had not yet been touched. But Elazar had no way of knowing this, and he was faced with the possibility that a new offensive would collapse from a lack of ammunition.

He ignored this new threat just as he ignored the fact that the troops in the Sinai were near exhaustion. Elazar took a daring step, one that ran counter to his instincts. He called Major General Yitzhak "Haka" Hofi, commanding the Golan Front, and told him to continue his defensive deployment and prepare to send one of his two tank formations south to the

Sinai Front. Offensive operations in the Golan were to be avoided with one exception: the recapture of Mount Hermon, which had to take place in forty-eight hours. Elazar shrugged off Hofi's bristling response. The imminent prospect of peace was now dictating both strategy and tactics.[8]

One disadvantage that an authoritarian government encounters in its propaganda campaigns is that events sometimes require that the truth be told, regardless of the information provided in the past. Such was the case in Moscow, where the Israeli cross-canal operation had been successively ignored, denied, then minimized. On October 18 Soviet newspapers mentioned dismissively that the Israelis had tried to put a small force of tanks across the canal but failed, "losing three of them." On the following day, it was acknowledged that a regiment of Israeli forces had crossed the canal but "was liquidated."

The men behind the headlines in the Kremlin knew better. Further, they knew that the Yugoslavian attempts to get a cease-fire resolution in the UN Security Council had run into difficulties with, surprisingly enough, the nonaligned nations. Therefore, they welcomed a cable from Ambassador Dobrynin suggesting that Henry Kissinger be invited to Moscow to "review the situation."

It was a touchy issue, a veritable minefield of adverse outcomes. First and foremost, a visit from Kissinger could signal the bankruptcy of Soviet diplomacy such that they had to seek out the assistance of the Secretary of State of its principal enemy. And they had to accept that Kissinger might decline the invitation for personal reasons or reasons of state. If the world learned of such a refusal, it would be an intolerable humiliation for Brezhnev.[9] Dobrynin had indicated that he would not, but the Soviets regarded Kissinger with the awe due a conjurer. He had impressed them in 1972, when he, then National Security Adviser, made a secret visit to Moscow, concealing his presence even from the U.S. embassy and State Department. Such an irregular action was unthinkable in the Soviet scheme of things, and thus no one could be sure of what he was capable. If the invitation was refused, for whatever reason, the Soviet Union would then have to suggest that it send a delegate to Washington, another humbling admission of helplessness. And that suggestion might be refused as well.

The questions of personality also arose. Kosygin was out of the question as an emissary to the United States. Brezhnev's distaste and Kosygin's failure in Cairo saw to that. But protocol prohibited sending Foreign Minister Gromyko to the United States after Premier Kosygin had been sent to Cairo. It would be a blatant insult, showing that relations with Egypt were regarded more highly than relations with the United States, the very last thing that Brezhnev wished to convey.

This left only Brezhnev as a candidate for the trip, and it was not one he wished to make. Kissinger had been handling all the negotiations, and Brezhnev was not ready to go to the United States merely to meet with the Secretary of State. Worse, even if the trip was totally successful and a cease-fire was arranged, the results were not going to be favorable for the Soviet Union.

In the end, the men in the Kremlin came to believe that Dobrynin would not have risked his career on the recommendation if Kissinger had not solicited the invitation himself. The deciding factor was that both Brezhnev and Gromyko, despite being ardent anti-Semites, liked and admired Kissinger—even if they did not trust him.

Brezhnev decided to have a message sent to President Nixon asking that Kissinger be *sent* to Moscow. To emphasize the gravity of the request and to maintain the appearance of being in control of the situation, Brezhnev suggested that Kissinger arrive the next day. Although quickly written, the message was carefully worded. It was not an invitation to

Kissinger to come—it was a request from one head of state to another, asking that a subordinate be sent. Kissinger, however, insisted on viewing Brezhnev's message to Nixon as a personal invitation and denied having solicited it. He saw at once that he could now delay any joint U.S./Soviet proposal for a cease-fire by as much as three days. This would give Israel enough time to improve dramatically its position on the ground—but not enough time to destroy the Egyptian armies. The invitation was in fact a nearly perfect solution to the cease-fire issue.

Kissinger spent the time before his departure explaining the purpose of his trip to Israel, other Arab states, and China. Everyone was informed, more than once, that his purpose was in response to a Soviet request and that his desire was to see that there was peace in the Middle East. He made sure in all his messages that he was going as a problem solver and not as a supplicant. And, in the classic fashion of double-edged diplomacy, he also used his secret channel with Hafiz Ismail to convey his position to Sadat. Of all the people receiving the information, it was Sadat who was most pleased. He desperately needed a cease-fire, and the hope that it might come quickly made him more inclined to defend his territorial gains to the last.

As might be expected from such a tangled web of diplomacy, events in the Middle East rapidly began to unfold with all the bizarre twists of a techno-thriller. The world's two superpowers were now embracing a joint diplomatic policy, one embodied in the visit of Henry Kissinger. Further, although the policy was joint, the results could not be, for there was no version of the cease-fire scenario that would benefit the Soviet Union.

Kissinger's visit would have a double effect. On the one hand, it provided a way out of the war for the Arab nations without their total collapse. On the other, it would drive them into the arms of the United States, for Soviet assistance in the future would be seen as fundamentally flawed. The leaders of the Soviet Union knew this very well and accepted it as the lesser of two evils, for the complete military humiliation of Arab states fully equipped with Soviet weapons would be intolerable.

Oddly enough, the Soviet acquiescence to Kissinger as peacemaker carried within it the germs of nuclear escalation. The Soviet military regarded Brezhnev's obliging treatment of Kissinger as too soft. Brezhnev himself would believe that a greater degree of understanding had been achieved than was in fact the case. When subsequent events disappointed him, it led to a series of escalating military actions that reached the nuclear threshold with bewildering speed.

Departing for Moscow, Kissinger would leave behind a domestic situation in shambles, for the Watergate scandal was now approaching its zenith. Just as his plane touched down, the "Saturday Night Massacre" exploded, in which the President fired independent counsel Archibald Cox and was then left hanging when Attorney General Elliot Richardson and his deputy, William Ruckelshaus, resigned in protest. Nixon, now having to focus almost entirely on his domestic problems, conferred upon Kissinger the full authority to conduct negotiations—the very last thing Kissinger wanted.[10]

9   *Seizing the Cease-Fire*

AROUND MIDNIGHT, THE Minister of War and Commander in Chief of the armed forces, General Ahmed Ismail Ali, made an urgent—almost frantic—request for Anwar Sadat to visit Center Ten.

The Chief of Staff, General Shazli, had returned bone-weary from his tour of command at the front and was in a black mood. He had seen the Egyptian army fighting to its physical limits and claimed to have the hard figures that proved the situation was becoming desperate. One example he cited was the elite 21st Armored Division and the 16th Infantry Division, which had been ground down to a total of only sixty tanks between them. Losses of officer personnel had been extremely high, and these men could not be immediately replaced. The only bright spot, one important to Sadat, was that the troops were still fighting well, despite their many losses and being short of food and ammunition.

A political pro, Sadat had met Shazli's message of doom with that standard military substitute for a kangaroo court, a council of war. Along with Shazli's ideological opponent, Ismail Ali, others present included General Hosni Mubarak, chief of the air force; General Muhammad Abdel Al Ghani Gamasi, the director of operations; and Major General Muhammad Ali Fahmi, the chief of the air defense. Sadat did not run things democratically, but it was obvious that if any vote was taken on which course of action to follow, Shazli would lose.

Despite his last encounters with Sadat and despite opposition from Ahmed Ismail Ali, Shazli still insisted that most of the Egyptian forces on the east bank of the canal be returned to the west bank to deal with the growing Israeli threat. In terse sentences, Shazli showed that the Egyptian counterattacks had failed and the EAF had been unable to take out the Israeli bridges. Then he came to his two main points. First, there were not enough Egyptian forces to halt an Israeli attack to the north on Cairo. Second, an Israeli advance to the south would cut off and surround the 3rd Army.

Sadat allowed each man present to put forward his own views. Ahmed Ismail Ali disagreed with Shazli as usual, this time for a humiliating reason. He feared that if the Egyptian 3rd Army was ordered to withdraw to the west bank it would be a repeat of 1967, when the retreat became a debacle, with the soldiers unwilling to stop and fight. The others present concurred, either from conviction or from their knowledge of what Sadat wanted them to say.

In his memoirs, Sadat describes Shazli as a "nervous wreck," unable to see the "true dimensions" of the situation. With an amazing disingenuousness, given the events that would occur over the next four days, Sadat records that all but Shazli were of his opinion, which was that "there was nothing to worry about."

Accordingly, Sadat ordered that there be no withdrawal at all—"not a soldier, not a rifle, nothing"—from the east bank. Egypt held some territory there, and Sadat intended to keep it, his hopes nurtured by the knowledge that Kissinger was in Moscow.[1] Although Sadat failed to advise his military commanders, he had already decided to accept a cease-fire in place. One of the deciding factors had been the deadly efficiency of the Maverick missiles that Operation Nickel Grass had supplied the Israelis. These air-to-surface missiles used a television guidance system to wreak havoc on the Egyptian missile sites and armor. To Sadat, this exemplified the folly of fighting America.

Immediately after the meeting, Sadat summoned the Soviet ambassador, Vinogradov, to urge rapid action on the cease-fire. Sadat also sent a message to Syria's President al-Assad saying: "I have accepted, with a heart that bled, the call for a cease-fire. I am willing to fight Israel no matter how long, but never the U.S.A."[2]

With that cable, Sadat established the true effect of the U.S. airlift. It had not only provided the weapons that were decisive in modern war; it was the obvious symbol of the U.S. commitment to Israel.

The Egyptian president had followed the classic pattern of military headquarters of rejecting information from the front on the grounds that the bearer of bad news did not "see the whole picture." The same thing was done regularly in Tel Aviv and, indeed, in most countries in most wars. Yet Sadat's decision was a self-inflicted Stalingrad. He gambled the Egyptian 3rd Army, exposing it to be outflanked, surrounded, and, if the war continued, exterminated. In the coldest manner, Sadat calculated that if a military victory was no longer feasible, the possible destruction of the 3rd Army was a risk worth taking in the hope that he could still pull off a diplomatic coup.

Given the political situation, it was not a bad gamble. Sadat had mistrusted the Soviet Union since the 1967 war, and he had a pressing desire to align himself with the West. For the moment, he was placing his faith in Henry Kissinger and hoping for the establishment of new and better relations with the United States. That hope would be severely tested in the next week.

This final argument at Center Ten was the end of the road for Shazli, whom Sadat relieved as Chief of Staff, replacing him with the director of operations, General Muhammad al-Ghani Gamasi.

By October 20, the Israeli high command was beset by desires that conflicted with the harsh reality of two weeks of unrelenting conflict. The probable date for the cease-fire resolution had continued to recede but now seemed almost certain to come by October 22 or 23 at the latest, given the bizarre turn of events that had placed Kissinger, the U.S. Secretary of State, in Moscow to bend the wishes of the Soviet leaders to his own ends.

The entire Israeli chain of command now thirsted for the maximum victory and the maximum territorial gains possible. Working against that desire was the combination of the IDF's near exhaustion and the continued stiff resistance by Egyptian forces. The Egyptian army was proving once again that while it might not have the offensive capability of the IDF, it fought superbly when entrenched in good defensive positions. By now, 60 percent of Egyptian armor was established on the west bank of the canal. Two armored divisions and parts of a mechanized brigade, all admittedly reduced in strength, were deployed in an arc around the southern flank of the Israeli bridgehead. Despite their losses, the Egyptians had managed to bring their artillery into position and were well stocked with ammunition. They may not have liked their Soviet mentors but followed their doctrine without question and sent a constant barrage of fire into Israeli positions.

Elazar was also concerned that the Egyptians, driven by the same desires for more territory, might from some unknown well of reserve strength launch a surprise attack to recoup their losses. To guard against this, Israeli offensive measures had to be conducted prudently, with solid lines of defense established before they moved.

The Chief of Staff was also concerned by Dayan's increasing tendency to issue orders directly to the field, short-circuiting the normal chain of command. To counter this, Elazar told Gonen to take orders from him alone.[3] It was difficult, for since October 16 Dayan had been visiting the generals at the front every day, and orders from him, on the spot, were difficult for even independent-minded generals such as Sharon and Adan to refuse. Dayan was shrewd, and the orders he gave were often the orders that the generals wanted but could not get from Gonen or Elazar.

Bren Adan was emerging as the leading figure among the

generals, and his drive south continued, knocking out ten missile batteries, one after another. The missile sites were miniature fortresses, easy enough to damage by artillery fire but difficult to overrun and hold. Each missile site featured an earthen mound as the center point. It sheltered the large fortified bunker housing the two trailers that contained the electronic controls. A ring of four missile launchers surrounded the mound, and an outer ring of machine-gun and antitank missile nests circled the complex. The captured sites were still well stocked with missiles, on the launchers and in cases at their side. The Egyptian soldiers defending the sites fought hard and well, turning the sites into miniature forts, not unlike the "hamlets" of South Vietnam. Few prisoners were taken, and subsequent Israeli units were struck by the number of bodies that littered the sites.

While some of Adan's forces were reducing the missile sites, other columns reached out to overrun Egyptian supply trains. These desert convoys were slow and stopped in huge traffic jams. They presented ideal targets. One brigade commander was heard to moan, "There are thousands of vehicles here, but I can't destroy them all." The IDF's policy was in fact not to destroy them all, for it wanted to avoid cluttering the road and to preserve the vehicles for future use.

Elazar now gave Adan orders to capture three commanding positions that controlled the road from Ismailia to Suez and the road leading to Cairo. Once these were in hand, they would provide a starting point for a later offensive. It was a question of strength and stamina; the IDF was now like an athlete in the last event of a decathlon, trying to summon up from some deep inner resource one last major effort.

When the positions were captured, Adan was to push south along the west shore of the Great Bitter Lake, aiming for the canal. To achieve this he had to make sure that he did not run out of fuel or tanks and that his valiant soldiers did not fall in their tracks from sheer exhaustion. But once the encirclement was complete, the fate of the Egyptian 3rd Army would be sealed. Instead of a threat to the Sinai, the 3rd Army would become an even more important bargaining chip than captured territory.

Armed with generally optimistic reports, Elazar traveled to Southern Command Headquarters to visit Bar-Lev and to stiffen Gonen's spine in regard to refusing Dayan's orders. They had just begun talking when the defense minister himself popped into Southern Command Headquarters.[4] Tanned and dusty, Dayan was nonetheless positively ebullient. The day before he had been under heavy artillery fire and had been extensively photographed doing so, and this kind of valorous photo op was always a tonic for him. That day he had visited all three of the generals commanding divisions across the canal—Adan, Sharon, and Major General Kalman Magen, who had replaced Mandler. While there, Dayan had given them all the information he had on Kissinger's visit to Moscow and what the probable cease-fire date might be.

In what had become a recurrent style, Dayan now squared off with Elazar and Bar-Lev. He had already ordered Adan to proceed to capture the west bank of the canal all the way to the city of Suez, insisting that this was absolutely necessary for political reasons. Dayan also wanted some of Adan's forces to move close enough to Cairo that the sound of their artillery would be heard in the city. (In truth, Dayan wanted the sounds of the cannons to be heard by Henry Kissinger in Moscow.)

Politically, Dayan's ideas were sound, but in this instance his orders had bypassed both the Chief of Staff and the Southern Command. It was an intolerable situation in terms of military discipline and resented bitterly by Elazar and Bar-Lev. Gonen would have resented it as well, had it not impinged upon Bar-Lev's position. He was glad to see his usurper squirm.

As this strange grouping of squabbling politicians and soldiers had done so often in the past, they compromised. Adan would strike out for the canal with one contingent of his division, keeping the rest in reserve to rest as much as possible on the far slopes of the Geneifa Hills.

Adan's division did just that, moving forward until nightfall, when, once again, heavy Egyptian resistance forced it to stop and regroup for an attack the following day. The brightest news, besides the elimination of so many missile sites, was the capture of the Fayid airport. Within hours, Israeli crews would prepare it to serve as an advanced supply base, bringing in the most necessary equipment—and flying out the steady stream of wounded.

Late in the evening, Elazar returned to Tel Aviv to report directly to the cabinet on the changing situation. By 10:00 P.M. word had come that Adan's division had enlarged the bridgehead from a relatively precarious twelve-to-eighteen-mile-wide area to a genuine salient almost thirty-six miles long. The continuing battles had reduced Egyptian tank strength near the bridgehead to fewer than two hundred tanks, and it was apparent that the enemy no longer entertained any ideas of an offensive to clean up the bridgehead.

At this point, Elazar's principal concern was the need for enormous quantities of artillery ammunition. His advancing forces were now using 175mm cannons to soften enemy positions, and the logistics of moving the huge 175mm shells over the tangled terrain on the west bank were immense. Fortunately, the only suitable paved road through the Geneifa Hills had been captured or seized by Adan and helped to solve the problem of ammunition supply.

The shortage of artillery and artillery ammunition stemmed from poor Israeli planning and from the Egyptian missile defense, which until the last two days had stopped the IDF from performing its "flying artillery" function. Never in the past had the IDF required so many shells, and all future armament calculations had to include not only more artillery, even at the expense of armor and perhaps even aircraft, but also quantities of shells on a scale never before considered possible.

The fifteen-hour-long flight to Moscow, across seven time zones, was always tiring, but this one was made especially difficult for Kissinger by messages from the White House that boded ill for the conference. One of these brought news of the decision by Saudi Arabia to embargo oil sales to the United States. Then he learned that Nixon had dispatched a message to Brezhnev conferring full authority upon Kissinger and stating that the Soviet leader could look upon his commitments as Nixon's own. It was an attempt by Nixon to free himself from concern about the negotiations in Moscow so that he could concentrate on the boiling Watergate problem.

On the surface, it might seem that a diplomat might like to have such authority, but it was poison to Kissinger, who was thus deprived of the opportunity to stall for time by "seeking approval" from the President. Nixon, who had become accustomed to his messages being altered after his drafting them, had taken the unusual step of appending a hand-written message to this one reading: "Mrs. Nixon joins me in sending our best personal regards to Mrs. Brezhnev and to you." Whether it was Nixon's intent or not, the postscript prevented any alterations in the basic message before it was delivered to the Soviet embassy.

The Soviets were quick to see their advantage in the letter and responded cordially, agreeing that they understood that Dr. Kissinger had full powers. In a graceful gesture that has been characterized as "unprecedented in Soviet diplomatic practice," Brezhnev also appended a hand-written note to his reply, sending his and his wife's regards to the Nixons.[5]

Immediately after his landing, another Kissinger ploy was foiled. He had made it a condition of his visit that no meetings would be held until the morning of October 21, to enable him to recover from jet lag. The Soviets thought otherwise, however, and the meetings began at 9:15 P.M.,

Moscow time. It was convened at Brezhnev's suggestion and started even before the obligatory huge welcoming dinner was given. Notably absent from the meeting was Kosygin, another slap on the wrist for his failure to achieve Brezhnev's goals in Cairo.

The long meeting was followed by the dinner, and it was after midnight before Kissinger could get to bed. Before he retired, however, he was handed two more surprises from Washington. In the first, Nixon directed him to agree with the Soviets on the imposition of a peace plan, a complete reversal of Kissinger's plan to seek only a cease-fire in Moscow. In the second, in a conversation with General Alexander Haig, the President's Chief of Staff, Kissinger learned for the first time of the Saturday Night Massacre, which would itself place limits on his flexibility and his credibility.

The sought-for invitation to Moscow had suddenly turned from triumph to minefield.[6]

The Pentagon carefully assessed the results of each day of the war, comparing reports from the combatant nations with its own independent intelligence sources. By the fourteenth day of the war it was apparent that both sides had lost heavily and that the results of these losses would be felt most severely in trained personnel. It was possible for the United States and the Soviet Union to replace aircraft quickly. Training pilots took far longer and presented each side with different problems.

For the Israelis, the task was to train pilots to the high standards of the IAF, then inculcate them with the aggressive spirit that characterized it. Doing this took many hours of flying. For the Arabs, the training was also long and difficult, but they faced the additional problem of overcoming the deep-seated sense of inferiority that destroyed morale and reduced the aggressiveness essential for combat operations. They had already lost the majority of their most talented leaders and were now at a much greater qualitative disadvantage than they had been at the start of the war.

The exemplar of the high standards of Israeli pilots was about to make history. On October 20, Giora Epstein, a veteran of the Six-Day War, shot down four MiG-21s southwest of the Great Bitter Lake. This brought his victory total to fourteen, nine of which had been scored in the Yom Kippur War. Four days later, he would add another three MiG-21s to his record, becoming the leading jet ace in the world and the only one to have shot down a total of nine MiG-21s. In standard IAF fashion, reserve Colonel Epstein's name and victory record were kept secret for more than twenty-five years.

The devastation to both sides was staggering. Syria had lost 149 fighters, mostly MiG-21s and Sukhoi Su-7Bs, and also six helicopters. Egypt had lost sixty-four MiG-21s, twenty helicopters, many of them loaded with highly trained commandos, one Tupelov Tu-16 bomber, the type that carried the Kelt missiles, and twenty-eight other aircraft. Iraq, which flew far fewer sorties than its Arab allies, lost twenty-one fighters, including both the elderly Hawker Hunters and the modern MiG-21s.

Israel admitted to losing 105 aircraft, including fifty-two of the Douglas A-4 Skyhawks shot down in their relentless close air support attacks into the storm of Egyptian missiles. Twenty-seven (some sources say thirty-three) of the valuable McDonnell F-4E Phantoms had been downed, some on long-range penetration missions and others in the close air support role. In addition, eight Dassault Mirage IIICs, five Dassault Super Mysteres, and three of the indigenous Neshers were destroyed. Almost all of the Israeli aircraft had been shot down by SAMs. Only about ten had fallen in air-to-air combat, and fewer than a dozen or so had crashed in noncombat accidents.

Most of the Arab air-combat losses had come from the Israeli heat-seeking missiles, the Sidewinder and the Shafrir. The Sidewinder was the U.S. AIM-9 and had been developed extensively over the years. The Shafrir was a product of the Rafael Armament Development Authority in Israel, and while it derived from the Sidewinder, it was slightly bulkier—and much cheaper, costing only about $20,000 per copy.

The vital resurgence of the IAF after two weeks of constant warfare came about for two reasons. The first of these was the success of Adan's tanks in overrunning the missile sites. The second was the introduction of three types of missiles that generated successful results in the battle against Arab armor. All three of these—the TOW, the Maverick, and the Shrike— really helped turn the tide of war, and all three of them were the fruit of the airlift. The TOW, used by surface forces, has been described previously. The Maverick was an air-to-ground missile for use against tanks and other installations, while the Shrike was an air-to-ground missile designed to suppress the radar at SAM sites.

The successes of the Maverick had considerably impressed Sadat, who was intrigued by the fact that it used television guidance in its technology. This seemed so quintessentially American to him that it bathed the Maverick with a special aura and caused it to be cited frequently in his protestations about "not fighting the USA." For the Israeli pilot, the great advantage of the Maverick was that it was a "fire-and-forget" missile, meaning that he did not have to keep boring in on the target after the missile was fired, exposing himself to anti-aircraft or SAM fire.

Technically, the AGM-65, the Maverick, was part of a family of Hughes missiles that shared the same aerodynamics as other missiles (including the earlier Falcon and the later Phoenix) but was adapted to a variety of guidance systems.[7] Although later Mavericks used a laser designation system, the AGM-65As being used by the Israelis used television guidance. The idea was not new, having been tried by the Germans in World War II, but it was very effective. Its use did require both training and skill, however, for many actions were required in the few seconds during which a launch was conducted. The Maverick carried a video camera in its nose, and the pilot of the attacking aircraft had an instrument that displayed what the Maverick's camera was viewing. The pilot would either use his gun sight to line up on the target or place the crosshairs of the video display on the target. When the target was acquired, he would then lock onto it. The missile could then be fired, and its automatic homing guidance system would track to the target while the aircraft departed the area.

While the Maverick was a desirable addition to the Israeli arsenal, the Shrike proved to be absolutely vital. The Shrike's mission was to destroy the radar used by SAM sites by homing in on the radar transmissions.

Designated the AGM-45, the Shrike was a large missile, ten feet long and weighing almost 400 pounds. It carried a 145-pound warhead and was capable of Mach 2 speeds and a range of eighteen to twenty-five miles. The crews who flew the Shrike missions put themselves in harm's way, for they had to fly into the very heart of enemy defenses. As soon as the Shrike radiation seeker locked onto the SAM's probing radar beam, it was fired. It would follow the beam exactly, striking the radar antennae and often blowing up missiles still in the launch rack.

In Vietnam, the enemy defenses became very sophisticated in dealing with the Shrike and developed tactics that made the U.S. defense suppression efforts ever more difficult. In the Yom Kippur War, however, the Shrikes mastered the Egyptian defenses swiftly, and the defenders never had a chance to develop new tactics.

These three missiles arrived in large quantities and just in time, thanks to the airlift. Their success, while gratifying, was also a tremendous embarrassment to the Israeli leadership, for it pointed out the glaring deficiencies in pre–October 1973 Israeli doctrine and procurement practices, particularly in the matter of suppressing enemy air defenses.

This failure is difficult to understand, in the light of the severe U.S. losses to SAMs in Vietnam and the equally high losses the IAF suffered from them during the War of Attrition. The capabilities of the SAMs were well known, and Israeli intelligence knew the vast numbers that the Soviet Union was supplying. An alarm should have gone off in Israeli headquarters, signaling the need for new weapons and the extensive application of the new tactics developed during the War of Attrition. In retrospect, the failure of the IDF to take appropriate action can only be attributed to two factors, the Israeli hubris resulting from the victory in the Six-Day War and the predilection that the Israeli high command had for tanks. It was ingrained in Israeli thinking that fast columns of tanks would always be enough to throw the Arabs into panic. There was also a "gunslinger" attitude within the IAF, the pilots feeling that their virtuoso airmanship would overcome any enemy opposition. The IAF failed to realize that a new generation of air warfare, in which electronic equipment dominated, had arrived.

Credit must be given to Anwar Sadat for recognizing that SAMs could take the place of air superiority for limited ground actions. Had he held to this tactic and not attempted a breakout to relieve pressure on Syria, the war might have had a different ending.

Just after midnight on the sixteenth day of the war, Dado Elazar received the stunning news that on the ground floor of the fallen electronic outpost at Mount Hermon forty Israeli troops were still holding out. It seemed almost impossible, but the report happened to coincide perfectly with the planning going on to recapture Mount Hermon the following day. If the news proved to be true, it would be a massive boost to Israeli morale.

The recapture of Mount Hermon was especially important now because of the impending cease-fire. Both the former Israeli position and the corresponding Syrian facility were slated to be captured. The operation was assigned the code name Operation Dessert in the typical Israeli manner of giving a hint at what the operation might be, for the taking of Mount Hermon at the end of the war would be considered a just dessert.

A complex and daring plan was swiftly laid out, using helicopters to place paratroops north of the position on the slopes of the mountain while other forces attacked from the south. Given the importance of the operation and the combination of prestige and revenge involved, Elazar decided to go to the Golan and personally supervise every step.

Before leaving for the Golan, the Chief of Staff analyzed the series of reports placed before him and realized that the news from all fronts was generally good, with the exception of the Egyptian stronghold at the Missouri position, which remained as was the case at the bridgehead. The Israelis had tried for six days to conquer it, and it remained in place, apparently impervious to both ground and air attack. The Missouri position was Sadat's best argument for the fact that he had created a new Arab soldier, able to take adversity and keep on fighting.[8]

The turbulent feud between headquarters and Arik Sharon now reached a new height. Sharon was ordered—again—to eliminate Missouri. He reacted in a boiling rage, sputtering that it was insanity to waste time, money, and munitions on a contained element of the front. He urged instead that he be unleashed to bypass Ismailia from the west, swing north to Kantara, and thus cut off the Egyptian 2nd Army. By the end of the day, he argued, it was possible that both the 2nd and 3rd Armies would be surrounded, giving Israel a bargaining position of incredible strength.

In his memoirs, Sharon waxes eloquent over the error. He had already watched an Israeli attack on the Missouri position by Colonel Tuvia Raviv's armored brigade, the only brigade Sharon had on the west bank. Raviv's assault began with forty-five tanks but ran into "a torrent of RPB, Sagger and tank fire" that destroyed twenty tanks, killing twenty-four men, including eight officers. The attack was suicidal, and Sharon resented being ordered to repeat it. Once again he used the inflammatory ploy "come on down to the battlefield and see for yourself." It was an insulting message and he knew it, for it implied a lack of bravery on the part of a group of men who had demonstrated their courage many times.

When Sharon protested that his brigade did not have the strength to take Missouri, he was told to order an armored brigade back from the west bank. Once again he pleaded that he not be ordered to mount a frontal attack against Missouri and that instead he be allowed to use the two brigades on the west bank to move to the north. Once again he was refused and ordered to reduce Missouri.

Sharon fought back, certain that the order was more than bad generalship—it was a demonstration of politics in action. He was convinced that Elazar and Bar-Lev were ensuring that he would not win a tremendous victory that he could use in his subsequent political campaigns, even though that insurance would be obtained at the cost of hundred of Israeli lives.

In the end, Sharon found a political solution to his dilemma. He went over Elazar's and Bar-Lev's heads, with a phone call to Dayan explaining the situation. Dayan reciprocated, bypassing the Chief of Staff and Bar-Lev again and ordering Gonen to call the attack off.

Sharon added insult to injury four days later when he told an interviewer that if headquarters wanted to override his decision as a field commander, they were obligated to be there on the spot to "assess our forces, the enemy forces, the terrain, morale—everything." He then stated that had they done that and disagreed with him, he would have accepted their decision. Sharon then plunged himself into further hot water by saying that it was his intention to disobey their order and accept a court-martial for disobedience, rather than waste lives in attacking Missouri.[9] The interview provoked a storm of controversy and seemed at the time to be a fatal political error, but his position was upheld in a subsequent investigation by the Agranant Commission, of which more later.

Time was now the enemy; no one was certain what was happening in Moscow, but in the Sinai the emphasis was on the race to trap Egyptian forces. In the north, Sharon's brigades pushed north and west, sweeping to within sixty miles of Cairo and being halted only at the gates of Ismailia by very heavy Egyptian resistance. In the south, Adan pushed out a three-pronged attack. One was to sweep along the routes edging the Little Bitter Lake. It was to be paralleled by a second attack that moved along inland. A third attack was sent along the main Cairo–Suez road.

During the early part of the attack, all three arms had moved with only partial protection from the IAF, which was fully occupied in supporting Colonel Raviv's ill-starred attack on Missouri. Later in the afternoon, however, the IAF provided close air support, breaking up Egyptian strong points, as the three arms of the attack converged in a pincer movement. The Egyptians continued to resist, contesting every advance and periodically throwing in a counterattack with small groups of tanks.

Adan's goal was to reach the canal, effectively surrounding the Egyptian 3rd Army. Behind the Egyptians, a mixed force under the command of Colonel Israel Granit had moved to block any attempts by the enemy to move farther to the east. In the meantime, Magen's division had moved to the west and then south, covering Adan's flank and eventually moving on south of the city of Suez to the Gulf of Suez itself.

On balance, October 21 had not gone brilliantly for the Israelis. In the north, Sharon's two brigades had not made the progress desired. In the south, the Egyptian commanders opposing Adan's forces could see that the fate of the 3rd Army rested on their shoulders.

Theirs and those of the redoubtable Henry Kissinger.

———

In the north, the Syrians were trying new tactics. A counter-attack was launched south of Tel Sham, with Syrian tank crews being promised a prize of ten thousand Syrian pounds and a promotion in rank for every Israeli tank destroyed. Despite the incentives, the attacks petered out, unable to overcome the stout Israeli defensive fire.

In the meantime, the Israelis were putting the finishing touches to an elaborate plan created under the supervision of Major General Yitzhak Hofi to seize both the Syrian and the captured Israeli positions on Mount Hermon. Hofi was to use two forces to strike suddenly on the afternoon of October 21. The first of these was the Golani Infantry Brigade, which had suffered grievous losses during the early days of the war. It was commanded by Colonel Amir Drori. The second was the elite 317th Parachute Brigade, commanded by Colonel Chaim Nadel. The latter unit was facing a minor morale crisis, embarrassed because they had not yet been tasked to do enough fighting. This was the opportunity they had been waiting for.

The Israelis consolidated their positions around the base of Mount Hermon, bringing up artillery and tanks. The Golani Brigade was to launch a general assault, well supported by artillery and aircraft and intended to focus Syrian attention on the base of the mountain.[10]

The crucial battles would have to be conducted the way the Syrians had operated on the opening day of the war: an assault landing by paratroopers on a position at 7,500-feet altitude. This was inherently dangerous, for helicopters are less efficient in the thinner air and vulnerable to the severe turbulence associated with the mountains. The Israeli helicopters took off at 2:00 P.M. to fly for more than an hour to reach their landing zone, much of the time in Lebanese airspace, subject to a variety of attacks, from antiaircraft guns, to missiles, to the Syrian fighters hungry for an easy target. The IAF, with the danger from SAMs much reduced, was able to intervene to protect the helicopters by shooting down seven Syrian fighters.

The helicopters of the lead assault element finally edged into the narrow landing zone, coming under Syrian artillery fire as they did. When the paratroopers exited they could actually look *down* on dogfights between Israeli and Syrian aircraft. The Israelis kept the pressure on, landing reinforcements every fifteen minutes.

The Syrians reacted quickly, dispatching their own Mil-8 helicopters carrying troops to reinforce their Mount Hermon position. Israeli fighters swept in to shoot three down; two escaped back to their home base. At 5:00 P.M. the Israeli paratroopers began their first assault on the outlying Syrian positions. The attack succeeded with only one casualty and was rewarded in less than an hour by the capture of a convoy of seven Syrian trucks, carrying mortars and ammunition.

The next eight hours were spent in carefully reducing resistance on the way to the Syrian observation post. The excellent Soviet infrared spotting scopes enabled the Syrian snipers to inflict heavy casualties on the Israelis. Shrugging off losses and using hand grenades to shower any sniper whose position was revealed by a muzzle flash, the Israelis pushed on, yard by yard. When they finally arrived at the Syrian facility, they found that the defenders had run away.

Now there remained the task of recapturing the former Israeli outpost. Once again the Golani Infantry Brigade pressed ahead, supported this time by eight Centurion tanks and by artillery fire. The battle went on all night; not until 10:53 the following morning did the Syrians formally surrender. The rumor that forty Israeli soldiers had survived in the fortress proved to be just that, but the truth did not in any way diminish the sweetness of the victory.

In Henry Kissinger's memoirs there are frequent references to the fact that the Israelis always played diplomatic hardball, even with their only patron state. Now that he was in Moscow, intent on furthering Israeli interests within the parameters that he had set, the Israelis continued to be difficult. Kissinger had begged Ambassador Dinitz to continue sending him up-to-date information on the progress of Israeli arms, so that he could use the knowledge to his advantage in the negotiations with Brezhnev. Yet no briefings were forthcoming from Dinitz or any other Israeli source, except for a radio broadcast from Defense Minister Dayan, who stated that while the IDF positions were continuing to improve on the battlefield, Israel was still receptive to a cease-fire. Kissinger was forced to rely on reports from the CIA, and these he found to be outdated upon receipt.

At noon on Sunday, Kissinger's meeting with Brezhnev began, clouded by the knowledge that the Soviet Union had earlier put seven airborne divisions on alert for possible use in the Middle East. Brezhnev undoubtedly regarded the alert as simple prudence on the part of his military commanders, preparing for alternative action in case negotiations failed. To Kissinger, it appeared to be a heavy-handed threat, one that would ultimately lead to the United States flexing its nuclear muscles in less than seventy-two hours.

Despite this background of bluff and bluster, the meeting went amazingly well. After the usual formalities, Kissinger then submitted a three-point proposal that he had, with his assistant Joseph Cisco, prepared overnight. The first point called for a cease-fire in place. The second called for the implementation of the UN Security Council Resolution 242, which had heretofore been instantly rejected by the Soviets. The third point was a weasel-worded reference to immediate negotiations "between the parties concerned" to be conducted under "appropriate auspices."

Kissinger was nonplussed when Brezhnev and Gromkyo agreed almost immediately.[11] Over the next three hours, with some minor editorial tweaking, they hammered out a final agreement. Then came the discussion of when the matter could be brought before the United Nations. Brezhnev wanted an immediate submission, as it was now 4:00 P.M. in Moscow and 9:00 A.M. in Washington.

Kissinger did not wish things to proceed with too much haste—he wanted to give the Israelis time to improve their position. He argued that it was impractical to send the document to the United Nations at that moment because it would require two hours to transmit the document to Washington and have it translated. It would then require discussion with the UN Security Council and, of course, Israel, Egypt, and Syria.

As an alternative, Kissinger proposed that the Soviet and U.S. representatives at the United Nations request a Security Council meeting for 9:00 P.M. New York time. He further stipulated that the cease-fire would not go into effect until twelve hours after the United Nations had adopted the resolution. In effect, he had chiseled out an extra twenty-four hours for Israeli operations.

Once in play, however, things moved swiftly, if not entirely smoothly, and the very next day at 12:50 A.M., New York time, their final product became the UN Security Council Resolution 338 of October 22, 1973. This resolution put some time constraints on the combatants, commanding "all parties to the present fighting to cease all firing and terminate all military activity immediately, no later than 12 hours after the moment of the adoption of this decision, in the positions they now occupy." The language of the resolution is confusing; it meant that all military activity was to be terminated twelve hours after the adoption of the decision—the word *immediately* was misplaced.

And as important as Resolution 338 was, it had a fatal flaw, for it did not call for any peace-keeping force to monitor its implementation. Agreement on such a force would have taken time, and even if the UN observers still in the area had been immediately available, there would have been difficulties. From the Golan to past the Suez Canal, there were still hundreds of small groups of soldiers who were cut off and continuing to fight, and communicating with them would take time. In addition, most of the UN observers had been caught in Cairo by the emergency, and their sympathies were suspected by both the Israelis and the Egyptians. However, in the absence of any supervision, the cease-fire was more than fragile; it was doomed to failure.

Kissinger had in this single four-hour meeting achieved remarkable results. He had met the cease-fire needs of all concerned, while leaving a twenty-four-hour loophole in which Israeli troops could do their best to extend their influence. He had avoided humiliating Anwar Sadat and in fact established the basis for closer U.S-Egyptian relations. He had avoided forcing the Soviets to make a choice between watching Israel defeat the Arab nations and intervening militarily on their behalf. Most important, he had achieved a cease-fire resolution that could serve as the basis for a peaceful settlement in the Middle East.

As soon as the meeting was concluded, Kissinger sought to secure agreement on the proposed resolution by preparing a flurry of letters for President Nixon to send explaining the settlement to Israel, Egypt, Iran, Jordan, and the U.S. representative at the United Nations, John Scali. Each of the letters was couched in terms that highlighted the advantages to the recipient and minimized the advantages to the recipient's adversary.

The letter to Golda Meir was laden with the most courteous and congratulatory terms. Nixon said that "we believe that this is a major achievement for you and for us and supportive of the brave fighting of your forces." He went on to note that the agreement would leave Israeli forces in place "right where they are" and that there was no mention whatsoever of the word *withdrawal.* Nixon took care to point out that the cease-fire resolution he was now proposing was enormously different from anything that Sadat had previously indicated he would agree to. Nixon went on to emphasize that for the first time

in history the agreement called for direct negotiations between the Arab nations and Israel. He concluded with the
promise that the United States and the Soviet Union would
make "our joint auspices" available to Israel and to the Arabs
to facilitate the peace process. It was an excellent letter, one
that outlined terms that would have seemed scarcely believ-
able to the Israelis only ten days before.

Yet Murphy's Law or Soviet intelligence had intervened.
The U.S. embassy had been tasked to send the letters through
its supposedly secure radio facilities, but Kissinger's staff
found that the embassy's procedures were too time-
consuming. A decision was made to use the presidential aircraft that had flown Kissinger to Moscow as the transmission
site, using a satellite hookup to the White House. The messages got through securely—but were so garbled as to be
unreadable. Kissinger's staff, now in a dire panic, first tried
to convey guarded messages via an open telephone line and
finally fell back on the embassy and its frustratingly slow
procedures. In British terms, it was a royal cock-up, and messages were delayed for as long as four hours. Later investigation indicated that the problem might have been caused by
atmospheric interference, but there was a strong body of opinion that it was nothing less than Soviet jamming that caused
the problem.

The suspicious delay in transmission and the general relentless haste of Kissinger's mission to Moscow had ruffled
Golda Meir's feathers. She felt that Kissinger had presented
Israel with a fait accompli. Faced with the deadline set for
the submission of the resolution to the United Nations, she
reluctantly accepted the decision. In addition, she requested
that Kissinger come to Tel Aviv from Moscow—the initia-
tion of what later became known as "shuttle diplomacy."

The Arab nations suddenly had divergent views. Egypt
would accept the cease-fire, effective at 5:00 P.M. on October
22. Syria, which had so ardently sought a cease-fire at the
start of the war, now made no statements concerning it and

instead was obviously preparing for an offensive—one that included the use of Iraqi forces. (President Assad would not accept UN Resolution 338 until 5:00 A.M. Syrian time on October 23.) Meanwhile, Israel continued to fight.

Sweat-stained and constantly coughing from the combination of a serious head cold and the smothering tobacco smoke, Dado Elazar assessed the news that Israel had accepted the cease-fire at 6:20 A.M., Tel Aviv time. The Israeli attack still had momentum, and there was still time to advance farther against the Arab forces before the cease-fire came into effect. But once combat ceased, the Arab forces, with their inexhaustible supplies of manpower, would be able to recover more swiftly than the weary IDF. Israeli intelligence believed that the Soviets had actually delivered, by air and sea, more supplies than the Arabs had lost and that, relatively speaking, with the possible exception of tanks they had more equipment than was available at the beginning of the war. If fighting resumed after a ten-day truce, the Israelis might not be able to contain a second Arab assault.[12] This time, the Iraqi and Jordanian forces would undoubtedly be thrown into the battle, opening yet another front. And, most dangerous of all, a ten-day respite would give the Arabs time to completely reinstall their SAM defenses.

Elazar's concerns were shared by his staff and the commanders in the field, even the contrarian, Sharon. After soberly assessing the IDF's strength, Elazar decided that the main effort would be to surround the 3rd Army, which would also present an implicit threat to capture Cairo. There were simply not enough forces available to also encircle the 2nd Army. Both the 2nd and the 3rd were now trapped in place, unable to move because most of their supply lines were cut, and were forced to rely on the fuel and the ammunition that they had with them.

With plans set, Dado went to the government "guest

house," an austere building under tight security where the meeting with Kissinger was to take place at 2:30 P.M. The U.S. Secretary of State, weary but exhilarated, had flown into the war zone in the Boeing transport that served as *Air Force One* when the President was aboard. A flight of U.S. Navy aircraft from the 6th Fleet acted as escort. Kissinger was driven directly in to the government guest house, which was kept under extreme security with machine gun—armed guards at the access gate, more stationed along the winding road, and then an inner security gate with more armed guards. Antiaircraft guns surrounded the house, and both U.S. and Israeli secret service agents combed the house and grounds.

Kissinger met three times with Golda Meir. The first meeting was private, and the Israeli Prime Minister demanded assurances that the United States had not made a private agreement with the Soviet Union to return Israel to its 1967 borders. Her suspicions were reasonable, given that the Soviets had agreed to the language of UN Security Council Resolution 242, something they had never done before. In return, Kissinger might have given away all of Israel's conquered territory as a bargaining chip. He assured her that no such agreements had been made.

Kissinger and Meir had great personal rapport, based on respect for each other. There is a story told, possibly apocryphal, that Kissinger once tried to stress to the Prime Minister that he was an American first, the Secretary of State second, and a Jew third. Meir reportedly responded, "That's all right, sonny; we read from right to left." True or not, the story captures both the mutual respect and the personal understanding they shared.

The second meeting took place in a more relaxed atmosphere, over lunch, with members of her cabinet. When the news arrived that Egypt had accepted the cease-fire, Meir displayed her keen political sense by stating that Sadat was now a hero to the Arab world, because against all odds he had dared to attack Israel. In this she showed more understanding than some of the Arab leaders themselves.

Later in the afternoon, Kissinger met again with Meir and her military advisers, including Dayan and Elazar.[13] Kissinger was impressed with all of their bravery, their weariness, and their tacit acceptance of the fact that despite the victory, they were at the end of their respective political and military careers. Israel had barely survived, and the great surprise attack of October 6 had come on their watch—all knew they would not be forgiven, despite the fact that the military situation was now almost restored. The Arab armies were unable to move from their positions, pinned down by Israeli airpower and denied the fuel and ammunition they needed to fight.

In spite of the gloomy atmosphere, Kissinger reemphasized that for the very first time in history an Arab nation had agreed to negotiate with Israel. He also pointed out that the word *auspices* in the resolution had been officially interpreted as meaning that the negotiations between the Arabs and the Israelis would take place with the active participation of the United States and the Soviet Union. It was a significant element of the agreement, for it meant that Israel would have the negotiating powers of the United States at its side, at a time when the Arab world also wished to build ties with the United States.

As an unusual courtesy, Colonel Strobaugh from the ALCE had been summoned to the guest house.[14] There he met Kissinger, who introduced him once again to Golda Meir and then to Foreign Minister Abba Eban, Dayan, and the U.S. ambassador, Kenneth Keating. Kissinger expressed the appreciation of the State Department for the monumental effort and success of the MAC airlift. Meir and Dayan then asked Strobaugh to pass on their gratitude to all the MAC people who were working so hard to supply Israel with arms.

Meetings over, Kissinger then stepped into a limousine that drove in a convoy of security automobiles straight through Tel Aviv at 60 mph, right to the airport. There he boarded his aircraft for departure to another war zone: Washington, D.C., where the cry to impeach President Nixon was growing louder. Strobaugh was dropped off back at his office. Since it was only two hours until he was supposed to come on shift again, he stayed there, putting in another twenty-four-hour day.

Egyptian resolve now began to crumble all along the front, with the troops, at long last, fleeing in disorder. What the Israelis had been hoping for since October 8 finally began. At Adan's field headquarters, actions were based on intercepted Egyptian radio transmissions. In one of the first of these, at 11:30 A.M. on October 22, the commander of the 3rd Army, Major General Wassel, reported to Minister of War Ismail that the front-line situation was fluid and the enemy was breaking through.[15] Confirming Ismail's earlier fears, Wassel went on to say that the brigade commander "is behaving like a frightened rabbit," condemning him for being some eight miles behind the brigade instead of leading it.

The retreating Egyptians were also feeling the full force of the IAF, now responding to a forward air controller (FAC) acting as personal liaison to Adan in his drive south. The FAC would give Israeli fighter-bombers instructions on the location of Egyptian strong points, and they would pry these points open with rockets, bombs, and napalm.

As Adan's forces moved south, the 3rd Army's radio reports became more frantic, complaining that the Israelis had cut off the Cairo–Suez road and that they were now trapped. Further reports indicated a breakdown in the Egyptian command structure, as some units no longer responded to instructions while others simply ceased responding at all, preferring to retreat in silence.

At 3:00 P.M., aware that he had just over three hours to complete his mission of reaching the Suez Canal from the west, Adan ordered a pell-mell charge forward, leaving only scattered light forces to cover the territory they had already captured. Within two hours his tanks were thundering toward the line of the canal, impeded by thousands of fleeing Egyptians. A problem reminiscent of 1967 arose—the Egyptian soldiers simply did not know that the protocol of surrender included laying down their arms. They would stand, hands up, one hand holding a rifle. Capturing them proved to be dangerous—the Israelis never knew when an Egyptian might decide to take one last shot. The result was as expected: Israeli soldiers shot first and asked questions later.

Adan's forces approached the canal minutes before the cease-fire came at 6:52 P.M. In his immediate front, many units of the Egyptian 3rd Army had disintegrated, leaving large numbers of individual soldiers walking about aimlessly, awaiting capture. Both the Egyptian and the Israeli commanders had received similar orders, that is, "Obey the cease-fire, but if the enemy shoots, fire back."

The killing and the hardships of the past seventeen days lingered on, and despite the cease-fire, both sides continued to shoot. When placed in defensive positions that still had stocks of fuel and ammunition, the Egyptians continued to fight well, using their firepower to inflict heavy damage on the Israelis. After losing more than forty armored vehicles, including thirty-two tanks, the Israelis had to regroup to gather their strength.

Well before the Yom Kippur War began, Anwar Sadat had been pleased and made confident by the installation of Soviet-built and -operated Scud missiles. They gave him the sense that there was a counter to Israel's long-range air superiority. The Scuds were governed by a Soviet-Egyptian military agreement that placed them virtually under Soviet military control. They were guarded by Soviet military units and could only be fired with Soviet approval, much to Sadat's dislike.

Sadat had threatened their use more than once, the last time being during a speech on October 16. And in fact, during the course of the war, the Egyptians had applied to the Soviets to use them several times but had always been turned down by the Politburo. Gromyko, in particular, had opposed using the weapon, fearing that it would infuriate the Americans.

As the hour of the cease-fire drew closer, Sadat was filled with mixed emotions. It was the political solution he'd sought to a growing military dilemma, but the continuing advance of Israeli forces filled him with indignation. According to his memoirs, he entered Center Ten and ordered that two Scuds be fired at Deversoir, near the Missouri charnel house, warning "Israel that such a weapon was indeed in our hands, and that we could use it at a later stage of the war."[16]

The facts of the case were a bit less dramatic, if a little more comic. Sadat's request sent the usual spasm of response up and down the Soviet chain of command. Ambassador Vinogradov called the Foreign Ministry, expecting Gromyko to once again refuse permission to fire the missiles. Gromyko was not in, however, and with the pressure of the cease-fire creeping ever closer, the call was referred to the Minister of Defense, General Andrei Grechko. Grechko, a tough individual who had advocated that the Soviet armies overrun Europe during the 1960s, responded in a typically belligerent mode to Vinogradov's inquiry, saying, "Go the hell ahead and fire it."[17]

Within minutes, two Scuds had soared, breathing flames across the Cairo sky, and headed for Deversoir. Notoriously inaccurate, neither Scud hit anything but the sands of the Sinai.

But the incident was not over. Within minutes, Gromyko was on the hot line to Vinogradov, demanding to know why he had crossed bureaucratic channels and talked to the Minister of Defense. When Gromyko learned what Vinogradov had asked of Grechko, he became enraged and forbade the firing. It was too late, and Vinogradov slipped a notch lower on the Kremlin's diplomatic scale.

More important than Gromyko's wrath, however, was the interpretation placed by the United States on the incident. It was well known that the Scud missiles could not be fired without Soviet approval and without the active participation of Soviet troops. A single misguided gesture had changed the character of the war: Soviet troops were now engaged in combat, and this tilted the world closer to nuclear conflict.

I O *Approaching Armageddon: The Nuclear Alert*

FROM MIDNIGHT ON, OCTOBER 23 saw light weapon and artillery fire flickering across the Sinai. An observer could tell nothing about the disposition of the opposing forces from the flashes, for the fire came from all directions. The Egyptian and Israeli forces were melded together in the dark, with small units blazing away at each other and with many losses to friendly fire.

The news of continued fighting did not surprise the sleep-deprived Elazar, who was determined to use any Egyptian infraction of the cease-fire as an excuse to cover the ongoing Israeli efforts to achieve further gains. Before his departure, Kissinger's sense of almost imperial power had let him make a remark to the effect that he would understand if there were a "few hours slippage in the cease-fire deadline."[1] Elazar interpreted this to mean Kissinger would look the other way if Israel continued fighting.

Despite their difficult circumstances, many of the Egyptian units continued to battle on as long as they had munitions. Only a few sectors, usually those occupied by service or support forces, gave up easily. An Israeli tank battalion had attempted to break through to the Suez Canal immediately after the cease-fire had officially started. The attack raged until after midnight, with nine tanks being lost and the rest driven back. Opposition was strong on the east bank as well, with the 3rd Army holding its positions against constant Israeli pressure. Ironically, Israel's position was in fact as precarious as that of the Egyptians and equally susceptible to a massive counterstroke. The single lane through Deversoir was all that connected the Israeli forces on either side of the canal. The war remained a fairly even match. The Israeli forces were more

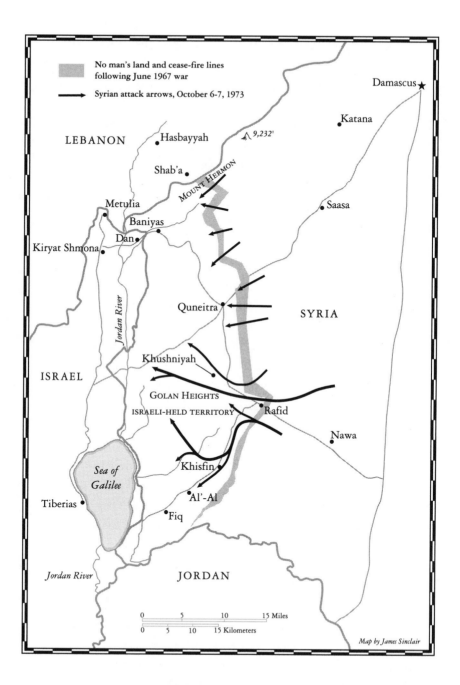

No man's land and cease-fire lines
following June 1967 war

Syrian attack arrows, October 6-7, 1973

LEBANON

Hasbayyah

Shab'a

MOUNT HERMON

9,232'

Damascus ★

Katana

Saasa

SYRIA

Metulia

Baniyas

Dan

Kiryat Shmona

Jordan River

ISRAEL

Quneitra

Khushniyah

GOLAN HEIGHTS

ISRAELI-HELD TERRITORY

Rafid

Nawa

Khisfin

Sea of
Galilee

Al'-Al

Tiberias

Fiq

Jordan River

JORDAN

0   5   10   15 Miles
0   5   10   15 Kilometers

Map by James Sinclair

extended and far wearier, but the Egyptian high command was too centralized and too slow to coordinate its much larger forces.

Elazar usually ignored the chain of command, given Dayan's abuse of it, but this time he sought to cover himself.[2] He telephoned Dayan, reporting that the Egyptians had destroyed nine more tanks and asking for "freedom to act" in the 3rd Army's sector. Dayan agreed at once and an announcement was immediately drafted for public consumption blaming the Egyptians for continuing to fight. And there was truth in this, for the Egyptian forces did fight on, in one instance massing a sizable amount of armor for an attack. The Egyptian reaction really did not matter, as the Israelis would have pushed on in any event.

Formal instructions were sent out to Adan and Magen to push on to the canal and the Gulf of Suez. Elazar was specific on one point: the fighting had to take place where the armor had a chance to maneuver. Israel could not afford to get into large-scale infantry firefights—too many men had already been killed. Strangely enough, the initial momentum of the Israeli attack, which began at 5:20 A.M., would delude them. Instead of obeying Elazar's instructions about fighting only where armor could maneuver, they instead plunged their tanks into the quagmire heart of a defended city.

With SAM opposition virtually nonexistent, the IAF was tasked to provide massive support of these final efforts. As battered as the IAF was, it was still able to mount more than 350 sorties on the day following the official cease-fire, with many aircraft armed with munitions that had only days before been in U.S. depots.

Dado Elazar was desperately aware of how difficult the situation was for Israel, both politically and militarily. There were already reports of complaints from the United States about Israeli military activity and a demand to "return to the positions of the 22nd." Elazar discounted this to a degree— no one could say for certain where those positions had been, and he felt comfortable with Kissinger's wink and nudge about the slippage of the cease-fire. But Elazar knew better than anyone else how much Israel now depended upon the U.S. airlift, and continued fighting in the Sinai jeopardized that crucial support.

In his morning staff briefing, Elazar stated, "Our readiness to accept a cease-fire is a function of our dependence on the United States. *Every morning, we shoot off what arrived the previous night.* [author's italics]. The same is true of planes. We lost one hundred and two planes in the war, and forty Phantoms and thirty-two Skyhawks have been supplied to us to date. And the matériel continues to come in. As a result of this dependence, the relationship that has developed between us and the United States makes us somewhat beholden to them. That is why we accepted the cease-fire the United States decided upon."[3]

The remarks about accepting the cease-fire were ingenuous, of course, given that Israel had by the morning of October 23 almost reached the city of Suez and had its artillery sited on the ramps the Egyptians had built on the west side of the canal, able to fire into the 3rd Army troops on the east bank. Other forces had trundled south into Ras Adabiyah, on the Gulf of Suez, surrounding the 3rd Army.

Back at the Kremlin the hostile relations between Gromyko and Grechko resulting from the Scud firings were closely observed. Their quiet ill will was long established, but their newly inflamed animosity would contribute in less than two days to a totally unforeseen nuclear alert. Their argument also formed a backdrop on the contest over Brezhnev's drive to assume sole power. A failure of the Middle East cease-fire or, worse, a rupture in U.S./Soviet relations could derail Brezhnev's efforts and place his enemies in the Politburo—and he had many—back in contention. Even the phlegmatic Kosygin seemed to lick his lips at a possible reversal of fortune.

Notwithstanding the Scud firing and the continual politicking, Leonid Brezhnev for a brief period on October 23 felt immensely satisfied by the cease-fire, telling Gromyko, "What Kosygin could not achieve in three days of negotiations in Cairo with our friend Sadat, I could achieve in four hours with our adversary, Kissinger."[4] Brezhnev's good mood was soon eroded by the news of continued advances by Israeli forces. The Politburo analysts drew upon information from the military attaché in Cairo and corroborated it with intelligence gained from satellite data and MiG-25 photos. The experts soon discovered that the Egyptian 3rd Army was indeed essentially cut off and that the Israelis had succeeded in recapturing Mount Hermon. It was evident that there was still fighting going on at many points, and the major question became how to force both sides, especially Israel, to comply with the cease-fire.

The Soviet leader's mood grew worse with repeated reports from Ambassador Vinogradov that Sadat wanted the Soviet Union to do something to stop the Israeli violations of the cease-fire. Sadat insisted he had accepted a cease-fire only because Kosygin had told him that there was a joint Soviet/American guarantee that it would be enforced. Although Sadat did not bother to mention the fact to the Soviet ambassador, Brezhnev now knew that Sadat was working both sides of the street and anticipated that he would also urge Nixon to intervene.

For his part, Kosygin added to Brezhnev's discomfort by insisting that the Soviet Union and the United States had indeed agreed to carry out the UN Security Council's Resolution 338 and should get on with it. Kosygin proposed that the United States and the USSR each send 250 observers to the Middle East immediately. When someone suggested that the UN peacekeepers already in place in Cairo be used, Kosygin dismissed them with a classic Russian characterization, saying, "Those observers are dead souls," meaning that Israel would object to them as being biased.

The Israelis' continued advance, provoked or not, put Brezhnev in a difficult situation. He desperately wanted to maintain a joint Soviet/U.S presence in the armistice and peace negotiations, yet had to put pressure on Nixon to force the Israelis to stop.

Writing Nixon had increasingly become an ego problem for Brezhnev. He felt he had already diminished his own position by writing twice as many messages to Nixon as he had received from him. The October 23 response from Nixon to a previous letter was particularly troubling, for the U.S. President seemed to downplay the seriousness of the situation and even had the temerity to suggest that Brezhnev press Syria and Egypt to comply with the cease-fire, when it was evident to him that Israel was the primary culprit in violating. When Brezhnev discussed the contents of Nixon's letter with the Politburo there was a general sense that it was a ploy, that Nixon was trying to trick them. The tone of subsequent messages became increasingly hostile.

Despite his displeasure with the Nixon message, Brezhnev still did not want détente to slip from his grasp. The most obvious solution, a request to have UN troops monitor the cease-fire, was distasteful to him because it removed the Soviet Union from the forefront of the process. Further, the knowledge of Kissinger's communications with Sadat had shaken Soviet confidence in the U.S. Secretary of State. Where Brezhnev once had a kindly—if wary—attitude toward Kissinger, he was now convinced that the Secretary of State had lied to him in Moscow before flying to Tel Aviv to make a deal with Prime Minister Meir.

This feeling of betrayal began to permeate the Politburo and combined with the militant mood that had grown out of arguments over the Scud firings. There was suddenly a growing sentiment to take a firm stand toward both Israel and the United States. This quickly resolved itself into a catch phrase—"making the Americans live up to their commitments."[5] The feeling soon spread to the floor of the United

Nations, where the USSR and its satellite nations railed against U.S. and Israeli disregard for the UN-sanctioned cease-fire.

Meanwhile, at the White House, the Israelis' continuing success after the hour of the cease-fire placed Kissinger in an invidious position. He had promised the Soviet Union that the Israelis would honor the cease-fire, and they had not. Worse, the continuous flow of supplies being brought in by the MAC airlift made it apparent to all that the United States was in fact providing the means by which the Israelis could continue their offensive. Yet the airlift could not be stopped; the Israelis needed to be supplied until the cease-fire was effective and their stocks, including reserves, were replenished. Otherwise they would be at the mercy of another Arab attack.

The morning of October 23, Kissinger staggered into his office, jet-lagged and weary from the long trip to Russia and Israel. Over the next eighteen hours, he would be besieged by a blizzard of messages reflecting the flagrant nature of Israeli breaches of the cease-fire.

The first two messages were contradictory, yet both promised trouble. One was from Hafiz Ismail, complaining in the most genteel fashion about the Israelis' breaking the cease-fire and occupying new positions. The second was a hard-edged missive from Golda Meir, insisting that the Egyptians had been the first to break the cease-fire and that she had ordered the Israeli army to continue fighting until the Egyptians stopped. Kissinger did not expect her to say otherwise. In his memoirs he indicates that he felt a trace of guilt, realizing that some of his remarks during his visit might have been interpreted by Israel as sanctioning violations of the cease-fire agreement. Given his chess player's insight into the importance of diplomatic nuance, this is ingenuous; he undoubtedly had given an unofficial go-ahead to Israeli efforts.

The importance of the first two messages was immediately trumped by a third cable from Brezhnev himself, a violation of custom, for he almost always addressed his own remarks to the President. This one informed Kissinger that Soviet MiG-25 reconnaissance aircraft had tracked the movement of Israeli troops south along the canal's west bank. He suggested a meeting of the UN Security Council to reconfirm the cease-fire and to order a withdrawal of all forces to the positions they had occupied when the October 22 cease-fire resolution passed.

Brezhnev's tone was so urgent that Kissinger immediately inferred that the Egyptian 3rd Army was in dire straits. This meant he had to act at once, for it would be impossible to conduct reasonable peace negotiations if the Israelis completely destroyed the 3rd Army. The Arab world would never tolerate such a humiliation, and the conflict would escalate.[6]

A quick succession of telephone calls to the Israeli ambassador, Dinitz, and to Golda Meir herself confirmed the problem. They admitted that the IDF had now virtually cut off the Egyptian 3rd Army and was prepared to destroy it by shell fire or starvation. The heavy casualties and the Israelis' indignation at the Arab sneak attack on their most solemn religious holiday had allowed an irrational element of revenge to permeate their thinking. Meir refused to consider making even the token gesture of withdrawing a few hundred yards from the current front lines.

Brezhnev then upped the ante with a wire to President Nixon that blasted the Israelis while guaranteeing that the Arabs would observe the cease-fire. He called upon Nixon to join with him in taking "decisive measures" to impose the cease-fire and ensure that the Israelis withdrew to their previous lines. The message, stern but essentially innocuous, was nonetheless another important step toward a U.S./USSR nuclear confrontation.

Kissinger did not see the cease-fire as a problem, for both sides were reaching the point of exhaustion, in any event. The withdrawal to an earlier position was troublesome because the Israelis would refuse to do so and, in any case, no one could say where those positions were. To finesse this, he made an agreement with Yuli Vorontsov, the Soviet chargé d'affaires, to agree on the cease-fire and leave the line to which the forces would withdraw to direct negotiations between Egypt and Israel.

The agreement was not satisfactory to Golda Meir, who responded vehemently that Israel would not comply. It was apparent that revenge was now uppermost in the minds of the Israelis and the possible destruction of the Egyptian 3rd Army seemed like a fitting way to punish Sadat for starting the war.

Sadat himself now entered the mix with the first direct communiqué he had ever sent to Washington. Sadat sent Nixon a frantically worded complaint that the United States had "guaranteed" the cease-fire and was now obliged to intervene with force to make good its guarantee. It was an unprecedented, almost surreal moment in diplomacy, for Egypt had not had direct diplomatic relations with the United States for six years.[7] Yet now Egypt was in essence calling upon the United States to take up arms if necessary against its longtime ally, Israel, by requesting troops "on the ground." It was clear that sharp political bargaining was beginning to give way to panic in Cairo.

Despite the bizarre nature of the request, the U.S. response was firm but tactful, stating only that while it had never guaranteed the cease-fire, it was prepared to support the UN resolution that required a cease-fire.

Desperately aware of its own army's fatigue, Israel ended October 23 on a more positive note, with Prime Minister Meir pledging Kissinger to honor the cease-fire if Egypt would do so also. The fact that the 3rd Army was cut off from most of its sources of food and water made Meir's concession easier. Nonetheless, the upbeat note continued when word came of Syria's acceptance of the cease-fire. The Syrian forces had suffered terribly, losing some 1,150 tanks plus 100 Iraqi and 50 Jordanian tanks.

Syria's acceptance enabled the UN Security Council to pass Resolution 339, which stated that the council

1. Confirms its decision on an immediate cessation of all kinds of firing and of all military action and urges that the forces of the two sides be returned to the positions they occupied at the moment the cease-fire became effective.

2. Requests the Secretary-General to take measures for immediate dispatch of United Nation observers to supervise the observance of the cease-fire between the forces of Israel and the Arab Republic of Egypt, using for this purpose the personnel of the United Nations now in the Middle East and first of all the personnel now in Cairo.

The second cease-fire was scheduled to go into effect at 7:00 A.M., Cairo time, on October 24. Things had apparently cooled down, but they would soon heat up on another front as suspicion, misunderstanding, and hubris combined to nudge the world toward a nuclear crisis.

The early morning of October 23 saw Bren Adan absolutely determined to press ahead, without regard to the cease-fire. He had seen too many Israeli soldiers die to stop now, on the verge of a great victory, the complete capture of the forty-five thousand troops of the Egyptian 3rd Army. As soon as dawn broke, his tanks had moved forward and overrun a number of small Egyptian logistics bases, capturing almost five thousand soldiers without much of a fight. There was no question in Adan's mind about the legitimacy of the cease-fire order. Despite this or perhaps seeking to protect himself, he queried General Gonen about it. The sharp rejoinder was not to his liking. Gonen, grumpy as usual, told him, "We in the army take orders. It was the Government of Egypt that decided to launch this war and the Government of Israel that decided on the cease-fire. And we in the army accept both orders."[8]

This was not what Adan wanted to hear, and he rejected Gonen's orders, informing him that since the cease-fire was not being observed (this was true—Adan himself was not observing it) he was going to continue fighting. When a brigade commander was heard asking about checking with the Egyptians to see if the cease-fire was on, Adan burst in with a salvo of criticism and an order: "Do not make me any armistice here—fire back and go into action."

Adan's forces were stretched thin, particularly in infantry, but they pressed ahead, with the armor taking positions and, when absolutely necessary, stopping to do the mopping up that was the infantry's normal task. Personnel were so short that Egyptian officers and noncommissioned officers were ordered to command convoys of their own troops and take them to designated detention areas in the desert, a sort of prisoner-of-war trustee system.

Late in the afternoon, Adan launched a two-brigade attack, with one reaching the Suez Gulf, on the outskirts of Suez City. The IAF, so near the "red line" just a few days ago, wreaked havoc on Egyptian armor and artillery. The IAF was particularly effective in taking out all of the Egyptian crossing equipment, preventing further withdrawal of forces from the east to the west bank.

The 7th and 19th Egyptian divisions that made up the bulk of the 3rd Army were now in desperate straits on the east bank, with Israeli forces deployed across their rear. Another Israeli brigade continued south to the port of Adabiah, opening it to Israeli patrol boats whose task was to prevent the Egyptians' supplying the 3rd Army by ship.

The trap was made complete by Adan's next order, which was to cut off the last of the water and fuel pipelines that supplied life to the 3rd Army. With their ammunition and fuel depots already captured, the Egyptians were now faced

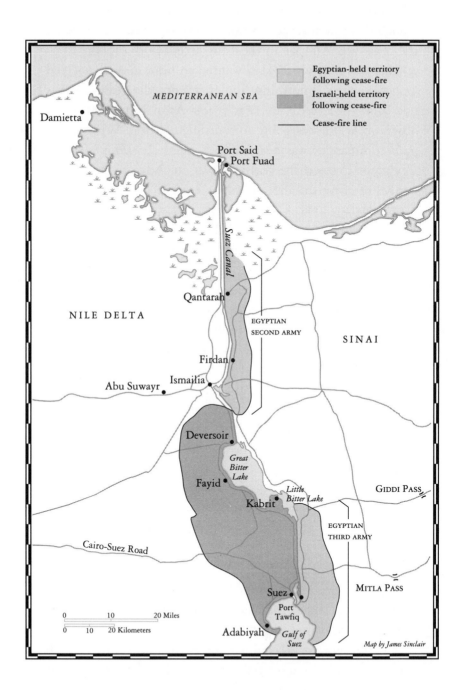

MEDITERRANEAN SEA

Egyptian-held territory
following cease-fire

Israeli-held territory
following cease-fire

Cease-fire line

Damietta

Port Said
Port Fuad

Suez Canal

NILE DELTA

Qantarah

EGYPTIAN
SECOND ARMY

SINAI

Firdan

Abu Suwayr   Ismailia

Deversoir

Great
Bitter
Lake

Fayid

Little
Bitter Lake

Kabrit

GIDDI PASS

EGYPTIAN
THIRD ARMY

Cairo-Suez Road

MITLA PASS

Suez

Port
Tawfiq

0   10   20 Miles
0   10   20 Kilometers

Adabiyah   Gulf of
Suez

Map by James Sinclair

with the very tragedy that Shazli had warned about. An immediate shortage of blood for transfusions to wounded soldiers developed, and this would become an international cause célèbre over the next few days. The 3rd Army was still able to defend against Israeli attacks, but its strength would continue to wane as the supplies on hand became exhausted. There was no Egyptian force to rescue it, and it could not break out. Morale sank and rumors ran rampart, with forlorn hopes being pinned on an intervention by an outside force— the United Nations or, if possible, the airborne troops of the Soviet Union.

Flushed with success, Adan now asked Gonen for permission to push on and seize the city of Suez. Gonen replied, "If it is empty, okay. If it is strongly held, no." Adan took that for an unqualified yes.[9]

Israeli plans for treating the new cease-fire, set to go into effect at 7:00 A.M. on October 24, were simple. Air attacks and artillery barrages would begin at 5:20 A.M., with armored forces attacking with as much mass as possible. At 7:00 A.M. the air attacks would cease, demonstrating Israeli "compliance" with the cease-fire, but the land battle would go, using the classic excuse of their "inability to disengage" as a cover story.

Unfortunately for Adan, the cover story proved to be the real story as his attempts to seize the city of Suez turned into a bloody debacle. Far from being empty, Suez turned out to be a wasps' nest of Egyptian defenders who had been transferred over from the east bank. The main problem for the Israelis was the narrow streets of the city. One Israeli armored column of twenty-one tanks and fifteen APCs stretched for more than a mile, in part surrounded by buildings as much as seven stories high. It was the custom for Israeli tank commanders to stand in the open hatches of their tanks, so that they could survey the battle better. All hell broke lose when the Egyptians unleashed a barrage of fire from the buildings. Antitank weapons were fired from lower floors while machine-gun fire and hand grenades rained down from above. Within minutes, only four tank commanders were left, the rest having been wounded or killed. The column dissolved as the vehicles, or sometimes just the crews, fled the scene, unable to fight back. In addition, two contingents of paratroopers had been cut off in separate sections of the city, and repeated attempts to rescue them had failed. When it became dark, the survivors made their way in small groups through the city streets and alleys back to Israeli lines.

By the end of October 24, Adan was forced to retreat from the city, having lost forty tanks and suffered two hundred casualties, eighty of them killed in action. It was a stupid and unnecessary action, one that Elazar deplored.

Meanwhile, Israeli forces captured the forward headquarters of the Commander of the 3rd Army, Major General Wassel. The General himself escaped into the desert.

It might have been some consolation to Adan that Sharon was doing no better in the north. It had long been Sharon's claim that he could sweep to the north and trap the Egyptian 2nd Army, providing Israel with an almost perfect situation for conducting peace talks. However, when his paratroopers moved toward Ismailia they ran into heavy resistance and suffered many casualties. Egyptian commando forces, which had fought well throughout the war, stymied Sharon's advance and, with familiar tactics, used Saggers and RPGs to stop his tanks. Sharon, for his part, was now very willing to observe the cease-fire.[10]

Détente and his personal relationships with Nixon and Kissinger were the things that Brezhnev prized above all others, and all three seemed to be on the road to disaster. The Israeli success on October 24 was exactly what the Politburo had predicted eighteen days before, but its belated arrival brought far greater problems than anticipated. Sadat's messages had not been confined to Nixon and Brezhnev; he had beat the drum throughout the Arab world and with all the nonaligned nations, calling for solidarity and demanding that both the United States and the Soviet Union stop the Israeli advance.

Brezhnev was being pushed into a corner, forced to believe that Israel would not have twice dared to ignore the UN call for a cease-fire unless it had the implicit backing of the United States in doing so. The strain on Brezhnev was compounded by the fact that the Kremlin's Hall of Congresses was the site of the World Congress of Peace Forces, a huge rally opening on October 25 and intended to establish his position as a world leader who worked for peace. It was not a simple "show" meeting, orchestrated by Politburo propagandists, like the May Day parade. There were more than three thousand delegates from 144 countries, many of them heads of influential international organizations. Brezhnev had worked hard to bring the congress about, expecting to shine with a long speech laying out a road map for peace throughout the world. A successful congress would strengthen his political position and weaken those of his enemies in the Politburo.

Yet with the Middle East still at war and with relations with the United States deteriorating, Brezhnev was stymied. He could not make a speech that might be overtaken by a total disaster of Soviet foreign policy in the Middle East. He stalled, electing not to make the opening address and leaving the timing of his speech open.[11]

As October 24 wore on, Sadat continued his volley of messages. In the early afternoon, he made a formal appeal to both Brezhnev and Nixon to dispatch troops. The message to Brezhnev was distinguished by an additional paragraph requesting that the Soviet Union act *separately* if the United States did not agree to send troops. Sadat knew full well that the United States would intercept his message to Brezhnev. He wanted this to happen, for he wanted the added pressure to be placed on the United States. He knew that the idea of the Soviet Union alone sending troops to the Middle East was totally unacceptable. Nonetheless, his central goal was to have both nations send troops. The last thing Sadat wanted was unilateral Soviet military action that would result in Egypt becoming dependent upon the USSR.

Moscow's first reaction to Sadat's request was surprisingly positive. It was decided to send fifty observers and twenty interpreters to Cairo, to act as peacekeepers. But then the Kremlin's simmering militant mood began to boil and serious discussions began on the option of sending troops. The prospects were not encouraging. Establishing an agreement with the United States so that the forces could be deployed jointly would take a great amount of time, and if the Israelis kept going at their current pace, Cairo and Damascus conceivably could be captured.

As discussions went on, the necessity of avoiding a situation in which Sadat had to surrender became paramount. It was absolutely unthinkable that such a debacle could take place while the World Congress of Peace Forces was in session in Moscow.

It should be noted that at no time, despite their increasing irritation and their ever bolder threats, did the leaders in the Kremlin envisage any sort of direct military confrontation with the United States. Brezhnev restated his resolve not to become involved in the Middle East war under any circumstances, and the Soviet General Staff had not yet created any operational plans to do so. However, as a matter of routine there was increased military activity (much of it on the authority of subordinate units) that included the alerting of seven airborne divisions, dispatching nuclear material by ship through the Dardanelles, sending additional naval forces to the Mediterranean, and firing the Scuds. Incredible as it may seem, the crafty Kremlin leaders, all veterans of years of political infighting in both domestic and international arenas, simply did not understand that their clumsy reactions to the situation could and would be interpreted as steps toward war.

In his first message of October 24 to Nixon, Brezhnev had been firm but polite, asking that the United States put an end to Israel's "provocative behavior" and merely inquiring as to what steps the United States intended to take to ensure Israel's compliance with the cease-fire.

While Brezhnev was waiting for the response to this message, Kremlin tempers continued to rise. Later in the day Brezhnev decided to up the ante in another message and promptly made a mistake that is as fatal in diplomacy as it is in poker: he began to bluff when he knew he did not have the wherewithal to call. He decided that a message should be sent to the United States indicating that if it was not ready for joint action, the Kremlin would not exclude the possibility of unilateral action in the Middle East. These remarks were intended to intimidate the United States and to force it to agree to joint action. The second message began with the routine complaints about Israeli aggression and remarks on the need for mutual understanding between the Soviet Union and the United States. It went on to suggest that both nations should accede to Sadat's appeal for military contingents to be sent to ensure implementation of the cease-fire. There followed two sentences that contained the threat. Brezhnev declared that "I will say it straight that if you find it impossible to act jointly with us in this matter, we should be faced with the necessity urgently to consider the question of taking appropriate steps unilaterally. We cannot allow arbitrariness on the part of Israel."

Brezhnev was the author of the last two lines; even at the height of the coming crisis, he would never recognize that it was his words that caused the U.S. reaction and plunged the world toward nuclear war.[12] Instead, Brezhnev and his colleagues in the Kremlin felt satisfied that they had struck just the right notes of friendship, firmness, and threat. It did not occur to them that the United States might interpret this as more than another move in the Middle East chess game. The Soviets had continued to discount the importance of the Watergate crisis and the effect it might have upon the internal workings of the U.S. government. What they all considered to be a sound, if very firm, diplomatic message was sent early in the morning of October 25, Moscow time, and would arrive in late afternoon of October in Washington.

The message was one of the great blunders in diplomatic history, one that characterized perfectly the inability of the leaders of one nation to understand the mind-set, reasoning, and motivations of another. Brezhnev, who prided himself on his friendship with Nixon and knowledge of Kissinger, placed his nation's life on the line. He appeared to be completely unaware of how the cumulative actions of the USSR would form an ominous backdrop to a threatening letter. No one had considered the limited number of alternatives the United States had with which to respond. It could acquiesce—or it could escalate.

Henry Kissinger began October 24 at 8:00 A.M. sharp functioning as a go-between. Waiting on his desk was the first message of the day, from his "secret" correspondent, Hafiz Ismail, charging the Israelis with breaking the cease-fire and resuming attacks all along the battlefield. Kissinger sought to verify the charges but could not reach the Israeli ambassador, Simcha Dinitz, until 9:22 A.M. These were the first of an avalanche of telephone calls, messages, and meetings, a staccato barrage of events, lies, and threats that would escalate the bitter Mideast war to the very brink of a global nuclear conflict.

Dinitz did the usual diplomatic tap dancing at which he was so adept, insisting that the Israeli army was not breaking the cease-fire but only blocking new Egyptian offensives. Kissinger had just hung up on his unsatisfying conversation with Dinitz when a highly charged message arrived for Nixon from Sadat, who demanded that the United States intervene on the ground to force Israel to comply with the cease-fire, saying: "That much you have promised."

Kissinger relayed the message to Dinitz, stressing that if

Egypt's charges were true and the Israelis did not desist, it would cause a U.S.-Soviet confrontation, one with catastrophic effects upon the cease-fire. Dinitz made the usual meaningless diplomatic concession: Israel would allow U.S. military observers into the Sinai to monitor the cease-fire. What he did not say was that in the intervening twenty-four hours before the observers could possibly be in place Israel would continue to violate the cease-fire.

Disappointed in Dinitz, Kissinger next issued a message under Nixon's name to Sadat, saying only that the United States opposed offensive actions, Israeli or Egyptian. The message was sweetened, however, by the suggestion that Kissinger would get in touch with Ismail about a visit to Egypt.

Dealing with Dinitz and Sadat was difficult. Kissinger assumed that the Arab claims of Israeli cease-fire violations were correct and Dinitz's responses were patently false. Even so, Kissinger had to reply to both parties with substantively neutral messages that kept the lines of communication open and still permitted negotiations for peace. In the meantime, he used photographic reconnaissance from Lockheed SR-71 Blackbirds for hard data on the military situation.

Wanting to know the Soviet view of the situation, Kissinger called Ambassador Dobrynin at 9:45 A.M. and explained the situation as he knew it. Dobrynin was noncommittal, saying that he had no instructions from Moscow but would call when he received them. At 10:10 A.M. an impatient Kissinger called Dobrynin again, the second of many calls that day, this time letting him know of Israel's "concession" about allowing U.S. military observers at the front.

When the telephone rang next at 10:19, it was Dobrynin, stating that a message from Brezhnev to Nixon was en route. As previously noted, it was calculated by Brezhnev to be stern but fair, but it was interpreted by Kissinger as a bombshell, for it began simply "Mr. President" rather than the usual "Esteemed Mr. President." Words count, and nowhere more than in the language of tough diplomacy.

Dismayed as he might be by the tone of the letter, Kissinger saw that the message had utility: he could use it to impress Israel with the growing seriousness of the crisis. After another long series of exchanges, he was able to extract from the Israelis a promise that they would not respond to Egyptian provocations and would "try" not to advance any farther. Golda Meir had made his task more difficult by a speech before the Knesset that she closed with the words: "If Egypt keeps on fighting, Israel will not be able to remain still." All of this information had to be distilled into a soothing answer to Brezhnev in the hope that it would assuage the obvious growing hostility in the Kremlin.

And it was not easy to be soothing when Kissinger was boiling with rage. He was dismayed at the Israeli actions and had even made some threats himself, letting Golda Meir know that if the fighting did not stop immediately he might have to "disassociate himself" from Israel. This was enormously serious, for the Israelis had one friend in the world, the United States. If Kissinger turned his back on them, they would be isolated. But continued fighting by the Israelis could be even more serious for the world; there was no way to predict what the Arab reaction would be and still less insight as to what the Soviets might do if all of Kissinger's efforts were seen as a sellout to Israel.

The message to Brezhnev was dispatched at 1:00 P.M., imparting all Kissinger knew of the current situation, including Israel's assurances about not beginning new offensive operations. Almost immediately thereafter, there was a private message from Sadat stating that he was going to formally request Soviet troops be sent to the Middle East. It was a gambler's bold move that threatened all of Kissinger's plans for mediating peace negotiations after the cease-fire finally lurched into effect. The United States, its morale still grievously wounded by the long ground war in Vietnam, was not going to either send troops to the region or allow the Soviet Union to do so.

Given that the United States was not going to send troops, stopping the Soviets from doing so left only one tactic: the threat of nuclear war. There were no intermediate steps, no alternatives, no third parties to call on. By 1:00 P.M. on October 24, the war in the Middle East had somehow become exactly what both superpowers feared most: a nuclear trip wire.

Kissinger was calling the shots, and from his point of view, the United States absolutely would not act jointly with the Soviet Union in placing troops in the war zone. Doing so would of course alienate Israel and also the moderate Arab nations who distrusted and feared the USSR. It would in fact exactly reverse the current situation, in which Israel was beholden to the United States—and Egypt wished to be.

There was a lull in the communiqué wars until 3:35 P.M., when Kissinger received a call from Dobrynin relaying a message from the foreign minister, Gromyko. Kissinger interpreted it as a conciliatory sign that it was from Gromyko rather than Brezhnev, but the message was clear and severe. Gromyko charged that Israel was stepping up its military operations and simply lying about it. Kissinger asked Dobrynin to come to his office at 4:00 P.M. and, while waiting, checked with Dinitz, who again asserted that there was no Israeli offensive action going on in the Sinai.

Kissinger and Dobrynin were personal friends who obviously liked each other and enjoyed each other's company. Yet at moments like this a grave diplomatic dignity prevailed. Instead of stating baldly that the United States would use force to oppose the introduction of Soviet troops into the Middle East if it became necessary to do so, Kissinger merely informed Dobrynin that the United States would veto any UN resolution calling for sending of troops to the Middle East by any of the permanent members of the Security Council (China, France, Great Britain, the United States, and the USSR).

Dobrynin was conciliatory, pointing out that it was now

11:00 P.M. in Moscow and that it might be prudent to do nothing till morning. Kissinger agreed and suggested that they begin to think about a Middle East peace conference. Things seemed to be cooling off.

Until 7:05 P.M. Washington time, when Dobrynin called to present a bombshell. He stated that someone—presumably the representative from Egypt—was going to introduce a resolution in the UN Security Council calling for the dispatch of U.S. and Soviet troops and that the Soviet Union would support the resolution.

As important as this information was, Kissinger had to ask Dobrynin to excuse him; he was being interrupted by an urgent call from a distraught Richard Nixon. On the point of a nervous breakdown, near tears, Nixon rambled on about not just being forced out of office but actually being killed by his political opponents. Convinced that he was going to be impeached, he wanted Kissinger to plead his case at a meeting scheduled for congressional leaders the following morning. Further, he wanted Kissinger to call several important senators on his behalf. Nixon tasked Kissinger to convince the senators that he, as President, had performed an important role in the Middle East and that his continued leadership was essential to the country.

After quickly agreeing to comply with Nixon's request— an agreement he failed to keep—a saddened Kissinger called Dobrynin back at 7:15 P.M. telling him again that the United States would veto a UN resolution calling for the dispatch of troops to the Middle East.

As the minutes ticked away, Kissinger sprang into action, ordering John Scali, the U.S. representative at the United Nations, to veto any resolution calling for the introduction of troops from the United States or USSR. Scali was also to inform the Chinese ambassador, Huang Hua, of his instructions.

At 7:25 P.M. Kissinger spoke to Dobrynin once more, strongly and directly urging him to see that the United States was not pushed further on a matter to which it could not agree. This was followed by a call to the British ambassador urging that Great Britain also veto the resolution. Ten minutes later, Kissinger briefed Dinitz on the growing crisis.

The cautionary words may have had effect. Egypt did not introduce a formal resolution but instead voiced Sadat's demand for the dispatch of troops. And while Yakov Malik, the UN representative of the Soviet Union, spoke supportively of the Egyptian position, he did not formally endorse it. He did, however, increase tensions by impugning the United States and Henry Kissinger personally. Malik demanded that the United States "check the adventurers in Tel Aviv" and went on to say, "The honor and the dignity of the United States and international trust in the new United States Secretary of State, Mr. Kissinger, are now being subjected to searching scrutiny." Malik could not have made this personal attack without direct instructions from Brezhnev. Once again, the Soviet leader had badly miscalculated. What he intended as merely conventional diplomacy, whipping up some additional pressure in the UN forum, was interpreted quite differently by the United States. To Kissinger and the State Department, Malik's fiery statements on the UN floor were a clear signal that Brezhnev was raising the ante.

As he was digesting this, Kissinger sent a message to Sadat in Nixon's name stating that if the resolution was formally introduced, the United States would veto it. And he salted the message with the threat that the introduction of the resolution would probably force the cancellation of any visit to Cairo by Kissinger.

There was time for a brief meeting with Alexander Haig, the President's Chief of Staff, at 9:32 P.M. The two men agreed that things were approaching crisis proportions. Nixon, totally worn out and well fortified with scotch, had gone to bed.

Their sense of urgency was heightened at 9:35 P.M., when Ambassador Dobrynin called with Brezhnev's second message of the day to Nixon. If the previous message had been a bombshell, this was a nuclear blast. The letter that Brezhnev had so carefully crafted to be a thinly veiled threat was viewed in Washington as an ultimatum. Just as the Gromyko-Grechko quarrel over the firing of Scuds had poisoned the atmosphere in the Kremlin, so had the Watergate crisis poisoned the atmosphere in the White House. The ominous creep in Soviet military preparations—now heightened by an alert in the East German forces—combined to make what Brezhnev considered a stern warning a threat of war.

The key words in Brezhnev's message were translated in convoluted English, but their meaning seemed clear: "It is necessary to adhere without delay. I will say it straight that if you find it impossible to act jointly with us in this matter, we should be faced with the necessity urgently to consider the question of taking appropriate steps unilaterally." The note went on to demand "an immediate and clear reply," in the tone of Hitler hectoring Poland.

Aghast at both the tenor and the content of the note, Kissinger was further appalled at its suggestion that the two powers impose a final settlement on the warring parties. He decided immediately that the note would have to be rejected in such a manner that the Soviet Union would be shocked into halting any unilateral movement.

Kissinger discussed the matter with Haig at 9:50. Haig at first thought the message was a bluff but came around to Kissinger's view that it was a naked threat. They then debated waking the President for the meeting. Haig suggested that Nixon was too upset to participate and that it was better if he slept.

At 10:00 Kissinger called Dinitz, to inform him of the gravity of the situation and to ask for Israel's views. This was followed fifteen minutes later by another call to Dobrynin, cautioning him that the Soviet Union should not take any unilateral action until the United States had a chance to reply to Brezhnev's letter. He insisted that the USSR not pressure the United States into action.

Kissinger called an emergency meeting of the Washington Special Actions Group (WSAG) for 10:30 P.M. in the White House Situation Room. Chairing it not as Secretary of State but in his capacity as Assistant to the President for National Security Affairs, Kissinger brought together some very talented and seasoned leaders. The group included Haig; Secretary of Defense James Schlesinger, Kissinger's old airlift nemesis; the Director of the CIA, William Colby; the Chairman of the Joint Chiefs of Staff, Admiral Thomas Moorer, who had been so diligent about getting the airlift under way; the Deputy Assistant to the President for National Security Affairs, Brent Scowcroft; and Kissinger's military assistant, Commander Jonathan T. Howe.

It is incredible that the President did not attend, although Kissinger's memoirs state that "no one present thought it unusual that he did not do so now." While Nixon did not normally attend WSAG meetings, these meetings normally did not discuss the possibility of a nuclear alert and all the potential complications that might ensue. Haig again maintained that it was better for the President to sleep, given the stress he was under with the Watergate crisis, and told Kissinger that he would relay the results of the meeting to the President. This suited Kissinger perfectly, for the last thing he needed was a lachrymose president attempting to show that he was in command. The rest of the WSAG members were probably grateful to Haig as well, for everyone could speak more openly with the President absent.

After a detailed briefing and intense discussions, the group reached consensus. The United States would raise its military alert status from Defense Readiness Condition (DefCon) IV to DefCon III, which indicates a state of increased readiness but not a determination that war is likely.[13] The group knew that the import of the raise in alert status would be known immediately by the Soviet Union. What they did not and could not know was how the Soviet Union would understand the action and, more important, how it would react.

The decision to go to DefCon III had immediate effect upon U.S. combat forces, and all around the world coded teletype circuits and scrambler telephones began to crackle with the information. Nowhere was it more important—or more closely monitored by the Soviet Union—than in SAC, where the effect was instantaneous. SAC's designated battle staff, composed of high-ranking and very experienced officers, was summoned to the Command Center, a closely guarded seven-story building with four of the most important stories underground. An immediate check was made of the readiness of SAC's strike force of more than a thousand aircraft, including 422 B-52s and 71 General Dynamic FB-111s. The change from DefCon IV, the norm since the Cuban Missile Crisis, to DefCon III meant an increase in the number of bombers on alert status. Bomber crews immediately began updating their target folders while on the flight line more aircraft were "cocked," that is, made ready for instant start-up. At the remote missile silos around the country, the usual hectic tenor of life was edged up a notch as 970 Minuteman and 57 Titan missiles were brought to an even greater state of readiness. All across the country, leave and training were canceled, aircraft maintenance was rescheduled, and everything possible to get the maximum number of aircraft and missiles ready was done. The same feverish activity was taking place on the same scale in every combat arm of the Air Force, the Navy, and the Army. Like a cracking whip, the chain of events accelerated as it moved down through the chain of command. At each subordinate level, as the still Top Secret steps necessary to go to DefCon III were executed, preparations were made to ease the transition to DefCon II and, if necessary, DefCon I, if the order came. All around the world, the U.S. military was aroused from its usual—and often boring—Cold War routine and made ready to go to war.

In the meantime, Kissinger unleashed a sequence of orders that gave teeth to the alert and indicated that the United States was deadly serious. At 12:20 A.M. the 82nd Airborne

Division, the elite fire brigade of U.S. military policy, was alerted for possible movement to the Middle East, the sleepy soldiers filing through hastily erected tents to get their inoculations updated. At 12:25 two aircraft carriers, the *Franklin Delano Roosevelt* and the *John F. Kennedy,* were ordered to join the *Independence* in the eastern Mediterranean. These were immensely powerful forces, giant nuclear carriers equipped with strike aircraft capable of carrying a wide variety of nuclear arms.

By 12:30 enough signals had been sent to allow drafting a reply to Brezhenv's inflammatory letter, which was to be dispatched in about five hours' time. The letter rejected every Soviet demand but did agree that the United States might participate in a UN truce supervisory force composed of noncombat personnel. It emphasized that the United States could not accept unilateral action and that such action "would produce incalculable consequences which would be in the interest of neither of our countries and which would end all we have striven so hard to achieve." In short, such action meant the end of Brezhnev's greatest achievement, détente.

Prior to the letter being sent, Kissinger informed only the British ambassador of the serious nature of the unfolding events; other allies were deemed too likely to leak information to the Soviets.

The WSAG meeting was concluded around 2:00 A.M., but Kissinger still worked on, his last military action being directing the Joint Chiefs of Staff to order at 3:30 A.M. the return of some seventy Boeing B-52s based at Guam to the United States.

Kissinger's orders and the titanic military reaction they invoked were intended as a signal to Brezhnev. Kissinger hoped that he would get the message and back off. This was extraordinarily optimistic thinking. The Soviets had rarely "got the message" in the past. Instead, they might easily have responded with a full-scale alert of their strategic forces, which in turn might have pushed the United States to DefCon

II, the situation where war is deemed imminent. And there existed the most ghastly possibility of all: the buildup might convince the Soviet Union, with its great missile capability, that now was the time to execute a first strike. A first strike, a preemptive nuclear attack with all its missile and bomber forces, was an integral part of Soviet doctrine and an ever-present danger.

Yet so desperate was the political climate in the United States that the response to Brezhnev's perceived ultimatum was prepared in Nixon's name without his approval or authority and transmitted by messenger to Ambassador Dobrynin at 5:40 A.M. on October 25 (12:40 P.M. Moscow time). It was the most dangerous message Kissinger ever delivered— and it was an unprecedented usurpation of presidential power, one that somehow went unchallenged politically or in the media.

When Nixon awoke on October 25, Haig gently informed him of the meeting and the message. Later, at 8:00 A.M., Kissinger gave Nixon a more detailed briefing. Still desperately preoccupied with his own survival, he approved the actions automatically. In his memoirs published in 1978, Nixon saved face by writing that he had given Haig and Kissinger instructions to hold the WSAG meeting, for "we needed action, even the shock of a military alert."

"Fat, dumb, and happy" is not an elegant expression, but it might be applied to the Politburo on the morning of October 25 as it waited for the response to Brezhnev's last message to President Nixon. Discussions in the Soviet Foreign Ministry centered around the United States' probable response, with most feeling that Nixon would reject the Soviet request for bilateral military action and put sufficient pressure on the Israelis to make them observe the cease-fire.[14] No one speculated about the unilateral movement of Soviet forces to intervene in the Middle East, for despite the alerts sent to the airborne divisions, no plans had been made by the Politburo for such an event. (The alert of the airborne divisions had been a routine military response, not originating within the Kremlin. As centrally controlled as the Soviet armed services were, they were so large that such delegation of authority was inevitable.) Brezhnev's threat had been pure rhetoric, and everyone in the Kremlin not only knew it but agreed with it as a reasonable diplomatic ploy.

These rather naïve pipe dreams went up in smoke as word spread like wildfire about the U.S. reaction. Soviet intelligence had reported immediately that the U.S. armed forces had gone to DefCon III. By 1:20 P.M., Moscow time, the U.S. military alert was known worldwide, thanks to the announcements trumpeted by the American media. The Soviet media ignored the fact, despite the fact that Moscow was abuzz with rumors and many of the foreign delegates to the World Congress of Peace Forces had received information from their own sources.

The October 25 meeting of the Politburo had begun at 11:00 A.M. Normally Politburo meetings had a long agenda filled with a variety of issues. Today the meeting was devoted solely to the Yom Kippur War. When "Nixon's" message from Washington was received just before 1:00 P.M., Brezhnev and his colleagues were stunned. To them the U.S. nuclear alert was absolutely inexplicable. They were still completely blind to the fact that it was Brezhnev's message that had precipitated the U.S. response, and they looked in vain for other causes. A general indignation pervaded the group, which felt the U.S. action violated the Soviet-U.S. treaty of 1972 for the prevention of nuclear war. As they searched for a response to the alert, they vented their feelings about Kissinger's presumed treachery and his undoubted preference for Israel's interests. But behind their grousing there was one underlying unanimous agreement: there should be no war. Egypt and Syria were not deemed important enough to cause a war. Above all, the Politburo unanimously wished to avoid a nuclear exchange.

The problem was how to answer the U.S. alert with a strong action that would not escalate the tension. The genuine degree of the danger of runaway escalation can be found in the response of the aggressive Grechko, who had authorized firing the Scuds. Grechko felt that the USSR did not have to ask anyone's permission to send troops to the Middle East if they wished to do so. He suggested a partial mobilization of troops and the dispatch of the fifteen hundred Soviet troops presently in Syria to occupy the Golan Heights, regardless of the consequences.

Mercifully, others disagreed, with Kosygin arguing that the United States would match any troops that the Soviet Union sent to the Middle East, whether it was one division or five. Gromyko agreed with Kosygin for once, asking academically, "Where is the brink, the line between peace and a new, nuclear war?" It was a line that had to be found, and swiftly.

The arguments dragged on until the author of the problem, Brezhnev, came up with a solution.[15] He suggested that the best thing would be to not make any response at all to the American nuclear alert. Instead, they would let "Nixon cool down" and, in the meantime, have Gromyko contact Kissinger with a message that would de-escalate the confrontation.

Brezhnev's suggestion was approved, and he managed with this single idea not only to recover from the debacle of the "misunderstood" message but also to preserve his cherished concept of maintaining détente with the United States. It strengthened his position in the Kremlin and gave him the opportunity to speak on October 25 as a reasoned advocate at the World Congress of Peace Forces.

The Soviet leader's position was further enhanced when President Nixon's response to his letter arrived at mid-afternoon on October 25. In it they noted that Nixon discarded the idea of a bilateral insertion of troops as infeasible but continued to express the hope that there could be Soviet/ U.S. cooperation in effecting a genuine cease-fire. Nothing in the message could be construed as a rationale for having declared the DefCon III alert.

Despite the failure to explain the heightened alert status, Brezhnev felt that Nixon's letter had done him well in the Politburo, and before the meeting concluded he provided a quick summary of his view of the situation. He felt that the record would show that the Soviet Union had always strongly supported joint Soviet/U.S. action. He had only stated that the Soviet Union would take unilateral action if the United States rejected joint action. President Nixon's letter indicated that he was now willing to send a group of U.S. and Soviet observers to Egypt. This clearly was joint action and made unilateral Soviet action unnecessary. Nixon's message also promised to secure Israel's full cooperation with the Security Council's decision on the cease-fire. Finally, Brezhnev expected to receive a full explanation from the United States on the reason for the nuclear alert.

The meeting was adjourned with a collective sigh of relief.

The long seven-hour time difference between Moscow and Washington had always complicated negotiations and never more so than during the last crucial days of the Yom Kippur War. A decision reached at 6:00 P.M. in Washington on Wednesday would arrive in Moscow at 1:00 A.M. Thursday morning. In a similar way, a 12:00 noon decision in Moscow on Wednesday would arrive at 5:00 A.M. in Washington. In both cases, there were only the lower-level duty personnel on hand to receive it—the higher-ranking men who would make the final decisions were in bed, exhausted. But world crises make even exhausted great men early risers, and Kissinger was back at work on October 25 after only three hours' sleep, aghast that the media had already informed the American public about the heightened alert status and wondering what effect this would have on solving the crisis.

What he soon found was that all sides had recognized the seriousness of the situation and cooler heads were prevailing. Sadat sent his second message to Nixon, this one acknowledging that there would be no Soviet/U.S. peacekeeping force but instead informing him that an international force had been requested from the UN Security Council. This was an immediate plus for the United States, for UN forces traditionally excluded troops from the five permanent members—China, France, Great Britain, the United States, and the USSR. This was exactly what Brezhnev did not wish to happen.

Kissinger, Haig, and Nixon then spent the morning reassuring congressional leaders. There was general approval, although reservations were expressed about any solution that would involve sending U.S. troops to the Middle East, for neither the Congress nor the public had recovered from Vietnam. A short WSAG meeting was held at 10:15.

At the noon press conference, Kissinger was asked if the alert was what would have been called in a later administration a wag-the-dog war, an action designed to divert attention from the Watergate morass. He denied this with vigor, as might be expected, for in his mind the crisis was real.

It was so real that briefing Nixon, informing legislators, and dealing with the media had less importance. What counted was the next drop of the shoe from the Soviet Union. When it fell, it was not a military jackboot but a diplomatic slipper. Dobrynin relayed Brezhnev's astute reply in mid-afternoon. It avoided, as he had ordered, any mention of the nuclear alert and simply informed President Nixon that the Soviets were going to send seventy observers, not military personnel, to check on the observance of the cease-fire. The message, as innocuous as the previous one had been belligerent, concluded on an optimistic note suggesting continued cooperation.

The threat of nuclear escalation was over. It had collapsed so swiftly that some suspected there had been no need for a nuclear alert in the first place. Some attributed the declaration of DefCon III to have been showboating on Kissinger's part, an attempt to emphasize just how closely he had come to assuming presidential powers. Others returned to the theory that Nixon was the culprit, willing to risk nuclear war to escape the heat of Watergate.

In the end, it did not matter. By great good fortune no further grand mistakes were made by either party, and there was no "assassination at Sarajevo" incident to cause things to run out of control. But it had been a close call, and the avoidance of war came about not because of any leader's brilliance but instead because the "right" mistake had not been made.

There was one bathetic afternote. Nixon once again called Kissinger to plead that he make the case that it was only Nixon's indispensable leadership that saved the day. He wanted the pitch to be made to the media, to Congress, and in particular to Jewish leaders.[16] In his memoirs, Kissinger notes that Nixon's request was "pathetic but accurate." Nixon had in fact taken the ultimate responsibility for the actions that had saved Israel and kept the Soviet Union from placing its troops on the ground in the Middle East. These facts notwithstanding, Kissinger declined to do what Nixon asked, on the basis that the specter of Watergate might corrupt future diplomatic actions.

By October 25, there was grim satisfaction in Tel Aviv knowing that the 3rd Army, cut off now for three days from its supplies, was beginning to suffer from the lack of food and water. That satisfaction was diminished by the knowledge that Washington was demanding that corridors be created through Israeli lines by which vital supplies could be transported to the 3rd Army.

Israel had taken Kissinger's threat to "disassociate himself" from her interest seriously. In Elazar's mind, Kissinger wanted the siege of the Egyptian army to be lifted not as a means to temper Soviet action but rather as a way of currying favor with the Arab world. The same sort of heated conversations that had boiled through the Kremlin over "Kissinger's treachery" and in Washington over Brezhnev's letter now percolated feverishly in the Pit and the Israeli cabinet.

The greatest concern had been raised by the various proposals that had called for a return to the positions held on October 22. By early morning, Elazar had convinced himself that the aim of the United States was not just to relieve the 3rd Army from being surrounded but also to ensure that it was sent back into battle as a vital fighting force. He was certain that any relief provided the Egyptians in the way of food, water, or the evacuation of the wounded would only serve to reestablish the 3rd Army's power. And with the Israelis so extended, the situation could abruptly reverse itself, with the Egyptians forcing the IDF into the final battle.[17]

In an impassioned briefing to the Prime Minister and her staff, Elazar outlined the dangers he saw, including the ever-present concern that during any truce the Egyptians would be able to reconstitute their SAM defenses and, in so doing, put the clock back to October 6. Egypt had lost the war militarily, he said; she must not be allowed to win it politically, particularly with the help of Israel's ally, the United States. Elazar advocated a compromise: both armies would fall back to the positions they held before the war started, but with each one a distance of ten kilometers from the canal itself.

Golda Meir, mentally and physically drained by the war, finally ended the discussions by calling the United States "the only real friend we have, and a very powerful one." It was her view that in this situation Israel had nothing to be ashamed of in giving in to Washington's demands. And these demands were unequivocal.

Yet by midafternoon an artful compromise had been

reached. Instead of withdrawing to the ephemeral "lines of October 22," the IDF allowed supply convoys through its territory. They were called humanitarian relief for the benefit of the press, but they were in fact a powerful bargaining chip, one that had left the military status quo intact. It was the first step in a long series of negotiations that would lead to the Geneva Middle East Peace Conference and ultimately to Anwar Sadat's historic visit to Israel in 1977.

Within a period of twenty-four hours, the world had gone from the brink of nuclear war to a seemingly genuine cease-fire in the Middle East.

On October 25, General Paul K. Carlton had reason to be pleased with the work of his people in MAC. Only two days before, the 200th MAC airlift aircraft had touched down at Lod International Airport. By coincidence it was also the fiftieth landing of a Lockheed C-5 Galaxy, which had completely proved itself in the airlift. The figures before him were interesting: on October 24, MAC had moved 4,500 rounds of 105mm armor-piercing shells, 6,500 rounds of 155mm high explosive, and 100 CBU-52 and 100 CBU-58 cluster bombs, plus 300 Rockeye bombs. During the first twenty-five days of the airlift, four M-60 main battle tanks and ten M-48 Pattons had rolled down the C-5 ramps and into battle. Many more would come after the cease-fire. It was first-class work.

Now, with the DefCon III alert, the airlift had taken on an entirely new dimension. A quick review of the fleet status showed that there were only forty-four C-141s and five C-5s available at their home bases for a brand-new mission, the transport of the 82nd Airborne Division to the Middle East—if necessary.

Moving the 82nd would take two massive waves of aircraft. The first wave, carrying 3,946 troops and 3,200 tons of cargo, would need 138 C-141 sorties and 16 C-5 sorties to do the job. The second wave would require 774 C-141 sorties and

86 C-5 missions to move 8,036 troops and 18,567 tons of cargo. And just as with Operation Nickel Grass, the choke point for moving the 82nd would be Lajes, which, after the month-long buildup, was maxed out with 6 C-5s and 36 C-141s a day.

Carlton began the long process of calling individual wing commanders and finding out what they could do to squeeze another few aircraft out of maintenance. By the end of the day, it looked as if MAC could handle the new workload, but only if another staging base was opened in Europe. Great Britain had already rallied to the U.S. side with a stiff message to Brezhnev about the dangers of placing troops in the Middle East unilaterally, so there was hope that a base would be made available in the United Kingdom.

It would be twenty-four hours before MAC's alert status would be reduced to DefCon IV, and not until October 28 would the requirement to move the 82nd Airborne be lifted. In the meantime, the conveyor belt of supplies kept on rolling to Lod,[18] where the DefCon III alert had not made a whit of difference to Strobaugh and his hardworking ALCE team. No matter what the alert status, there was nothing more that they could do to improve the by-now routine system of off-loading, refueling, and dispatching the endless stream of aircraft that moved like clockwork through Lod.

Strobaugh had things working so well that he could occasionally take time to drop by the El Al "Donut Dolly" shop and chat with the crews. He was compiling a journal, and the doughnut shop was an ideal place to exchange ideas and pick up anecdotes from his crews. The veteran navigator Harry Heist told Strobaugh about a previous trip when they were scheduled to take back captured weaponry. In this one, a captured Soviet T-62 tank had been delivered by an Israeli colonel, who demanded that they show him precisely where the tank would be positioned inside the airplane. When asked why he was so concerned, he said, "I've got to drive it exactly to the right spot because I cannot back up. The Russians take the reverse gears out so the Egyptians cannot retreat." It was almost certainly a joke—but there was no way they could prove him wrong.

The potential danger in the war had been driven home a few days before when the "Crippled Goose," a C-5A that had been chosen to lead the fleet in flying hours, was due in on a routine trip, carrying much-needed 105mm ammunition. While it was en route, a threat was received from the Egyptians that it was going to be shot down. The aircraft diverted to Crete, but the Israelis sent a fleet of helicopters to the fabled island. They loaded the ammunition into slings, then flew the helicopters low and slow across the Mediterranean to Israel.

The strangest event had also occurred on October 24, at the height of the alert crisis. An American scientist, one of the few working with Russian colleagues in the Arctic, had ruptured his esophagus and was bleeding to death internally despite the best that Soviet doctors could do for him. For some reason, his body was rejecting the blood the Soviet doctors were using in his transfusions. After seven days, it became apparent that the man would die, and a cry for help went out to the United States. A MAC Lockheed C-141 was pulled from its Nickel Grass duties and directed to fly directly to Moscow. From there, with Soviet navigators on board, it flew to Irkutsk to pick the sick man up and take him directly to Yokata Air Base, Japan. The aircraft was fully equipped with medical personnel, and as soon as the patient was on board, transfusions began that saved his life. The Soviet people encountered by the MAC crew were helpful but seemed utterly perplexed as to why the United States would send a big aircraft like the C-141 on a trip to save one ill citizen.[19] General Carlton observed that there had never been a similar instance of a U.S. aircraft making such a trip, particularly with no Soviet navigator on board.

A few days later, Strobaugh would hear the strangest story of all. On October 28, at about 10:00 P.M., Master Sergeant Henry Baker, a C-5 flight engineer, was going through the drill of off-loading his aircraft. It was his first trip to Tel Aviv, and he had been astounded by the welcome, with beautiful El Al stewardesses coming on board with huge bouquets of roses. He went aft, to help unload a helicopter that was being sent to Prime Minister Meir for her personal use. Baker was astonished to find Golda Meir herself in the C-5's cavernous hold, physically helping to manhandle the Bell helicopter out. She was laughing and gracious, obviously pleased with her present, in which she took her first trip the very next morning.

Not one hundred yards from where Strobaugh stood talking to the crews, Harry Cohen was carefully picking a long splinter from the palm of his hand, a souvenir of his pallet building. Cohen was tan and fit, hardened by the sheer physical labor of the last eighteen days, and, overall, content. He had flown no missions and had made no heroic contribution to the Israeli war effort. But he had been there; he had shared some of the hardships and, he liked to think, at least a modicum of danger. The morning's newspaper had been filled with news about Israeli advances, and the air base was buzzing with rumors of wild victories. Cohen glanced proudly around at the smooth, almost mechanical operation at Lod of which he had been a part. And as he slowly unwrapped the sandwich brought for his lunch, he decided it was time to go home. There was not much more he could do here, and he had memories for a lifetime.

For most others, the war ended as it had begun, in a welter of confusion and mistakes at the top, while at lower levels the soldiers, sailors, and airmen fought for their respective causes with courage and skill.

The cease-fire was violated on October 25 at numerous points in both the Golan and the Sinai, but at a relatively low level of intensity. The more vicious fighting went on at the diplomatic level, where the United States slowly hammered out its policies despite the intransigence of the Israelis, the stubbornness of the Arabs, and the overwhelming desire of the Soviet Union to somehow carve a place for itself in whatever negotiations would take place.

The most difficult task was removing the stranglehold that the Israelis held on the Egyptian 3rd Army, which was already suffering from a lack of blood and beginning to run short on food and water.

Despite the increasingly forceful demands of the United States, the Israelis refused to allow relief convoys to cross their lines, insisting that the Egyptians had adequate food and water. The Israelis were justifiably concerned that war might break out again without warning, and they wanted the 3rd Army to be as weak as possible in any event.

Aghast at the reported suffering of the Egyptian forces, the U.S. DOD suggested to Kissinger that the U.S. Air Force could begin another airlift, this one using Lockheed C-130s and helicopters to supply the 3rd Army with food, water, and medical supplies. Kissinger did not accept the suggestion but allowed the essence of the idea to get through to the Israelis. The result was that a convoy of supplies, carefully inspected to be sure that no arms or ammunition were included, was allowed to pass through the lines on October 26. (This event was extremely controversial in Israel, where most people felt that had the situation been reversed, the Arabs would not have been so merciful.)

In some ways, that convoy set the tone for the subsequent negotiations, for it relieved the Egyptians of an embarrassment and the Israelis of the onus of being unreasonably vindictive. Checkpoints were established between the opposing armies, and manned by a U.N. peacekeeping force commanded by the Finnish general Ensio Siilasvuo.

On October 28, for the first time in twenty-five years, military representatives of Egypt and Israel met, to begin talks on disengaging the forces.[20] Direct talks were conducted by Major General Aharon Yariv of Israel and General Muhammad abdel-Gamasi Alghani of Egypt, initially at the checkpoint at Kilometer 109 on the Suez City–to–Cairo road.[21] The talks began at 1:30 A.M. Cairo time on October 28 and were later moved to the Kilometer 101 checkpoint. From this dusty beginning there began an agonizing and attenuated peace process that would see partial successes and bitter, continuing, and ever more dangerous failures.

Epilogue

The war had opened with a series of swift surprise blows. The initial peace efforts were just the opposite—agonizingly slow negotiations with very few surprises.

The initial steps toward a cease-fire had begun in the arcane world of diplomacy that had seen the policies of the U.S. Secretary of State being adopted by the Soviet Union. After the cease-fire, both Egypt and Israel would turn to the United States for patronage and leadership, the Egyptians with what amounted to a charm offensive, the Israelis with their customary belligerent and uncompromising insistence on what they perceived as equity.

The Egyptians were first on the scene, sending the rotund Foreign Minister Ismail Fahmy to meet with Kissinger and Nixon on October 29. Fahmy was a consummate politician, able to present polished arguments in an agreeable style that revealed his considerable intellect. Fahmy conveyed that Anwar Sadat was eager to have improved relations not only with the United States but with Israel as well. He made a crucially important point: for the first time Sadat did not tie improved relations with Israel to resolving the Palestinian issue.

The tone of Golda Meir's visit on October 31 was markedly different. Although obviously stressed by the effects of the war and its casualties, she was defiant, demanding guarantees about the peace process that the United States—or any other nation—could not give. She was bitterly against any additional supplies going to the surrounded Egyptian 3rd Army and vehemently rejected any suggestion that Israel withdraw to the admittedly indeterminate lines of October 22. Kissinger recognized her strategy. Rather than make any concessions that would have to be explained to an increasingly hostile Knesset, she wanted to be able to say that the United States had forced her to yield, particularly on the question of continued relief to the Egyptian 3rd Army.

Kissinger then renewed his shuttle diplomacy, with quick visits to Morocco and Tunisia before a historic breakthrough meeting with Anwar Sadat in Cairo on November 7. As improbable as it might seem given their hereditary backgrounds, Kissinger and Sadat liked and trusted each other from the start. After the usual diplomatic civilities, Kissinger put forward the following six-point plan:

1. Both Egypt and Israel were to observe the UN cease-fire.

2. Discussions under the auspices of the United Nations would begin immediately on the return to the positions occupied on October 22.

3. The town of Suez would be supplied with food, water, and medicine, and all wounded civilians would be evacuated.

4. Nonmilitary supplies could be moved without restraint to the east bank.

5. UN observers would take over the Israeli checkpoints. Israeli officers could check the flow of supplies to the east bank to ensure that no military supplies were included.

6. As soon as the UN checkpoints were established, there would be an immediate exchange of all prisoners of war.

Sadat accepted this plan, emphasizing only that it was not an agreement with Israel but one with the United States. Kissinger immediately dispatched envoys to Israel, where after much deliberation and many counterarguments this plan was finally formally accepted on November 11.

Despite this agreement, the situation required Kissinger's close attention from January 11 to January 17, 1974, as he shuttled back and forth from Tel Aviv to Cairo to ensure that the critical agreement on the disengagement of forces was signed. On January 18, Israel agreed to withdraw all its forces from the west bank to a line fifty kilometers to the east of the Suez Canal. In exchange, the Egyptian armies were brought back to the west bank. For Israel, the most important result of the agreement was the immediate exchange of prisoners of war. Two hundred and forty-one Israelis were exchanged for 8,031 Egyptians.

Sadat was allowed to retain his greatest achievement, a six-to-ten-kilometer-wide zone on the east bank. Egyptian forces were to be limited to six batteries of 122mm artillery, seven thousand soldiers, and thirty tanks. A UN buffer zone thirty kilometers wide separated the Egyptian forces from Israeli units of similar size. The United States made regular reconnaissance flights in the area and distributed the information resulting from the flights to both Israel and Egypt. The following year, the Israeli forces were withdrawn to a line connecting the famous Gidi and Mitla passes, ranging from thirty-three to sixty-six kilometers farther east. (Israel agreed to this withdrawal in depth only after receiving a promise for, among other things, massive arms shipments that would include the McDonnell Douglas F-15 and General Dynamics F-16 fighters.)

Syria's Hafiz Assad proved to be far tougher to negotiate with than Sadat. The first and perhaps critical breakthrough came on February 27, 1974, when Assad agreed to provide the names of the sixty-five Israelis being held as prisoners of war—and gave assurance that all were alive and well. This news, so well received in Tel Aviv, ultimately led to a disengagement agreement on May 31, 1974, after another series of shuttle flights by Kissinger. Israel retained the Golan

Heights, but a buffer zone was established to separate the two opposing forces, which were to be limited and equal.

Sadat would expand upon his leadership role, risking Arab support by offering to visit Israel to make an address in Jerusalem. He did so on November 20, 1977, and while his speech offered no new proposals, it did prepare the stage for future negotiations. On September 17, 1978, Sadat, Israeli Prime Minister Menachem Begin, and U.S. President Jimmy Carter signed the Camp David Accord, which provided a framework for a peace treaty between Egypt and Israel, to be signed within three months. The accord called for Israel to withdraw all its armed forces from the Sinai, while Egypt agreed to allow Israel right of free passage of ships through the Gulf of Suez, the Suez Canal, the Straits of Tiran, and the Gulf of Aqaba.

The Camp David Accord was violently opposed by other Arab nations, but on March 26, 1979, Sadat and Begin signed a peace treaty at the White House. The treaty gave Israel full diplomatic recognition by Egypt and allowed Egypt to reoccupy, in stages, the Sinai, the last area being turned over in 1982. The treaty was a step forward, but much resentment remained, and the problem of Palestine has proved to be impossible to solve.

With the peace treaty signed, it became possible to assess the results of the October War. While it is not surprising that errors were committed both at the beginning and during the war, it is perhaps a little strange that when it finally ended most of the participants, whether combatants or superpowers, should draw the wrong conclusions about the results. Further, the war would have exactly the opposite effects on the governments of the participants than might have been predicted.

Among the participants, Anwar Sadat was the one man whose goals for the October War had been achieved, albeit at great cost and at tremendous risk. He had been aware of the military superiority of the Israelis, including their possession of nuclear weapons, and nonetheless had made a decision to go to war to achieve limited aims. Sadat's decision was so impressive that, as previously noted, during Kissinger's visit to Tel Aviv, Golda Meir called Sadat the hero for daring to begin the war with limited means and limited aims and to completely foil Israeli intelligence. Her assessment was exactly correct, for Sadat was the only leader of all the powers involved who saw the war achieve his aims, albeit at tremendous sacrifice.

Furthermore, Sadat had gone to war to establish the credibility of Arab arms by smashing the Israeli reputation for invincibility and, after seizing a limited strip of territory, to use the superpowers to force Israel into negotiations. To achieve this he did two bits of masterful planning. The first was the recognition that he could offset superior Israeli airpower and armor by relying on a superabundance of Soviet-supplied missiles. The second was the creation of a sophisticated plan that capitalized upon Israeli arrogance and their inability to believe that Sadat would attempt a war with limited aims.

Sadat made major mistakes as well, two with Syria. He erred in not telling Syria of his intentions to fight a strictly limited war. Within days he had lost all credibility with a man he greatly admired, Syria's President Assad. (For his part, Assad had surprised Sadat with his almost immediate request for a cease-fire.) More important, Sadat violated his own plan by attempting to aid Syria with the ill-fated October 14 offensive in the Sinai, important as this was to Arab solidarity after the war. Other major mistakes included his refusal to accept a cease-fire early on and his adamant order that "not a soldier, not a rifle" be withdrawn from the east bank to counter the Israeli crossing. Fortunately for him and for Egypt, he salvaged his errors by barely maintaining a presence on the east bank and simultaneously working both superpowers into achieving a cease-fire.

At the end of the war, Sadat was recognized throughout the Arab world as a leader who had done what Nasser had not. He had demonstrated the prowess of Arab arms and redeemed Arab honor. More important from the U.S. perspective, he had moved Egypt out of the Soviet orbit and under the wing of the United States. He had, at great cost, accomplished much of what he had set out to do.

In contrast, most of Israel's goals were not met, although the war had ended in a military victory. Israel had not wanted a war but had become so convinced of its own superiority that it did not do what was necessary to avoid war. In many ways, as Dr. George W. Gawrych has said, the overwhelming victory of the 1967 Six-Day War proved to be an albatross that almost doomed Israel in 1973. Gawrych, a distinguished historian on the faculty of the U.S. Army Command and General Staff College, asserts that the victory created a mystique of invincibility about the IDF that was believed not only by the military but also by the politicians and the public.[1]

As we have seen before and during that bloody October, Israeli hubris led to many errors. Fortunately for Israel, her citizen-soldiers fought magnificently to redress the balance, and Golda Meir captured their tenacity when she said that while the Arabs were fighting for conquest, the Israelis were fighting for a continuation of their way of life. In her heart, Meir knew that the Arabs were fighting for pride as well.

Syria, which had planned little more than a smash-and-grab raid on the Golan Heights, had been deceived by Sadat as badly as had the Israelis. Its armed forces fought much better than ever before, and it is probable that the issue on the Golan Heights might not have been settled as early as it was had there not been the Israeli threat to use nuclear weapons. Had Sadat responded positively to Assad's early request for a cease-fire, the postwar negotiations would have found the Arab world in a far stronger position than that on October 25.

The superpowers made an equivalent number of mistakes that were remarkable for their similarity. Neither the United States nor the Soviet Union wanted a war in the Middle East, and neither had any intention of intervening militarily. Both nations expected the Israelis to win another quick victory, and both were stunned by the Arab successes. Perhaps most important, and most inexplicable, was the fact that neither nation had a real conception of the other nation's internal political requirements in regard to the war and its outcome.

The rest of the world was not excluded from the privilege of making mistakes. It would have been wiser for NATO nations to have supported the United States and put on a united front in the face of the Arab oil embargo. Once they had sensed the panic, the OPEC nations knew that there was virtually no limit on their actions. They succeeded with the capitalist dream: cutting production to create a shortage, but raising prices so much that profits continued to increase. Yet the Arab nations were not able to control themselves, greed induced more production, and the oil embargo soon lost much of its effect.

At the political level, the results were just the opposite of what might have been expected. Sadat and Assad had once again been defeated, but they had lost gloriously and were more firmly in power than ever. Sadat would, in the sad fashion of Arab politics, lose his life to assassination in 1981 but he would be succeeded by the man he had picked to be his Vice President, Hosni Mubarak. Assad would remain firmly in control until his death from natural causes on June 20, 2000, and was succeeded by his son, Bashar.

Things went less well for Israeli leaders. A commission of inquiry headed by the president of the Israeli Supreme Court, Shmuel Agranat, was established one month after the cease-fire. The commission deliberated for four months and submitted a preliminary report to Golda Meir on April 1, 1974. The voluminous report, later called the Agranat Report, was classified and only released in part.

The commission took direct aim at the IDF high command but skirted criticism of the political leaders. It stated that the responsibility for the surprise attack and the inability to quickly mobilize reserves centered on two senior officers. The first was the intelligence chief, Major General Eli Zeira, whose blind adherence to his own conception of enemy action prevented him from seeing the obvious preparations for attack. Zeira was criticized for his overconfidence and his method of presenting a single opinion rather than a range of possible alternatives and his monopoly on the intelligence business. The commission recommended that Zeira and his principal assistants resign and that the intelligence function be taken out of the supervision of the IDF. Zeira and his staff were ousted, but the latter recommendation was ignored.

Lieutenant General David Elazar also was found guilty of negligence, having acted with insufficient caution on the basis of the information that he had. The commission believed that Elazar should have ordered a partial mobilization as early as October 1 and claimed that he failed to coordinate the plans of the IDF and the IAF. He was also censured for the slow pace of the initial mobilization.

The Agranat Report had some kind words for Elazar as well, stating: "He served the state with devotion and distinction for many years and had a record of glorious achievements in the Six-Day War and earlier. It is public knowledge that, despite the critical situation during the first stages of the fighting, the chief of staff led the IDF through the containment battles on to the enemy's doorstep."

Nonetheless, Elazar resigned immediately. He would die less than two years later of what his many loyal friends said was a broken heart.

Golda Meir (of whom it was said that she regarded herself as "the only virile man in her cabinet") was even more emphatic in her praise of Elazar. She backed him all through the war and said that she believed that he never made an error in the conduct of operations.

The commission made a point of looking into charges that Major General Ariel Sharon had been undisciplined and even insubordinate. They found that the charges were unsubstantiated and that he had performed exactly as an officer should have performed under the circumstances. Their decision would have long-range implications for the twenty-first century, when the recalcitrant Sharon would become Prime Minister. Had they censured him, his political future would have been clouded forever. As it was, he suffered from the results of the Israeli invasion of Lebanon in 1982, intended to prevent the Palestine Liberation Organization from staging terrorist raids. The Israelis were successful in defeating the Syrian-backed forces but ultimately had to withdraw in 1985.

Despite the commission's refusal to assign blame to the political leadership, public opinion was inflamed by the harsh treatment accorded the military leaders. There was particular criticism of Dayan for failing to resign along with Elazar, to show his support.

Meir was reelected before the Agranat Report was released, but her grip on her party was slipping, and she ultimately decided to resign on June 4, 1974. Her cabinet resigned with her, but the irrepressible Dayan would be rehabilitated, returning to serve as Foreign Minister under Prime Minister Menachem Begin in 1977.

In the United States, the successful conclusion of the fighting in the Middle East, in great part due to the efforts of Henry Kissinger, could do nothing to stem the tide of the Watergate scandal. President Nixon resigned on August 9, 1974. He was succeeded by Vice President Gerald Ford, who retained Henry Kissinger as Secretary of State.

In Moscow, the Politburo viewed the ending of the Middle East war as a triumph for Leonid Brezhnev's policies and consolidated his position, even though it recognized that Egypt had moved closer to the United States. It would take time, but by 1977 Brezhnev had demolished the troika by dismissing both Kosygin and Podgorny. He would hold supreme power until his death in 1982.

As for the competing airlifts, the Soviet Union and the United States both did well. The biggest difference was that the airlift to Israel was absolutely critical for its survival and eventual military victory, while the airlift to the Arab states was neither so vital nor so well utilized. The Arab states possessed more people and more resources and had been stockpiling for war, and their supplies, with the exception of tanks, were never so critically short as those of the Israelis. Most, if not all, of the Soviet-bloc replacement tanks came by ship rather than by air.

Operation Nickel Grass proved to be an outstanding success, although, paradoxically, once started, it was just business as usual for MAC. The operative words here are "once started," for the United States was so confident of a quick Israeli victory that an airlift seemed almost unnecessary, and certainly nothing to be rushed into. However, when the chips were down and the decision made, all resources were thrown into it. The airlift results were quite remarkable. Kenneth L. Patchin's recently declassified monograph *Flight to Israel* reveals that the airlift continued for thirty-two days, not ending officially until midnight on November 14, 1973. In that time, 567 aircraft off-loaded 22,300 tons of matériel at Tel Aviv. This compared with 935 Soviet missions that off-loaded about 15,000 tons to Egypt and Syria during a forty-day period. The average MAC aircraft had flown a total of 6,450 miles from on-load to off-load, with the last 3,145 miles being the important Lajes-to-Lod leg of the trip. Soviet routes averaged about 1,700 miles. Overall, the Soviets sent about 100,000 tons of war matériel to their Arab clients, some 85,000 tons by ship. The United States sent about 51,000 tons, and of this about 28,000 tons moved by ship.

The airlift cost the citizens of the United States just over $50 million. The cost of the matériel that was transported was perhaps $10 billion. While most of the airlift cargo consisted of munitions and other military consumables, about 10 percent, or 2,264 tons, was devoted to "outsize" equipment that could be accommodated by no airplane in the world except the Lockheed C-5A Galaxy. This outsize equipment included nineteen M-60 tanks, sixty-three M-48 Chaparral Guided Missile Systems, sixty-four Sikorsky CH-53 helicopters, and nineteen Douglas A-4 fuselage and tail sections. After years of controversy, the C-5A proved itself beyond all doubt and would continue to do so for decades to come.

Unfortunately, there is a tendency on the part of some contemporary Jewish historians to downplay the key role of the airlift in helping save Israel in the Yom Kippur War. This runs completely counter to the evaluations made at the time and later by such disparate individuals as Dado Elazar, Anwar Sadat, and Moshe Dayan. Perhaps the definitive characterization of the importance of the airlift was made by Golda Meir herself, in a meeting in Washington some three weeks after the cease-fire. She told a group of Jewish leaders that "for generations to come, all will be told of the miracle of the immense planes from the United States bringing in the matériel that meant life to our people."

The men of the airlift were proud of their accomplishments and went on to continue to lead productive lives. Before General Carlton retired in 1977, he used the lessons learned in Operation Nickel Grass to great effect within the USAF. Aerial refueling became an important component of MAC training, and the requirement for an en route stop such as Lajes was eliminated forever. He insisted that the jigs and tooling for the C-5 be preserved (such equipment is usually destroyed at the end of a production run), and this permitted the production of an additional vitally needed fifty C-5Bs in 1985. But his most important contribution was in using his knowledge to solve the communication problems, and a lack of central authority might have hopelessly compromised Nickel Grass if Carlton and others had not worked well together. Based on Carlton's recommendations, MAC was designated a "specified command," a title that meant the USAF had control of all joint forces within MAC, and Carlton was named the first Commander in Chief, reporting directly to the Office of the Secretary of Defense. This organizational change made any future Nickel Grass a much easier proposition.

Carlton retired in 1977 and became a consultant to both McDonnell Douglas and Martin Marietta. He looks back kindly upon Operation Nickel Grass as an expression of the United States, and the USAF at its best, being turned to in emergency situation and delivering the goods.

Don Strobaugh's sterling work was recognized with an important job at 21st Air Force Headquarters before his retirement on June 30, 1976. Strobaugh stayed fit and continued his parachuting exploits. He finally and reluctantly retired from the sport after forty-five years and jumps in fifty-three countries.

Strobaugh cherishes Operation Nickel Grass for the memory of working with people who were fighting for their lives. He once asked about the manner in which Israeli officers threw themselves into battle without regard for casualties and got the reply: "When you're in a battle and can look over your shoulder and see your home and family, it makes you fight a little harder." Strobaugh felt this sense of urgency, and never more so than when "that little graying ex–Milwaukee schoolteacher" Golda Meir herself came to see the "great planes."

Many of the airlift crews returned to their home bases, where they retired. Harry Heist had a successful career in real estate before returning to his real love—MAC. Harry was helpful in establishing the Air Mobility Command Museum at Dover AFB and now serves there as archivist and keeper of the corporate memory. (MAC was subsumed by the Air Mobility Command in a 1992 reorganization.) Henry Baker came back to Dover as well and converted his flight engineering experience into the sales and installation of precision tooling. Like Carlton and Strobaugh, both men look upon Nickel Grass as the high point in their flying careers. All four would, at the sound of the fire bell, leap into their flying suits and do it all again.

And while Harry Cohen never got to fly for Israel, he did extend his flying experience in the United States. In the process he became a successful photographer and filmmaker whose duties sometimes gave him the opportunity to fly in air force aircraft. He still wishes he could have flown in combat in 1973—but he would not have missed being in Tel Aviv, if only to assemble beds and build pallets for Operation Nickel Grass cargo.

Appendix: Born in Battle

IN DECEMBER 1946 THE LABOUR government in Great Britain referred the Palestine issue to the United Nations. Great Britain's mandate had Palestine divided into Jewish and Arab parts; Transjordan absorbed the Arab part, thereby denying the Palestine Arabs their own state. Egypt did the same with Gaza.

The United Nations, anxious to establish itself as a peacemaker, proposed a partition of Palestine into Jewish and Arab states, with the wan hope that they would join in an economic union. Predictably the major Arab nations protested, but 55 percent of mandated Palestine territory was allocated to Israel, about eight thousand square miles. Two thousand square miles were divided between Transjordan and Egypt. Great Britain set a date of May 15, 1948, as the end of its mandate. When that date came, Palestine would cease to exist formally, but all of the old resentments and tensions remained in place.

Some seven hundred thousand Palestinians became refugees. Some stayed in Israel and eventually became citizens of the Jewish state. Most, however, wound up in refugee camps in neighboring Arab states, while others emigrated to other countries, especially those in the Persian Gulf. Among the Arab states, only Jordan offered citizenship freely to the Palestinian immigrants, yet at the same time Jordan refused to recognize a Palestinian identity. All the other Arab states steadfastly refused to accept the economic burden implicit in absorbing a Palestinian population, preferring to keep the refugees in camps for generations rather than give up a reason to fight Israel.

Civil war broke out immediately in what had been Palestine upon news of the partition, and the ragtag Jewish military, thrown together and equipped with a startling miscellany of arms, fought successfully to crush the Palestine Arab military forces. On May 15 the state of Israel was proclaimed. It was recognized at once by the United States and immediately invaded by the regular armies of Syria, Transjordan, Lebanon, Saudi Arabia, Iraq, and Egypt. These armies were poorly trained and led but advanced in seemingly overwhelming numbers. Their goal was the eradication of the Jewish state on the day it was born. Further, the Arabs had to take the offensive, a more difficult military option than remaining on the defensive. As in all but one of the later wars, the Arabs attacks were not coordinated. The Israelis resisted bitterly and in just ten days were ready to counterattack.[1]

The War of Independence, 1948–49

In terms of equipment, the initial odds were formidable. The combined Arab armies had fifteen tanks, 130 artillery pieces, 105 armored cars, and about forty aircraft. Against this the Israelis could field only some homemade armored cars—just trucks with armor plate bolted on—a few small-caliber mortars, and some antitank weapons.

The situation was soon redressed as money flowed in from the United States to purchase arms from those who would sell them, mainly Czechoslovakia, Italy, and Yugoslavia. By early spring the Czechs had sold Israel twenty-five fighters, two hundred heavy machine guns, many rifles, and tons of ammunition. At the same time, and more important, the fervor of Jewish patriotism saw no fewer than ninety thousand men and women under arms in what was now termed the Israel Defense Force, compared to the sixty-eight thousand Arab soldiers in the field. The Israeli forces included a small contingent of foreign volunteers and also received a great deal of foreign aid, which the Arabs did not.

The mutual incapacity of the combatants resulted in an

episodic war, a series of fierce, bloody clashes, the longest of which lasted for about a month. Long truces intervened between battles, and during these each side geared up for further combat.

Over time there was a steady improvement in the IDF's equipment and munitions while the Arab armies ran out of supplies of every kind. Without a unified war plan and beset by their own internal animosities, the Arab forces made piecemeal attacks in a very orthodox manner. By March 1949, when the armistice agreements were signed, only parts of the Arab forces remained intact. Had the Israelis not decided otherwise for political reasons, all of the Arab armies facing Israel could have been utterly crushed.

Israel immediately began preparing for the next war, for although armistices had been signed, there were no peace treaties. The brand-new country was in a position of inferiority to the Arab nations in terms of geography and numbers and would have to be prepared to fight to survive.

Israeli training was tough and the raw amateurism of the initial war for independence was soon replaced by professionalism of the highest order. This was particularly true in the IDF/IAF, which had quite literally been "born in battle" as a miscellaneous collection of aircraft and foreign volunteers made their contribution in the War for Independence.

Israel was small, less than 270 miles long at its extreme points and less than 15 miles wide at its narrowest point. Its economic growth was hampered by the welcome but challenging influx of immigrants in the years after 1948.

The metamorphosis of the IDF from a collection of competing terrorist squads to a highly effective military force was fostered by the appointment of the daring Moshe Dayan as Chief of Staff in December 1953.

286 Appendix: Born in Battle

Operation Kadesh: The Suez Canal Fiasco

Gamal Abdel Nasser, the president of Egypt, sought to become the leader of the Arab world by maintaining constant
pressure on Israel and defying the once-great colonial powers
Great Britain and France. Nasser sponsored fedayeen terrorist
attacks against Israel, closed the Red Sea's narrow Straits of
Tiran, and effected a military alliance with Syria. His military
movements were buttressed by massive infusion of Soviet aid,
principally heavy weapons. In 1955 Egypt received 200 armored troop carriers, 100 self-propelled guns, 230 tanks, 200
warplanes, 500 artillery pieces, and a miniature navy of de-
stroyers, submarines, and patrol boats. Soviet technicians began training the Egyptians in the use of the equipment in
what was the first extensive Soviet foothold in the Middle
East. For Moscow it was a dream come true: a position in the
Mediterranean.

The newfound strength and the promise implicit in the
Soviet ally gave Nasser courage. When the United States reneged on its promise to fund the Aswan Dam, he announced
on July 26, 1956, the nationalization of the Suez Canal and
the abrogation of the Anglo-Egyptian Treaty.

The blow to Anglo-French prestige was insufferable, and a
decision was made to retake the canal by a military operation.
Britain and France were aware that Israel had been forced into
planning a preemptive attack on Egypt. In response, Egypt,
Syria, and Jordan formed a joint military command to fight
Israel.

It must be made plain that Israel was not an innocent by-
stander in the world of politics. Israeli agents had bombed
both U.S. and British installations in Egypt as a part of plot
to tarnish Nasser's image.

The Israeli leadership decided in July 1956 that war was
inevitable and that they would launch it sometime that year.[2]
France and Great Britain secretly invited Israel to cooperate

in a joint operation. To Israel, isolated so long and surrounded by hostile forces, the invitation was truly as manna in the desert.

Great Britain initially was reluctant to participate, and the plan was continuously changed. It was decided that the Israelis were to invade Egypt, removing the threat of the growing Egyptian army in the Sinai Peninsula. They would attempt to destroy the structure of the fedayeen terrorists and, finally, secure freedom of navigation through the Straits of Tiran. Great Britain and France would react by demanding that all combatant forces pull back ten miles from the Suez Canal, knowing that it would be politically impossible for Nasser to comply with the ultimatum. The Franco-British forces would react to Nasser's refusal by bombing Egyptian airfields and capturing the canal. The attack was sanctioned by the terms of the 1955 Anglo-Egyptian Treaty, which specified that in time of war Britain had the right to seize the canal by force.

Sir Anthony Eden, after waiting in the wings for decades, had at last on April 6, 1955, succeeded his longtime mentor, Winston Churchill, as Britain's Prime Minister. Eden had been terribly embarrassed by Nasser's nationalization of the canal. Nonetheless, in this, Eden's first major international confrontation, he was forced to allowed Britain to waver for weeks before committing to war, because Britain was not prepared militarily to undertake the mission. Eden did not wish to be perceived as anti-Arab by the Jordanians and Saudi Arabians. He also wished to avoid damaging relations with either the United States or the Soviet Union.[3]

By late October, Great Britain perceived domestic difficulties in both of the latter two states and decided that it would now be possible to proceed with France. The U.S. presidential election was only weeks away, and Eden felt comfortable that President Eisenhower would take no major international action that might prejudice his reelection bid. To the east, Eden believed that the Soviet Union was too busy suppressing the rising tide of nationalism in both Poland and Hungary to take active exception to Great Britain asserting itself in an area that had long been within its sphere of interest.

Israel masked its preparations by stepping up border activity against Jordan so sharply that it received a note of warning from Great Britain that any escalation would bring the Royal Air Force into action on the side of the Jordanians. In the meantime, Israel began a series of actions that forecast the next two wars in two important ways. First, it would bring into prominence the men who would guide Israel's military destiny. Ironically, the same men who would win the greatest victories would also place Israel in deepest peril in 1973. Second, it would establish the IDF's modus operandi, by which the officers and high-ranking noncommissioned officers set personal examples of courage and leadership by leading their men up front and under fire. Their casualties were high, but they forged an indomitable esprit de corps.

At 3:00 in the afternoon on October 29, in what was characterized as a "major reprisal raid" for terrorist actions, a flight of four Israeli North American F-51 Mustangs flew across the Sinai a few feet off the ground, cutting Egyptian telephone lines with their propellers and wings. It was a dangerous but effective tactic, cutting off most of the Sinai landlines. Two hours later, sixteen Douglas C-47s dropped 395 men of the crack 202nd Parachute Brigade at the eastern entrance to the Mitla Pass, deep in the central Sinai.

The A Battalion of the 202nd was led by Lieutenant Colonel Rafael ("Raful") Eitan, a tough veteran who would become a brigadier general and a division commander on the Golan Heights by the time of the Yom Kippur War and later Chief of Staff of the IDF. The 202nd was commanded by another colorful character, then-Colonel Ariel ("Arik") Sharon. The solidly built, willful Sharon would have a turbulent military and political career lasting into the twenty-first century, when his walk to the Temple would precipitate a new round of violence and ultimately lead to his becoming Prime Minister. Sharon would be distinguished by great victories and near disasters, both resulting from his headstrong actions and life-long habit of disobeying orders. During the Yom Kippur War motives were constantly questioned and he was assigned tasks as often for political as military reasons. Even his ability as a field commander was questioned because of the losses that had befallen troops under his command.

The Egyptians swallowed the Israeli ploy, allowing them twenty-four hours to build up a supply line across the hostile Sinai desert. In the meantime, other Israeli forces swung into action, attacking the Egyptian stronghold at Abu Agelia on October 31. Another future star emerged as Lieutenant Colonel Avraham ("Bren") Adan first stopped the Egyptian forces, then surrounded them in a move worthy of Rommel. Egyptian resistance was strong, particularly in their heavy artillery barrages, but by November 2, after heavy hand-to-hand fighting, the Israelis had captured the position.

Egypt now understood that it was at war and was prepared for the next Israeli attack in Gaza, another fortress surrounded by minefields and well equipped with artillery of all sizes. Here, on October 31, then-Colonel Chaim Bar-Lev would lead the 27th Armored Brigade, in concert with the 1st Golani Infantry Brigade. Bar-Lev, a Yugoslavian, was a serious, almost severe individual whose slow speech pattern camouflaged his quick, decisive mind. He would become Chief of Staff in 1968 and lend his name to the fortified defensive line that would play an important role in 1973.

A complex but well-coordinated plan saw the 27th Armored and 1st Infantry Brigades join forces on the morning of November 1, shattering the Egyptian forces and clearing the way for an advance to Romani, just ten miles east of the Suez Canal. The rest of the Gaza Strip was cleared by an intense battle on November 2, by which time the Egyptians were ready to surrender not only their armed forces but also governance of the strip.

Israel next saw to its own interests by sweeping down 150 miles along the Gulf of Aqaba and even farther along the Gulf of Suez to surround the Sharm al-Sheikh. By November 5, the Egyptians had surrendered, the Sinai had been conquered, and the Straits of Tiran were open. Israel had fulfilled its promises to Great Britain and France. It had also established the basis for what it would perceive to be an invincible military force, as first-rate leaders came to the fore and superb tactics were created for desert warfare.

The Anglo-French Debacle

The British and French governments had opened their part of the grand plan by presenting the ultimatum calling for a withdrawal of both Egyptian and Israeli forces from both sides of the Suez Canal on October 31. They then made a massive attack on Egyptian air bases, destroying more than a hundred aircraft. The Allied task force set sail from Malta on November 1. Paratroops were dropped on November 5, and the invasion took place the following day.

The UN Security Council attempted to bring about a general cease-fire, but such efforts were vetoed twice by both the British and French representatives, despite growing political opposition to intervention in Egypt in their home countries. Contrary to Eden's expectations, the United States and the Soviet Union vigorously expressed their strong disapproval of the Anglo-French action, and by the night of November 6 Anthony Eden saw his legacy go up in smoke as Great Britain agreed to a humiliating cease-fire. France followed suit, and the comedy of the Anglo-French attempted seizure of the Suez Canal was over.[4]

The inept performance by Great Britain and France even included bombing the Suez Canal, their lifeline to the East. Despite this, their entry into the war had ratified Israel's actions in many ways. The opening of the Straits of Tiran and the ending of the terrorist raids across the Egyptian border was of immense benefit. Most of the territorial gains were diminished when the United Nations decided that a UN Emergency Force would replace Israeli control of Gaza and the Sharm al-Sheikh.

What could not be diminished was the stature of the Israeli armed forces and the innate conviction of the people of Israel that they had more defendable frontiers.

Ironically, the big winner of the war proved to be President Nasser, whose successful defense against the hapless British and French gave him virtually unlimited stature and prestige in the Arab world. The losses to Israel were explained away as a minor result of the major effort against France and England.

The Six-Day War, June 1967

Israel's 1956 victory did not mean peace in the Middle East, for both sides encroached on border areas and the long cycle of violence continued. In the headlines, open warfare was replaced by stories of the brutal political infighting. In Iraq, a bloody revolution deposed King Faisal and allowed the introduction of Soviet influence into the country for the first time. Civil war broke out in beautiful Lebanon, once the garden spot of the Middle East, beginning its long spiral toward devastation. Nasser capitalized on his position as defender against the West on February 1, 1958, by forming, with Syria, the United Arab Republic. This lasted only until 1961, when Syria reasserted its independence, but for a time it gave Egypt a base for operations against Israel denied by the presence of the UN forces on the Egypt-Israeli border.

At an Arab League summit meeting in Cairo in 1964, Syria, Jordan, and Lebanon agreed on a plan to divert tributary waters from the Jordan River and thus drastically reduce irrigation water available to Israel.[5] Only fierce attacks by Israeli forces on the engineering equipment being used to divert the rivers forced the plan to be dropped. Syria retaliated by using its dominating position on the Golan Heights to rain artillery fire on Israeli territory and sponsoring the newly organized PLO in its attacks on Israel. A series of pitched battles followed, including aerial dogfights that seriously depleted Syria's air force.

By May 1967 the glow of Nasser's glory had dimmed considerably, and he found himself at odds with much of the Arab world, including Yemen, Saudi Arabia, and Jordan. His failure to move to the assistance of Arab states involved in border clashes with Israel had made him a hollow figure.

Nonetheless, Syria now feared an attack by Israel and sought Nasser's assistance. It was a clear case of put up or shut up, and in a move to reestablish his popularity Nasser complied, moving seven divisions, with close to eighty-five thousand men and hundreds of tanks, to Israel's border. He next demanded that the UN Emergency Force stationed along the Sinai and Gaza Strip border withdraw, and, quite cravenly, it did so. Then, as a clear act of war, Nasser again declared the Straits of Tiran closed to Israel. To remove any remaining doubts, Nasser challenged Israel to attack Egypt.

King Hussein of Jordan quietly placed Jordan's armed forces under Nasser's command, and Iraq followed suit. Other Arab states sent contingents to demonstrate their solidarity upon the one issue about which all agreed: the destruction of Israel.

In this struggle, as in every previous instance, no international action was taken to inhibit the Arab aggression. The United States, Great Britain, and France had guaranteed the Israelis that they would open the Straits of Tiran if they were blocked by Egypt but made no effort to do so. France, so long involved in a struggle against the Arab world in Algeria, had for many years been much more than merely a supporter and a supplier of arms to Israel. Now President Charles de Gaulle, having withdrawn from Algeria, sought to curry favor with the Arab nations by cutting off the supply of weapons to Israel.

It was a time of clear-cut crisis, and the new Israeli Minister of Defense, Moshe Dayan, saw the situation as worse than that in 1956.[6] Once again, overwhelming Arab forces were massed on Israel's borders, and this time Egypt possessed a Soviet-equipped and -trained air force of 385 combat aircraft. These included the MiG-17, MiG-19, and MiG-21 fighters. The MiG-21 was built in greater numbers than any other jet fighter in the world and proved to be a worthy opponent of the United States in Vietnam. The older MiG-17s and -19s were slower but more rugged and maneuverable. Egypt had also built up a jet bomber force of Tupolev Tu-16 and Ilyushin Il-28 aircraft that could reach Tel Aviv within minutes after takeoff.

Israel properly regarded Egypt's army as the main threat, for it had now grown to more than 100,000 men, equipped with 900 tanks and more than 1,000 artillery pieces. The Syrian and Jordanian armies actually mustered more men—120,000—but they were neither well equipped nor well coordinated. Their air forces were considered a negligible threat. The Jordanian forces were better trained, reflecting their long, if onerous, relationship with Great Britain, but the Syrian soldiery were not up to the standards demanded by their modern weapons.

Israel was in a precarious position in regard to its leadership. The Prime Minister, Levi Eshkol, seemed strangely reluctant to confront Egypt.[7] (Eshkol also held the post of Minister of Defense, which he later surrendered to Moshe Dayan—a key move in Israel's ultimate position as a nuclear power.) Some sources indicate that Eshkol's uncertainty stemmed from the IDF Chief of Staff, Yitzhak Rabin, who was undergoing a crisis of confidence in his own stewardship and was particularly concerned about Israel's ability to meet the Egyptian forces in the southeast. Overstressed, Rabin collapsed and called on the charismatic former head of the IAF, Major General Ezer Weizman, to take his place. Weizman, a swashbuckler idolized by his airmen, refused to do so formally but "temporarily" assumed the position and, in doing so, paved the way to victory. Rabin had planned a mild response to Egypt's provocations, an incursion into the Gaza Strip. Weizman wanted far more. Tall, handsome, and an excellent pilot, he had commanded the IAF from 1956 to 1966 and had full knowledge of its capabilities.

Israel's air force had leaders who believed in the strategy of the first strike. Weizman was chief of these, of course, and he had struggled long and hard to have his protégé Brigadier General Mordechai "Moti" Hod named to replace him. The two men and their staffs had developed a series of plans calling for preemptive strikes.

First Strike

At 0700 hours (8:00 Egyptian time) the first wave of forty of the French-built fighter-bombers took off. At ten-minute intervals, nine more waves of forty aircraft took off for targets in Egypt. They flew in flights of four, one flight for each of the ten most important Egyptian airfields. Over the target, they would attack in pairs. The timing was deliberately chosen to catch the officer personnel of the EAF en route from their homes to what was to have been another normal day at the "office."

In the north, the Israeli Dassault Super Mystere B2 and Mirage IIIC fighter-bombers had flown low over the Mediterranean to avoid Arab radar. In the south, IDF/AF Dassault Ouragan and Mysteres did the same by following the floor of the desert terrain. The first flights all achieved surprise, hitting their targets at 0745. They dropped their bombs, made several strafing passes, then departed to refuel and rearm. The first-wave bombs were directed primarily at cratering the runways to prevent Egyptian aircraft from taking off. Ten minutes later, the second flights arrived over each of the damaged bases, now fully alarmed and looking like kicked-over anthills as fire trucks, rescue crews, and mechanics swarmed over the smoldering wreckage.

With surprise lost, the Israeli aircraft saved time on the following missions by flying direct routes and adding radar and SAM sites to the target list. The attack process varied with the target. If the runways were sufficiently damaged, the fuel storage and ammunition dumps became the focus of the bombs, while the strafing remained concentrated on aircraft. All ten flights would follow the same pattern, with the later flights having to pick and choose their targets more carefully from the smoking, debris-filled airfields.

The initial strafing attacks concentrated on the Tupolev Tu-16 and Ilyushin Il-28 bombers that constituted a threat to Israel's cities and airfields. Next on the priority lists were the delta wing MiG-21 interceptors, Mach 2 aircraft that were nominally superior to anything in the Israeli inventory. The remaining combat aircraft became targets of opportunity, vulnerable on the ramps, in revetments, and in the hangars.

Israeli ground crews worked miracles fueling and rearming the returning aircraft, so that by the end of the day the 220-odd principal strike aircraft had flown more than 1,000 missions. The Israelis claimed 308 aircraft destroyed, 240 of them Egyptian, while admitting to the loss of 14 primary combat aircraft and a handful of ancillary planes. On other fronts, the IAF inflicted severe losses on both the Syrian and Jordanian air forces.[8]

The Six-Day War was essentially decided in the first three hours of the first day, for the almost complete destruction of Arab air forces gave Israel total air superiority. This allowed Major General Yeshayahu Gavish to lead his ground forces to victory in the Sinai once again. IDF armor smashed into the Egyptian positions, and the IDF/IAF wreaked havoc on the long lines of retreating enemy armor. As the main body of Israeli forces rolled across the Sinai to the Suez Canal, a smaller force occupied the Gaza Strip after a fierce fight.

Israel now turned its attention to Syria and Jordan. By June 7, Jerusalem had fallen and control of the West Bank had been secured. King Hussein, who had insisted on war with Israel, was now eager to accept the UN cease-fire. Syria, which had observed with horror the success of the Israelis against Egypt, made so little effort to fight that the Syrian leaders were denounced as traitors by King Hussein. By June 10 Israeli forces had swept over the Golan Heights and occupied a commanding position above the Damascus plain.

Faced with a military debacle of unprecedented scale and wishing to end it as soon as possible to prevent further defeats, the Arab nations sullenly accepted the UN-imposed cease-fire at 1830 hours on June 10. The Six-Day War was over.

Results . . . and Effects

For the first time in its history, Israel no longer faced the threat of being overrun in a single day of battle. Its frontiers were expanded tremendously to the west, where the Sinai, formerly harboring a growing Egyptian threat, was now a buffer zone, and the Suez Canal became the most effective antitank trap in history—until 1973. The occupation of the Golan Heights reversed the strategic situation with Syria, and the control of the West Bank gave Israel breathing room in the east.

The great geographic advantage attained carried some powerful baggage with it. In the past, Israeli strategy had all been placed on seizing the initiative, preemptively if necessary, and then conducting blitzkrieglike air and ground operations. Now, with so much space, it became possible to think in defensive terms—a mind-set with which many Israeli leaders were not comfortable.

The costs to the Arab nations had been great. Some 452 aircraft had been destroyed, and more than 18,000 Arabs had been killed. The Israelis lost 46 aircraft and suffered 785 deaths. Arab matériel losses dwarfed those of Israel, whose armored strength actually grew as a result of captured Arab vehicles.

A totally unexpected effect of the war was to move the Middle East center stage alongside Vietnam in the ongoing Cold War confrontation between the United States and the Soviet Union. The Soviets, with their customary clumsy diplomatic techniques, reinforced the Arab states' decision not to reconcile with Israel and immediately began to reconstitute the Arab forces. In September 1967, at the Arab Summit Conference in Khartoum, the infamous "three nos" resolution was passed. The Arab leaders pledged that there would be no negotiations with Israel, no recognition of Israel, and no peace with Israel. Nasser would later add another "no"—"no concessions on the legitimate rights of the Palestinian people." This was perhaps the most hypocritical of all the proclamations, for the Arab states had done almost nothing on behalf of the Palestinian people. In the course of time, the Palestinian problem would result in armed conflict between Syria and Jordan.

There were many effects upon Israel, internal and external. France's President, Charles de Gaulle, placed an embargo on the sale of all arms to Israel and suspended delivery of fifty new Dassault Mirage V fighters that had already been paid for. This and the increased Soviet presence in the Arab world ensured that Israel would look to the United States to be both its patron and its arms supplier. Israel also began to vastly expand its indigenous arms industry.

No one could have foreseen it at the time, but this change coincided with a remarkable improvement in the quality of U.S. arms. Israel benefited by the introduction of first the relatively inexpensive Douglas A-4H Skyhawk and later the McDonnell F-4E Phantom aircraft. (General Weizman used to joke that the *H* in *A-4H* stood for "Hebrew.") These aircraft could carry up to six times the ordnance loads of the French airplanes they replaced. (Major General Chaim Herzog, author of one of the best books on the Arab-Israeli wars, claimed that the Phantom was the most important single weapon and that its receipt probably postponed an Egyptian invasion.) In addition, Israel was supplied with advanced electronic countermeasures equipment and other sophisticated weaponry. Had Israel remained tied to French weaponry, it not only would have been far less well served; it also could have been defeated in 1973.

Israel also made remarkable efforts to create its own fighter industry, redesigning existing aircraft to take more powerful engines and undertaking the design of an indigenous fighter.

Perhaps the most important conclusion from the Six-Day War was that the Israeli military leaders who had earned their spurs in 1956 had proved themselves once again in even higher positions in the political and military chains of command. They now quite properly considered themselves masters of warfare in the Middle East. They and the people of Israel would feel an overwhelming pride in their accomplishments. They had defeated an enemy far stronger in personnel and equipment and done so with negligible losses. Unfortunately for the future, much of this pride would become hubris and render Israel vulnerable in 1973.

The measure of U.S. and Israeli friendship was tested severely in the deliberate attack by Israeli fighters on the U.S. electronic intelligence ship the *Liberty* on June 8, 1967. Thirty-four crew members were killed, and 164 were wounded. Israel denied that the attack was premeditated, and for reasons of state those denials were accepted, if not believed.

For the Arabs, the situation was just the reverse. President Nasser was totally humiliated, going so far as to make obviously specious charges that the Israeli air attacks had actually been flown by French, British, or U.S. pilots. The Arab military leaders were ashamed of their own performance and that of their troops. From this point on both their allies and their enemies would have doubts about the Arabs' military capacity.

Changing this impression became one of Nasser's major

goals. He sought to create a more reliable and efficient army by embracing the Soviet Union, its equipment, and its method of training.

Nasser and Egypt were not alone. All of the Arab nations learned from their mistakes and made serious efforts to improve their performance over the next decade and demonstrated their proficiency in what became known as the "War of Attrition." This almost continuous conflict varied in intensity from periods of calm to those of all-out warfare and lasted from July 1, 1967, until the August 8, 1970, cease-fire between Egypt and Israel.

The War of Attrition: July 1967 to August 1970

The bitter Spanish Civil War of 1936–39 had served as a testing ground for the weapons of Germany and Italy on the Nationalist side and the Soviet Union on the Republican side. During the War of Attrition, the Middle East served in a similar manner for the weaponry of the United States and the Soviet Union. For much of the time, this testing appeared to be of far greater benefit to the Arabs and the Soviet Union than to their opponent. Only in the most crucial moment of the later Yom Kippur War did the reverse prove to be true.

While individual incidents were reported in the media, the three-year-long War of Attrition attracted relatively little attention outside of the Middle East. The almost continuous flow of guerrilla raids, artillery barrages, and air raids blended in anonymously with the general background of violence in the Middle East. The United States in particular was almost totally preoccupied with the agonizing war in Southeast Asia, and there seemed to be little new in the protracted Arab-Israeli struggle.

In fact, there was much new. Warfare in the Middle East was being revolutionized with implications for the entire world. Almost every sort of weapon short of biological or chemical warfare was engaged. The Egyptians employed heavy artillery in accordance with Soviet doctrine, having been supplied with many cannons and lavish supplies of ammunition. A touch of the future was seen when Egyptian Komar-class patrol boats used Soviet-built surface-to-surface Styx missiles to sink Israel's largest warship, the destroyer *Eliat*. A subsonic missile with a twenty-eight-mile range, it carried a 1,102-pound warhead and had active radar terminal guidance.

An even more potent harbinger of the future was the Egyptian integrated defense network, the most efficient in the Middle East. It combined a continually growing number and variety of SAMs with radar-directed antiaircraft guns. New combat aircraft were employed, bringing the most advanced Soviet and U.S. aircraft into conflict. The Israelis upgraded their own tanks and equipped units with more than two hundred Soviet T-54 and T-55 tanks captured in 1967.

Each new weapon and each new incident triggered another hostile event, each time raising the ante, following a pattern that would lead to the brink of full-scale war. It was Israel's practice to respond to each Arab attack with a massive counterstroke. At first these produced the desired results, a temporary slackening of Egyptian provocations. When Egypt again attacked, Israel would retaliate once more at a level of intensity far surpassing the Egyptian. Eventually this seesaw process reached such an intolerable level that Egyptian leaders decided that, given the level of Israeli responses, there was no point in mere individual attacks and there might as well be full-scale warfare.

The War of Attrition ultimately proved to be immensely important, for it fundamentally altered the balance of power in the Middle East and almost led to the destruction of Israel. It introduced the Cold War directly into the middle of the Arab-Israeli hot war, and for the first time actions in the Middle East carried with them the very real possibility of escalation to a nuclear exchange between the United States and the Soviet Union. Less apparent but still starkly real was the potential for Israel to use its own nuclear weapons.

Further, the War of Attrition's series of actions and reactions tended to trigger unintended consequences important far beyond the Middle East. The leaders of both the Soviet Union and the United States were absorbed in the delicate diplomatic waltz leading to détente, and they were all too aware that problems in the Middle East could scuttle their efforts in an instant. They attempted to create a safety valve by backing the UN Resolution 242, passed on November 22, 1967, very early in this protracted conflict. Resolution 242 called for Israel to withdraw from captured Arab territory. In exchange, the Arab nations were required to acknowledge the existence of the state of Israel. Both sides were to solve the problem of the Palestinian refugees and to establish demilitarized zones. Resolution 242 had no appeal to either side but would be a key element in diplomatic maneuvers for many years to come.

The Soviets Move In, Bag and Baggage

An essential factor in the War of Attrition was the massive way the Soviet Union moved into Egypt and Syria, completely reequipping and reorganizing their armies so that they soon were as strong as they had been in the summer of 1967. As usual, the Soviet Union came with a heavy hand, demanding much for its assistance and doing little to adapt to the ways of a client state.

Just as the United States had raised the level of Israeli equipment, so did the new Soviet arms impart a higher level of technology to the Egyptians. Some 550 of the latest T-54 and T-55 tanks, considered by many to be the best in the world, were supplied along with more than 130 late-model jet fighters, mostly MiG-21s. More than 750 pieces of artillery, along with 200 mortars and a virtually unlimited supply of ammunition, provided Egypt with incredible firepower. By the spring of 1970, there were more than 20,000 Soviet military in Egypt, including those who manned the dozens of new SAM sites and about 150 "volunteer" pilots who flew the fighter aircraft.

The 1967 war had been immensely costly to Egypt, with estimates running as high as $800 million in damage and lost business opportunities. In the long run, this was more than offset by the $250 million in annual subsidies provided by the wealthy Arab states and the Soviet Union. The infusion of equipment, training, and wealth helped the Egyptian army recover its strength. Nasser soon put it to work harassing the Israelis all along the Suez Canal, formally announcing a "war of attrition" in the process. Given that the Arab nations outnumbered Israel by some 55 million to 3 million, attrition made sense.

The Egyptian army now used its powerful artillery to deluge Israeli positions along the canal with shell fire. The Israelis could not respond in kind, for they had emphasized procurement of tanks and aircraft as the preferred weapons, at the expense of obtaining adequate artillery and other supporting equipment such as APCs. Instead, after July 1969 the IAF launched thousands of sorties against artillery and radar installations and began long-range surgical strikes in the heart of the Nile Valley against bridges, electric power centers, and other important targets.

The Israelis had three mission objectives. The first was to destroy the radar sites and the artillery and SAM batteries. The second was to make comprehensive attacks on all elements of the air defense system, including missile sites and antiaircraft positions. Third, Israel wanted to develop intelligence on the Soviet systems being used by Egypt so that their capability could be assessed and effective electronic countermeasures be developed to defeat them.

Egypt attempted to counter by establishing an Air Defense Command,[9] equipped with thirty batteries of SA-3 SAM sites and more than a thousand antiaircraft guns. Several squadrons of MiG-21 interceptors supplemented these. And, unlike in 1967, the Egyptians now protected their aircraft in concrete shelters.

Initially, Israel's decision to use its air force as "flying artillery" in lieu of building up a more powerful artillery arm seemed to pay dividends. Daring raids deep inside Egypt disconcerted the Egyptian public and were said to be the direct cause of one of Nasser's heart attacks. Israeli aircraft flew more than three thousand sorties by April 1970, dropping eight thousand tons of ordnance, much of it near and around Cairo. The sheer weight of Israeli effort knocked out 80 percent of the Egyptian air defense system and secured air superiority. The Israelis could now fly almost with impunity throughout the length and breadth of Egypt. (Not without cost to the Israeli airmen, who, if captured, were sentenced on Nasser's orders to life imprisonment without the possibility of pardon. Egyptian prisons were not country clubs.)

This dominance permitted tactical excursions by Israeli armored forces to cross the Gulf of Suez and run riot down the Egyptian coast. In another instance, Israeli Sikorsky S-65C-3 helicopters were able to fly deep within Egypt and physically remove seven tons of the latest Soviet P-12 "Bar Lock" ground control and interception radar from Ras Ghareb on December 26, 1969. This coup was of immense value to the Israelis and to the United States and a haunting humiliation to the Egyptians and the Soviet Union.

To offset the Egyptian advantage in artillery, the Israelis had adopted a plan of static defense that was entirely foreign to their previous operations. Amid violent argument, a decision was made by Lieutenant General Bar-Lev to build a defensive system in the Sinai that would withstand the artillery attacks with minimum Israeli casualties. As usual, Major General Ariel Sharon opposed the plan, advocating the use of armor only, deployed in depth. He and his cohort Major General Israel Tal were overruled.

The system of fortifications that became known as the Bar-Lev line was the result of a study headed by Major General "Bren" Adan.[10] It was not a defensive position in the sense that the Maginot Line was, a barrier intended to repel all attacks. It was instead intended to provide observation posts that could watch the Suez Canal visually by day and electronically at night.

Nonetheless, it was the largest engineering project in Israel's short history, costing $500 million. It consisted of thirty-one fortifications located about seven miles apart and manned by fifteen to sixty troops. The forts were supported by patrol roads, earth walls, and underground control centers. Tank and artillery positions were sited for mutual support. Mobile armor formations were tasked to patrol between the forts, and reserves of armor and artillery were kept in depots in the rear. A sand barrier, sometimes thirty feet high, was erected along the Israeli side of the canal to prevent Egyptian amphibious vehicles from scaling the banks. The essential features of the line were completed by March 15, 1969, but work on its support systems continued from then on.

Israel was also pressed to defend its other frontiers. Lebanon, which had been peaceful for years, now provided a base for PLO terrorists. In Syria, the regular Syrian army conducted artillery barrages and the PLO mounted raids into Israel.

The Israelis reacted vigorously to the PLO incursions, but ironically, it would be Jordan's army that would put an end to PLO cross-border raids on Israel. King Hussein became increasingly concerned that the PLO forces had grown so strong that they constituted a threat to the monarchy. When the PLO hijacked three Western airliners, flew them to Jordan, and then blew them up, he knew he had to act or see Yasir Arafat take over his country. On September 15, 1969, Hussein ordered his artillery and tanks to fire on the PLO refugee camps, butchering them without mercy and sending the survivors to flee across the River Jordan to seek safety with the IDF.

Unintended Consequences

Both the Bar-Lev line and the relentless Israeli air attacks had unintended consequences. The other Arab nations were upset that Egypt had allowed the Israelis to fortify the east bank of the Suez Canal and openly expected Nasser to correct the situation. The Soviet satellite nations were disturbed that the same Soviet air defense equipment set up in their defense was unable to keep the Israeli aircraft from using Egypt as a bomb range. This forced the Soviet Union to furnish Egypt with an even greater supply of modern SAMs and radars.

The air defense problem was mitigated somewhat in April 1970 when the Israelis became aware that Soviet pilots had effectively relieved Egypt of its home defense mission. The IAF made a decision to stop its long-range incursions to avoid a confrontation. However, the Soviet pilots then began flying near the Suez Canal, becoming involved in a number of dog-fights with Israeli pilots.

Pressure from all sides was placed on Nasser to resolve the issue with a full-scale invasion. He agreed with this idea but wished to extend the increasingly elaborate Soviet air defense system so that it would protect the forces that would cross the canal. The plan was to have a complex array of SA-2 Guideline long-range missiles, SA-3 Goa intermediate-range missiles and radar-directed ZSU 23-4M antiaircraft guns placed far forward to protect the artillery emplacements along the Suez Canal and to provide coverage for any cross-canal operations. By July 1970 the new missile sites were in place and began exacting a heavy toll of Israeli fighters. Israeli intelligence indicated that the SA-3 sites were manned entirely by Soviet personnel, while the SA-2 sites were manned by Egyptians with Soviet supervision.

On August 8, 1970, a cease-fire initiated by U.S. Secretary of State William Rogers[11] was at last agreed to, and it brought about the first period of relative quiet since the Six-Day War.

During the War of Attrition, thousands of rounds of artillery shells had been exchanged. Thousands of Egyptians and hundreds of Soviets and Israelis had been killed or wounded. The Arab nations lost about 115 airplanes, to an Israeli loss of 35. Despite his signing the agreement, there is every indication that Nasser intended to invade Israel in the fall of 1970, fulfilling his promises to his Arab allies. This was not to be, for he suffered a fatal heart attack on September 28.

Nasser was succeeded by Anwar Sadat, a man relatively unknown in the West. Sadat was regarded by many as inadequate for the job and was expected to hold the position only until a stronger candidate came along. Instead, Sadat proved to be an extremely strong individual, with an excellent grasp of the situation, and perhaps the only Arab leader who could see a way to break Israel's hold on occupied Arab lands.

Relative quiet ensued for the next three years. Most people view the War of Attrition as a victory for Egypt, even though there were far more Egyptian than Israeli casualties. More than anything else, the War of Attrition was a training ground for the Yom Kippur War, one in which the Arabs learned much and one from which the Israelis failed to draw the correct conclusions.

Acknowledgments

THIS WAS FOR MANY REASONS A VERY difficult book to write, for there were almost as many points of view as there were sources. Each and every event was recorded in several ways and remembered in many more. On three separate occasions I told my fine and helpful agent, Jacques de Spoelberch, that I thought I would give up.

Fortunately, however, there were so many people helping me that each time I not only went on but also gathered more enthusiasm for the project, which represents not only war at its worst but people at their best.

There are a number of people whose help was absolutely fundamental. I owe a tremendous debt to the excellent work Kenneth L. Patchin did as a historian at what was then the Military Airlift Command in compiling *Flight to Israel*. This compelling and so-long-classified history of Operation Nickel Grass reveals not only the events of the airlift but also the various political hazards and motivations behind them. Ken also very kindly reviewed my completed manuscript. The *Flight to Israel* history was made available to me by Dr. James K. Matthews and Margaret Nigra of the U.S. Transport Command.

In a similar way, I was fortunate to have the original journal compiled by the USAF ALCE commander at Lod International Airport, Colonel Donald Strobaugh, and also his review of my manuscript. Thanks to Museum Director Michael Leister's help and the diligence of archivist Lieutenant Colonel Harry Heist, (Ret.) I was able to muster the full support of the excellent Air Mobility Command Museum at Dover Air Force Base, Delaware. Harry was particularly helpful in obtaining an excellent selection of photos and in commenting on the intricacies of high-speed navigation during wartime.

The indomitable Kenneth K. Robertson Jr., the author of the very fine monograph *Operation Nickel Grass,* not only gave me free access to his material but also arranged for several important meetings and briefings and then faithfully reviewed my manuscript. Ken is a true historian, and his interest in Nickel Grass has brought much to light over the years.

Harry and Ken arranged for me to meet many of the original crew members of the Yom Kippur airlift, and they very kindly provided me with memories, photographs, and fact checking. They included Lieutenant Colonel David Wilson, Kenneth Smith, and H. John Royston and Senior Master Sergeant Byron "Hank" Baker.

An excellent writer and historian himself, Lon Nordeen was extremely helpful in supplying difficult-to-obtain and only recently declassified material on both the Israeli and Egyptian forces, as well as providing free use of material from his own fine books *Phoenix over the Nile* (coauthored with David Nicole), *Fighters over Israel,* and *Air Warfare in the Missile Age.* Lon used a wire brush on my manuscript and saved me from several errors, for which I thank him.

I owe an equally great debt to Dr. George W. Gawrych, author of *The Albatross of Decisive Victory—War and Policy Between Egypt and Israel in the 1967 and 1973 Arab-Israeli Wars.* Besides steering me to material that I would not have found otherwise, George took time from his busy schedule to review my manuscript and make absolutely vital critical comments. I will be forever in his debt.

A colleague and collaborator for many years, Philip Handleman was kind enough to give me the benefit of his knowledge of the subject and to carefully and thoughtfully review the manuscript. Yosseff "Seffy" Bodansky, an international authority on foreign affairs, encouraged me with the book, provided me excellent sources, and reviewed my manuscript.

I also received significant help from interviews with General Paul K. Carlton, who commanded MAC during Operation Nickel Grass. In addition, I received valuable inputs from Walter Baade, Major Sam McGowan, Charles Simpson, and General Harley Hughes.

Dr. George Watson at Air Force History was, as always, extremely helpful in obtaining declassified but difficult-to-find material and commented on sections of the book. All of the people at the National Archives Still Photo Section were unbelievably helpful; if you ever want to see the best and most efficient of government operations, just avail yourself of their services. The people at the Israeli National Photo Collection were also very helpful and forthcoming. Major General Mahmoud Moawad, Egyptian Defense, Military, Air, and Naval Attaché, was extremely courteous and helpful. Wally Meeks, as always, had good suggestions and ideas. Also making valuable contributions were Colonel William Dickey and Charles Dickens.

Many words of thanks must go to the fine people at St. Martin's Press. My editor, Sean Desmond, made excellent suggestions, and his editorial cuts were always on the mark. Thanks also to Thomas Dunne and Pete Wolverton, who are always patient, courteous, enthusiastic, and helpful.

Many other people helped, and if I have forgotten to mention your name, please forgive me but know that I appreciate your assistance.

Notes

Chapter 1: Hubris and the October War

1. Martin Van Creveld, *The Sword and the Olive: A Critical History of the Israeli Defense Force* (New York: Public Affairs, 1998), p. 105.
2. John L. Frisbee, "The Military Balance, 1973," *Air Force Magazine*, December 1973, pp. 57–130.
3. George W. Gawrych, *The Albatross of Decisive Victory, War and Policy Between Egypt and Israel in the 1967 and 1973 Arab-Israeli Wars* (Westport, CT: Greenwood, 2000), p. 139.
4. Hanoch Bartov, *Dado 48 Years and 20 Days* (Ma'ariv Book Guild, Tel Aviv, 1981), p. 161.
5. Ibid., p. 191.
6. Brigadier General Yoel Ben-Porat, "The Yom Kippur War: A Mistake in May Leads to a Surprise in October," *Israel Defense Journal* 3, no. 3 (1987): pp. 32–61.
7. Christopher Chant, *Compendium of Armaments and Military Hardware* (London: Routledge and Regan Paul, 1987).
8. Anwar Sadat, *In Search of Identity* (New York: Harper and Row, 1977), p. 241.
9. Chaim Herzog, *The Arab-Israeli Wars: War and Peace in the Middle East from the War of Independence Through Lebanon* (New York: Vintage, 1984), p. 228.
10. Victor Israelyan, *Inside the Kremlin During the Yom Kippur War* (University Park: Pennsylvania State University Press, 1995), p. 11.
11. Van Creveld, *The Sword and the Olive*, p. 224.

Chapter 2: A New Kind of Arab Soldier

1. Jerry Asher and Eric Hammel, *Duel for the Golan: The 100-Hour Battle That Saved Israel* (New York: William Morrow, 1987), p. 115.
2. Chaim Herzog, *The Arab-Israeli Wars: War and Peace in the Middle East from the War of Independence Through Lebanon* (New York: Vintage, 1984), p. 241.
3. Donald Neff, *Warriors Against Israel: How Israel Won the Battle to Become America's Ally* (Brattleboro, VT: Amana, 1988), p. 151.

4. Hanoch Bartov, *Dado 48 Years and 20 Days* (Ma'Ariv Book Guild, Tel Aviv, 1981), p. 273.

5. Ibid., p. 276.

6. Moshe Dayan, *Moshe Dayan: The Story of My Life* (New York: William Morrow, 1976), p. 476.

7. Golda Meir, *My Life* (New York: G. P. Putnam's Sons, 1975), p. 426.

8. Victor Israelyan, *Inside the Kremlin During the Yom Kippur War* (University Park: Pennsylvania State University Press, 1995), p. 11.

9. Lon Nordeen and David Nicolle, *Phoenix over the Nile: A History of Egyptian Air Power 1932–1994* (Washington, DC: Smithsonian Press, 1996), p. 300.

10. Bartov, *Dado*, p. 286.

11. Nordeen and Nicole, *Phoenix over the Nile*, p. 272.

12. Herzog, *The Arab-Israeli War 3*, p. 287.

13. Walter J. Boyne, *Beyond the Horizons: The Lockheed Story* (New York: St. Martin's Press, 1998), p. 335.

14. Asher and Hammel, *Duel for the Golan*, p. 64.

15. Martin van Creveld, *The Sword and the Olive: A Critical History of the Israeli Defense Force* (New York: Public Affairs, 1998), p. 225.

16. Asher and Hammel, *Duel for the Golan*, p. 110.

17. Dayan, *Moshe Dayan*, p. 481.

18. Henry Kissinger, *Years of Upheaval* (Boston: Little, Brown, 1982), p. 486.

19. Bartov, *Dado*, p. 317.

20. Israelyan, *Inside the Kremlin,* p. 43.

21. Ibid., p. 45.

Chapter 3: Black Monday

1. Chaim Herzog, *The Arab-Israeli Wars: War and Peace in the Middle East from the War of Independence Through Lebanon* (New York: Vintage, 1984), p. 255.

2. Hanoch Bartov, *Dado 48 Years and 20 Days* (Ma'Ariv Book Guild, Tel Aviv, 1981), p. 341.

3. Donald Neff, *Warriors Against Israel: How Israel Won the Battle to Become America's Ally* (Brattleboro, VT: Amana, 1988), p. 180.

4. Bartov, *Dado*, p. 325.

5. Seymour M. Hersh, *The Sampson Option: Israel's Nuclear Arsenal and American Foreign Policy* (New York: Random House, 1991), p. 129.

6. Ibid., p. 120.

7. Ibid., p. 216.

8. Henry Kissinger, *Years of Upheaval* (Boston: Little, Brown, 1982), p. 493.

9. Lon Nordeen, *Air Warfare in the Missile Age* (Washington DC: Smithsonian Press, 1985), p. 153.

10. Kissinger, *Years of Upheaval*, p. 496.

11. Jerry Asher and Eric Hammel, *Duel for the Golan: The 100-Hour Battle That Saved Israel* (New York: William Morrow, 1987), p. 208.

12. Bartov, *Dado*, p. 374.

13. Edgar F. Puryear Jr., *George S. Brown, General, U.S. Air Force: Destined for Stars* (Novato, CA: Presidio, 1983), p. 246.

14. Kenneth Patchin, *Flight to Israel: A Historical Documentary of Strategic Airlift to Israel, 14 October–14 November, 1973* (Scott Air Force Base, IL: Office of Military Airlift Command History, 1976), p. 39.

15. Kissinger, *Years of Upheaval*, p. 496.

Chapter 4: Arab Euphoria

1. Hanoch Bartov, *Dado 48 years and 20 Days* (Ma'Ariv Book Guild, Tel Aviv, 1981), p. 400.

2. Ibid., p. 396.

3. Chaim Herzog, *The Arab-Israeli Wars: War and Peace in the Middle East from the War of Independence Through Lebanon* (New York: Vintage, 1984), p. 255.

4. Victor Flintham, *Air Wars and Aircraft: A Detailed Record of Air Combat from 1945 to the Present* (New York: Facts on File, 1990), p. 64.

5. Kenneth L. Patchin, *Flight to Israel: A Historical Documentary of Strategic Airlift to Israel, 14 October–14 November, 1973* (Scott Air Force Base, IL: Office of Military Airlift Command History, 1971), p. 37.

6. Jerry Asher and Eric Hammel, *Duel for the Golan: The 100-Hour Battle That Saved Israel* (New York: William Morrow, 1987), p. 227.

7. Ariel Sharon, *Warrior: The Autobiography of Ariel Sharon* (New York: Simon and Schuster, 1989), p. 307.

8. Christopher Chant, *Compendium of Armaments and Military Hardware* (London: Routledge and Kegan Paul, 1987), p. 67.

9. Victor Israelyan, *Inside the Kremlin During the Yom Kippur War* (University Park: Pennsylvania State University Press, 1955) p. 37.

10. Ibid, p. 72.

11. Patchin, *Flight to Israel,* p. 25.

12. Ibid., p. 34.

13. William H. Tunner, *Over the Hump* (Scott Air Force Base, IL: Military Airlift Command, 1964), pp. 43–222.

Chapter 5: Pushing the Red Line

1. Hanoch Bartov, *Dado 48 Years and 20 Days* (Ma'Ariv Book Guild, Tel Aviv, 1981), p. 429.
2. Chaim Herzog, *The Arab-Israeli Wars: War and Peace in the Middle East from the War of Independence Through Lebanon* (New York: Vintage, 1984), p. 257.
3. Henry Kissinger, *Years of Upheaval* (Boston: Little, Brown, Vintage, 1982), p. 507.
4. Victor Israelyan, *Inside the Kremlin During the Yom Kippur War* (University Park: Pennsylvania State University Press, 1995), p. 73.
5. Kissinger, *Years of Upheaval,* p. 512.
6. Donald Strobaugh, *Unpublished Journal of Operation Nickel Grass,* 1973, p. 2.
7. Herzog, *The Arab-Israeli Wars,* p. 297.
8. Avigdor Kahlani, *The Heights of Courage: A Tank Leader's War on the Golan* (New York: Praeger, 1992), p. 132.
9. Simcha Dinitz, "Diplomacy in War and Peace," and Nixon, "In the Arena," in P. R. Kumaraswamy, ed., *Revisting the Yom Kippur War* (London: Frank Cass, 2000), pp. 116, 336.
10. Kenneth L. Patchin, *Flight to Israel: A Historical Documentary of Strategic Airlift to Israel, 14 October–14 November, 1973* (Scott Air Force Base, IL: Office of Military Airlift Command History, 1976), p. 82.
11. Ibid., p. 41.
12. Herzog, *The Arab-Israeli War*, p. 301.

Chapter 6: Airlift and Breakout

1. George W. Gawrych, *The Albatross of Decisive Victory — War and Policy Between Egypt and Israel in the 1967 and 1973 Arab-Israeli Wars* (Westport, CT: Greenwood, 2000), p. 205.
2. Hanoch Bartov, *Dado 48 Years and 20 Days* (Ma'Ariv, Tel Aviv, 1981), p. 448.
3. Ibid., p. 471.
4. Henry Kissinger, *Years of Upheaval* (Boston: Little, Brown, 1982), p. 522.
5. Donald Strobaugh, *Unpublished Journal of Operation Nickel Grass,* 1973, p. 4.
6. Kenneth L. Patchin, *Flight to Israel: A Historical Documentary of Strategic Airlift to Israel, 14 October–14 November, 1973* (Scott Air Force Base, IL: Office of Military Airlift Command History, 1976), p. 129.
7. Victor Israelyan, *Inside the Kremlin During the Yom Kippur War* (University Park: Pennsylvania State University Press, 1995), p. 84.

8. Bartov, *Dado*, p. 474.
9. Ariel Sharon, *Warrior: The Autobiography of Ariel Sharon* (New York: Simon and Schuster, 1989), p. 312.
10. Israelyan, *Inside the Kremlin*, p. 90.
11. Patchin, *Flight to Israel*, p. 50.

Chapter 7: Back Across the Canal

1. Chaim Herzog, *The Arab-Israeli Wars: War and Peace in the Middle East From the War of Independence Through Lebanon* (New York: Vintage, 1984), p. 270.
2. Victor Israelyan, *Inside the Kremlin During the Yom Kippur War* (University Park: Pennsylvania State University Press, 1955), p. 104.
3. Herzog, *The Arab-Israeli Wars*, p. 275.
4. Donald Neff, *Warriors Against Israel: How Israel Won the Battle to Become America's Ally* (Brattleboro, VT: Amana, 1988), p. 240.
5. Israelyan, *Inside the Kremlin*, p. 103.
6. P. R. Kumaraswamy, ed., *Revisiting the Yom Kippur War* (London: Frank Cass, 2000), p. 4.
7. Herzog, *The Arab-Israeli Wars*, p. 303.
8. Kenneth L. Patchin, *Flight to Israel: A Historical Documentary of Strategic Airlift to Israel, 14 October–14 November, 1973* (Scott Air Force Base, IL: Office of Military Airlift Command History, 1976), p. 125.
9. Lon Nordeen, *Air Warfare in the Missile Age* (Washington, DC: Smithsonian Press, 1985), p. 163.
10. Lon Nordeen and David Nicolle, *Phoenix over the Nile: A History of Egyptian Air Power 1932–1994* (Washington, DC: Smithsonian Press, 1996), p. 294.
11. Ibid., p. 253.
12. Henry Kissinger, *Years of Upheaval* (Boston: Little, Brown, 1982), p. 526.
13. Herzog, *The Arab-Israeli Wars*, p. 274.
14. Ariel Sharon, *Warrior: The Autobiography of Ariel Sharon* (New York: Simon and Schuster, 1989), p. 319.
15. Ibid., p. 375.
16. Ibid., p. 376.
17. Avraham Adan, *On the Banks of the Suez* (Novata, CA: Presidio, 1980), p. 294.
18. Kissinger, *Years of Upheaval*, p. 535.
19. Israelyan, *Inside the Kremlin*, p. 109.

Chapter 8: The Kremlin Turns to Kissinger

1. Hanoch Bartov, *Dado 48 Years and 20 Days* (Ma'Ariv Book Guild, Tel Aviv, 1981), p. 507.
2. Avraham Adan, *On the Banks of the Suez* (Novata, CA: Presidio, 1980), p. 308.
3. Ibid., p. 319.
4. George W. Gawrych, *The Albatross of Decisive Victory — War and Policy Between Egypt and Israel in the 1967 and 1973 Arab-Israeli Wars* (Westport, CT: Greenwood, 2000), p. 223.
5. Henry Kissinger, *Years of Upheaval* (Boston: Little, Brown, 1982), p. 538.
6. Donald Strobaugh, *Unpublished Journal of Operation Nickel Grass,* 1973, p. 6.
7. Victor Israelyan, *Inside the Kremlin During the Yom Kippur War* (University Park: Pennsylvania State University Press, 1995), p. 114.
8. Bartov, *Dado,* p. 526.
9. Israelyan, *Inside the Kremlin,* p. 121.
10. Kissinger, *Years of Upheaval,* p. 547.

Chapter 9: Seizing the Cease-Fire

1. Anwar Sadat, *In Search of Identity* (New York: Harper and Row, 1977), p. 263.
2. Ibid., p. 264.
3. Hanoch Bartov, *Dado 48 Years and 20 Days* (Ma'Ariv Book Guild, Tel Aviv, 1981), p. 528.
4. Ibid., p. 529.
5. Victor Israelyan, *Inside the Kremlin During the Yom Kippur War* (University Park: Pennsylvania State University Press, 1955), p. 126.
6. Henry Kissinger, *Years of Upheaval* (Boston: Little, Brown, 1982), p. 552.
7. Christopher Chant, *Compendium of Armaments and Military Hardware* (London: Routledge and Kegan Paul, 1987), p. 505.
8. Bartov, *Dado,* p. 538.
9. Ariel Sharon, *Warrior: The Autobiography of Ariel Sharon* (New York: Simon and Schuster, 1989), p. 331.
10. Jerry Asher and Erie Hammel, *Duel for the Golan: The 100-Hour Battle That Saved Israel* (New York: William Morrow, 1987), p. 240.
11. Kissinger, *Years of Upheaval,* p. 554.
12. Bartov, *Dado,* p. 544.
13. Kissinger, *Years of Upheaval,* p. 565.

14. Donald Strobaugh, *Unpublished Journal of Operation Nickel Grass*, 1973, p. 10.
15. Avraham Adan, *On the Banks of the Suez* (Novata, CA: Presidio, 1980), p. 388.
16. Sadat, *In Search of Identity*, p. 265.
17. Israelyan, *Inside the Kremlin*, p. 143.

Chapter 10: Approaching Armageddon: The Nuclear Alert

1. Henry Kissinger, *Years of Upheaval* (Boston: Little, Brown, 1982), p. 569.
2. Hanoch Bartov, *Dado 48 Days and 20 Days* (Ma'Ariv Book Guild, Tel Aviv, 1981), p. 556.
3. Ibid., p. 559.
4. Victor Israelyan, *Inside the Kremlin During the Yom Kippur War* (University Park: Pennsylvania State University Press, 1995), p. 148.
5. Ibid., p. 160.
6. Kissinger, *Years of Upheaval*, p. 571.
7. Ibid., p. 574.
8. Avraham Adan, *Banks of the Suez* (Novata, CA: Presidio, 1980), p. 401.
9. Ibid., p. 409.
10. Ariel Sharon, *Warrior*, p. 333.
11. Victor Israelyan, *Inside the Kremlin During the Yom Kippur War* (University Park: Pennsylvania State University Press, 1995), p. 165.
12. Richard B. Parker, ed., *The October War, a Retrospective* (Gainesville: University of Florida Press, 2001), p. 212.
13. Henry Kissinger, *Years of Upheaval* (Boston: Little, Brown, 1982), p. 588.
14. Israelyan, *Inside the Kremlin*, p. 173.
15. Ibid., p. 182.
16. Kissinger, *Years of Upheaval*, p. 599.
17. Bartov, *Dado 48 Years and 20 Days,* p. 576.
18. Kenneth L. Patchin, *Flight to Israel: A Historical Documentary of Strategic Airlift to Israel, 14 October–14 November, 1973* (Scott Air Force Base, IL: Office of Military Airlift Command History, 1976), p. 166.
19. Ibid., p. 182.
20. Kissinger, *Years of Upheaval*, p. 611.
21. Parker, *The October War*, p. 8.

Epilogue

1. George W. Gawrych, *The Albatross of Decisive Victory — War and Policy Between Egypt and Israel in the 1967 and 1973 Arab-Israeli Wars* (Westport, CT: Greenwood, 2000), p. 144.

Appendix: Born in Battle

1. See Martin Gilbert, *Atlas of the Arab Israeli Conflict*, 6th ed. (New York: Oxford University Press, 1993), for a kaleidoscopic view of the changing borders and demographics of the Middle East.
2. Chaim Herzog, *The Arab-Israeli Wars: War and Peace in the Middle East from the War of Independence Through Lebanon* (New York: Vintage, 1984), p. 113.
3. Ibid., p. 139.
4. Seymour M. Hersh, *The Sampson Option: Israeli's Nuclear Arsenal and American Foreign Policy* (New York: Random House, 1991), p. 41.
5. Herzog, *The Arab-Israeli Wars*, p. 147.
6. Moshe Dayan, *Moshe Dayan: The Story of My Life,* (New York: William Morrow, 1976), p. 316.
7. Ibid., p. 348.
8. Lon Nordeen, *Fighters over Israel* (New York: Orion, 1990), p. 67.
9. Lon Nordeen and David Nicolle, *Phoenix over the Nile: A History of Egyptian Air Power 1932–1994* (Washington, DC: Smithsonian Press, 1996), p. 257.
10. Avraham Adan, *On the Banks of the Suez* (Novata, CA: Presidio, 1980), p. 17.
11. Herzog, *The Arab-Israeli Wars*, p. 219.

Bibliography

Public Documents

United Arab Republic (Egypt). Air Force Intelligence Study DIA-240-3-1-71-1NT, January 1, 1971. Washington, DC: Defense Intelligence Agency, 1971.

Arab Republic of Egypt. Air Force Intelligence Study D1-240-EC-74, October 1, 1974. Washington, DC: Headquarters, USAF, 1974.

Patchin, Kenneth. *Flight to Israel: A Historical Documentary of Strategic Airlift to Israel, 14 October–14 November, 1973*. Scott Air Force Base, IL: Office of Military Airlift Command History, 1976. Declassified 1993.

Strobaugh, Donald. *Unpublished Journal of Operation Nickel Grass*. 1973.

Interviews: Sr. M. Sgt. Byron "Hank" Baker; Walter Baade; Yossef Bodansky; General Paul. K. Carlton, Lt. Col. Harry Heist (Ret.); Michael Leister, Director, Air Mobility Command Museum; Maj. Sam McGowan; Kenneth Robertson; Lt. Col. H. Jack Royston; Lt. Col. Kenneth Smith; Col. Donald Strobaugh; Kenneth L. Patchin; Lt. Col. David Wilson.

Unpublished Source

Nordeen, Lon. *A Bad Investment: Soviet Support for Egypt*. 1989.

Published Sources

Adan, Avraham. *On the Banks of the Suez*. Novata, CA: Presidio, 1980.

Bartov, Hanoch. *Dado 48 Years and 20 Days*. Tel Aviv: Ma'Ariv Book Guild, 1981.

Asher, Jerry, and Eric Hammel. *Duel for the Golan: The 100-Hour Battle That Saved Israel*. New York: William Morrow, 1987.

Ben-Porat, Brigadier General Yoel. "The Yom Kippur War: A Mistake in May Leads to a Surprise in October." *Israel Defense Force Journal* 3, No. 3, (1987): 32–61.

Bokhari, Colonel Eas. *October 1973 War & Lessons for the Arabs*. http://www.defencejournal.com

Bowen, Wyn. "Living Under the Red Missile Threat." *Jane's Intelligence Review,* December 1996, pp. 560–64.

Boyne, Walter J. *Beyond the Horizons: The Lockheed Story*. New York: St. Martin's Press, 1998.

———. *Beyond the Wild Blue: A History of the United States Air Force, 1947–1997*. New York: St. Martin's Press, 1997.

———. "Operation Nickel Grass." *Air Force Magazine*, December 1998, pp. 54–59.

Chant, Christopher. *Compendium of Armaments and Military Hardware*. London: Routledge and Kegan Paul, 1987.

Cohen, Avner. *Israel and the Bomb*. New York: Columbia University Press, 1998.

Cohen, Eliezer. Israel's Best Defense: *The Full Story of the Israeli Air Force*. New York: Orbis, 1993.

Dayan, Moshe. *Moshe Dayan: The Story of My Life*. New York: William Morrow, 1976.

Dobrynin, Anatoly. *In Confidence: Moscow's Cold War Ambassador to Six Presidents*. New York: Random House, 1995.

Dupuy, Trevor N. *Elusive Victory: The Arab-Israeli Wars, 1947–1974*. 1978. Reprint. Fairfax, VA: Hero Books, 1984.

————. *Numbers, Predictions & War: Using History to Evaluate Combat Factors and Predict the Outcome of Battles,* rev. ed. Fairfax, VA: Hero Books, 1985.

Eban, Abba. *Abba Eban: An Autobiography.* New York: Random House, 1977.

————. Interview, Tel Aviv, May 13, 1997. http://www.hfni.gsehd.gwu.edu

Eshel, David. *Chariots of the Desert: The Story of the Israeli Armor Corps.* London: Brassey's, 1989.

Flintham, Victor. *Air Wars and Aircraft: A Detailed Record of Air Combat from 1945 to the Present.* New York: Facts on File, 1990.

Frisbee, John L. "The Military Balance," *Air Force Magazine,* December 1973, pp. 57–130.

Gawrych, George W. *The Albatross of Decisive Victory—War and Policy Between Egypt and Israel in the 1967 and 1973 Arab-Israeli Wars.* Westport, CT: Greenwood, 2000.

Gilbert, Martin. *Atlas of the Arab-Israeli Conflict,* 6th ed. New York: Oxford University Press, 1993.

Greenhut, Jeffrey. "Air War: Middle East." *Aerospace Historian,* March 1976, pp. 36–40.

Hart, Harold H. *Yom Kippur plus 100 Days.* New York: Hart Publishing, 1974.

Hersh, Seymour M. *The Sampson Option: Israel's Nuclear Arsenal and American Foreign Policy.* New York: Random House, 1991.

Herzog, Chaim. *The Arab-Israeli Wars: War and Peace in the Middle East from the War of Independence Through Lebanon.* New York: Vintage, 1984.

Hunt, Brigadier General Kenneth. "The Arab-Israeli War, Some Tentative Conclusions." *Air Force Magazine,* December 1973, pp. 51–58.

Israelyan, Victor. *Inside the Kremlin During the Yom Kippur War.* University Park: Pennsylvania State University Press, 1995.

Kahalani, Avigdor. *The Heights of Courage: A Tank Leader's War on the Golan.* New York: Praeger, 1992.

Kissinger, Henry. Interview by Karen Brutents, CNN. http://www.cgi.cnn.com

————. *White House Years.* Boston: Little, Brown, 1979.

————. *Years of Upheaval.* Boston: Little, Brown, 1982.

Krisinger, Chris. J. "Operation Nickel Grass: Airlift in Support of National Policy," *Airpower Journal,* Spring 1989, pp. 11–16.

Kumaraswamy, P. R., ed. *Revisiting the Yom Kippur War.* London: Frank Cass, 2000.

Laqueur, Walter, ed. *The Israel-Arab Reader.* New York, Bantam, 1976.

Meir, Golda. *My Life.* New York: G. P. Putnam's Sons, 1975.

————. *Statement to the Knesset, November 13, 1973.* Tel Aviv: State of Israel, 1973.

Morgan, David R. *Threats to Use Nuclear Weapons.* Toronto: University College, 1996.

Neff, Donald. *Warriors Against Israel: How Israel Won the Battle to Become America's Ally.* Brattleboro, VT: Amana, 1988.

Nixon, Richard. *In the Arena: A Memoir of Victory, Defeat and Renewal.* New York: Simon and Schuster, 1990.

————. *RN: The Memoirs of Richard Nixon.* 2 vols. New York: Warner, 1978.

Nicolle, David. "Holy Day Air War." *Air Enthusiast International*, May 1974. pp. 240–242.

Nordeen, Lon. *Air Warfare in the Missile Age.* Washington, DC: Smithsonian Press, 1985.

————. *Fighters over Israel.* New York: Orion, 1990.

Nordeen, Lon, and David Nicolle. *Phoenix over the Nile: A History of Egyptian Air Power 1932–1994.* Washington, DC: Smithsonian Press, 1996.

Parker, Richard B., ed. *The October War, a Retrospective.* Gainesville: University of Florida Press, 2001.

Podhoretz, Norman. "Israel and the United States: A Complex History." *Commentary,* May 1998.

Puryear, Edgar F., Jr. *George S. Brown, General, U.S. Air Force: Destined for Stars.* Novato, CA: Presidio, 1983.

Quandt, William B. *Decade of Decisions: American Policy Toward the Arab-Israeli Conflict, 1967–1976.* Berkeley: University of California Press, 1977.

Robertson, Kenneth K., Jr. *Operation Nickel Grass.* Dover, DE: Air Mobility Command Museum Foundation, 2000.

Sadat, Anwar. *In Search of Identity.* New York: Harper and Row, 1977.

Sharon, Ariel. *Warrior: The Autobiography of Ariel Sharon.* New York: Simon and Schuster, 1989.

Tunner, William H. *Over the Hump.* Scott Air Force Base, IL: Military Airlift Command, 1964.

Van Crevald, Martin. *The Sword and the Olive: A Critical History of the Israeli Defense Force.* New York: Public Affairs, 1998.

Weizman, Ezer. *On Eagle's Wings.* New York: Macmillan, 1976.

Weinraub, Lt. Col. Yehuda. "The Israel Air Force and the Air Land Battle." *Israel Defense Force Journal* 3, no. 3 (1987).

Yonay, Ehud. *No Margin for Error: The Making of the Israeli Air Force.* New York: Pantheon, 1993.

Index